As I Walk With God
Author: Todd Crawford

Copyright © 2019 by Todd Crawford.
First printing, 2019.

ISBN: 978-1660295982 (Paperback)

Editing Assistance by: Hannah Crawford

Cover Design by: Chin Crawford & iDesignArizona.com

Interior Layout by: iDesignArizona.com

To order copies email:
drmdc@comcast.net

AS I
WALK
WITH
GOD

BY: TODD CRAWFORD

"[Job said, and I agree] Oh that my words were written!
Oh that they were inscribed in a book!
That with an iron stylus and lead they were engraved in the rock forever!
And as for me, I know that my Redeemer [my vindicator, defender]
lives, and at the last He will take His stand on the earth. Even after my
skin is destroyed, yet from my flesh I shall see God."

Job 19:23-26

FOREWORD

Between late in 2007 and the first few month of 2009 I was going through a time of transition. I had been humbled and taken from my short career as a medical Dr. to jail for 8 months and then to working in a plastics factory-then later into ministry/discipleship where I am happy to be. Within that transition between my medical career and ministry there was a period of about 14 months that the Lord was revealing things to me in ways and frequency that was unusual (at that time) for me. I often refer to that period of time as "my training period". I feel compelled to record these and other insights, miracles, dreams and observations… because I want others to share in the great things that the wonderful Lord has shared with me. I write this book that others may **give thanks to the Lord, and learn to call upon Him, and to share His great deeds with others**.

"Oh give thanks to the LORD, call upon His name; make known His deeds among the people."
1ˢᵗ Chronicles 16:8

Please note that this is not an exhaustive compilation of the: insights, miracles, dreams and observations…during this time as the things that had and continue to happen are much too frequent and miraculous to ever document. I can appreciate the Apostle John's statement

"And there are also many other things which Jesus did, which if they were written in detail, I suppose that even the world itself would not contain the books that would be written."
John 21:25

A LONG WALK WITH A
WHEELBARROW OF GRAIN

The LORD can do so much with so little, all that seems to be required of us is our obedience.

I had a vision that I was pushing a wheelbarrow of grain-it was full to overflowing. I was on a dirt path and the grade varied with slopes of elevation followed by declines, and off I went down the path pushing a wheelbarrow full of grain. Along the path were people going about their business and it seemed that some of the people were familiar to me. As I pushed the wheelbarrow on the path the people along the path would randomly grab handfuls of grain from the wheelbarrow and some while mocking my mission. My destination was still a significant distance away and I was concerned that I was losing so much grain-but I continued to push my wheelbarrow along the path. As I walked the path I needed to control the wheelbarrow using both hands and I was unable to push past the people and hold them back as they took handfuls of grain from the wheelbarrow. My mission was to forge ahead and push the wheelbarrow to the destination regardless of how much grain was being taken from the barrel. This was a frustrating task to say the least. As I walked and pushed the barrel people grabbed and scooped the grain until I was pushing an almost empty barrel. I eventually arrived at my destination, I looked into the barrel and it seemed that I was delivering only one single kernel of grain. I arrived feeling discouraged and sorry for the small amount of grain that I had delivered. Upon my arrival I saw only the LORD's hand reach into the wheelbarrow and He plucked up the single grain of wheat as He said "Let Me show you what I can do with this". At that the LORD dropped the single grain onto the ground in front of me and as soon as it hit the ground I heard a whoosh sound and the landscape literally exploded with the growth of perfect and colorful wheat as far as I was able to see. The once barren field was now a lush wheat field of grain ready for a great harvest.

1

My interpretation of this vision was so clear. We are responsible for our effort and obedience while God is responsible for the outcome.

John 12:23-26

[23]And Jesus answered them, saying, "The hour has come for the Son of Man to be glorified.

[24]"Truly, truly, I say to you, unless a grain of wheat falls into the earth and dies, it remains alone; but if it dies, it bears much fruit.

[25]"He who loves his life loses it, and he who hates [disregards] his life in this world will keep it to life eternal.

[26]"If anyone serves Me [Jesus of Nazareth], he must follow Me; and where I am, there My servant will be also; if anyone serves Me, the Father will honor him [or her].

2

A VARIETY OF GIFTS-THE SAME SPIRIT-FOR THE COMMON GOOD OF THE BODY

I have had the opportunity to be involved in deliverance ministry. On one occasion there was a young man who was reported to "have demons". As this was my first experience in deliverance prayer ministry I was skeptical, however, that skepticism was short lived. A team of believers assembled and we met with the young man mid-week at a local church with the intention of dealing with the demons. As we assembled it was clear that the LORD was present. We were hearing conformational passages being shared as some had a word from the LORD, songs were spontaneously sung consistent with the things that we were quietly praying about, musical gifts were manifested. The music being shared seemed anointed and angelic, interesting connections with: names, places and people were made, even the sun as it was setting was pouring rays of light into the church sanctuary through a western window in a beautiful waterfall of light looking almost like volcanic lava pouring into the room. It was exciting to observe the Spirit of the LORD working through His people in so many ways-it stirred our anticipation. While praying for this young man I observed manifestations of the spirit. The man was violently lunging at the prayer team and growling, names of the demons were exposed, knowledge about the demons was elicited and information about the expulsion of the demons was shared as at least one of the team was gifted and experienced in dealing with demons. Clearly the spiritual realm was active and the LORD was moving. In the beginning of the deliverance I had a vision. **Prior to the demons being expelled (evidenced by violent coughing, vomiting and retching) I clearly saw a man locked in a dungeon, the dungeon looked old with hay scattered on the floor, he was crouched down on a western wall near the corner of the cell with his head between his knees, he looked**

3

hopeless. Perhaps an hour later, after several demons were identified and expelled; each expulsion was accompanied by violent vomiting and retching... We were exhausted and sweaty and the man that we were praying for was collapsed on the church floor exhausted, but peaceful. **About this time, toward the end of our session I saw a second vision of the same dungeon cell and the same man, however, the man that was once crouched over, looking hopeless was now standing near the door of the dungeon anticipating his released. He looked like a new man, a man with hope and empowered by authority with a vision for his future.** This vision seemed to be a very good sign, and it was good to see the Scriptures being played-out before our eyes.

1 Corinthians 12

Now concerning spiritual *gifts*, brethren, I [Paul] do not want you to be unaware... [4] **... there are varieties of gifts, but the same Spirit.** [5] **And there are varieties of ministries, and the same Lord.** [6] **There are varieties of effects, but the same God who works all things in all *persons*.** [7] **But to each one is given the manifestation of the Spirit for the common good.** [8] **For to one is given the word of wisdom through the Spirit, and to another the word of knowledge according to the same Spirit;** [9] **to another faith by the same Spirit, and to another gifts of healing by the one Spirit,** [10] **and to another the effecting of miracles, and to another prophecy, and to another the distinguishing of spirits, to another *various* kinds of tongues, and to another the interpretation of tongues.** [11] **But one and the same Spirit works all these things, distributing to each one individually just as He [YHWH, LORD God] wills.**

4

ALBANIA

In 1990, my wife and I were spending a lot of time with our good friends Greg and Karen. Greg is my wife Linda's brother and Karen is Greg's wife. Greg and Karen, Linda and I were seeking the LORD's will for us and we had a common burden for world missions. At that time, Greg, Karen, Linda and I lived a few blocks from each other-we shared our lives and almost all of our evening meals together, and we shared in intercessory prayer. At some point we sensed that the LORD was calling us to pray on a global sale. **Together we felt a common burden to pray for Albania. At that time the Albanian government was openly hostile to the Gospel of Jesus Christ** and was persecuting Christians. As a group we began to pray for the people of Albania to become open to the LORD, and, as far as we were aware, we were the only people praying for Albania. As I recall we had been praying for about one year and one evening we were all together at a mission's conference **when the speaker made the statement that the LORD was moving "millions of groups to pray for Albania"**. At that statement our heads turned toward one another, we looked at each other in amazement, little did we know that we were part of a world-wide movement of the Spirit to pray on behalf of Albania.

The Communist regime that took control of Albania after World War II persecuted and suppressed religious observance and institutions and entirely banned "religion" to the point where Albania was officially declared to be the world's first atheist state. Religious freedom has returned to Albania since the regime's change in 1992 roughly 2 years after our little group of four people and perhaps millions of little groups like ours were called to pray for the Spirit of God to move in the people of Albania.

⁵Thus says God the LORD [YHWH],
Who created the heavens and stretched them out,
Who spread out the earth and its offspring,
Who gives breath to the people on it
and spirit to those who walk in it,
⁶"I am the LORD, I have called You in righteousness,
I will also hold You by the hand and watch over You,
and I will appoint You as a covenant to the people,
as a light to the nations,
⁷To open blind eyes,
to bring out prisoners from the dungeon
And those who dwell in darkness from the prison.
⁸"I am the LORD [YHWH], that is My name;
I will not give My glory to another,
Nor My praise to graven images.
⁹"Behold, the former things have come to pass,
Now I declare new things;
before they spring forth I proclaim them to you."

ALL PEOPLE ARE: ON PROBATION, INCARCERATED AND SEX OFFENDERS

I was in prayer regarding our condition while here on earth in these mortal bodies; and as I recall I was talking to the LORD about: murder, probation, incarceration and sexual offenses. I believe that the LORD spoke to me and reveled to me that while we are on the earth we are all incarcerated as we are confined to this planet as well as to these earthen bodies, and we will not get off of this planet apart from Him. With regard to probation the LORD reveled that we are all on probation, as there are those watching us and our every move, and, they are taking meticulous notes on every detail of our lives, actions and thoughts. With regard to sexual offense I believe that the LORD revealed to me that we as humans are all sex offenders as we have all offended Him in some way with regard to our sexuality. Therefore, **we are all: incarcerated, we are all on probation, and we are all sex offenders.**

Romans 3

[10]**as it is written,**
"THERE IS NONE RIGHTEOUS, NOT EVEN ONE;
[11]**THERE IS NONE WHO UNDERSTANDS,**
THERE IS NONE WHO SEEKS FOR GOD;
[12]**ALL HAVE TURNED ASIDE, TOGETHER THEY HAVE**
BECOME USELESS;
THERE IS NONE WHO DOES GOOD, THERE IS NOT EVEN
ONE."
[13]**"THEIR THROAT IS AN OPEN GRAVE,**
WITH THEIR TONGUES THEY KEEP DECEIVING,"
"THE POISON OF ASPS IS UNDER THEIR LIPS";

[14]"WHOSE MOUTH IS FULL OF CURSING AND
BITTERNESS";
[15]"THEIR FEET ARE SWIFT TO SHED BLOOD,
[16]DESTRUCTION AND MISERY ARE IN THEIR PATHS,
[17]AND THE PATH OF PEACE THEY HAVE NOT KNOWN."
[18]"THERE IS NO FEAR OF GOD BEFORE THEIR EYES."

ASK HER HER NAME

I met a young married lady when I worked at a plastics factory, we had a language barrier as she spoke fluent Spanish and broken English; I spoke relatively decent English and almost no Spanish. When we talked we talked about the LORD as He always seems to find a way for us to communicate in spite of our language barrier. In one of our conversations this lady communicated that she was very unhappy and that she was considering leaving her husband. At that point I began to explain that marriage was very tender on the heart of the LORD, I was quite bold regarding my interpretation of the Scripture on the matter of divorce and remarriage, and I told her in no uncertain terms that "it is not God's will that you leave your husband". As I shared with her I began to have a thought in my mind "ask her what her name means", the voice was "still and small" and sounded like my voice; I felt that I was hearing from the LORD and as she continued to speak and defend her reasoning for wanting to leave I continued to hear the still and small voice say "ask her what her name means". I finally gently interrupted her and I asked her "what does your name mean?", and I repeated "your name, what does your name mean?" **At that point she seemed to have lost her resolve to leave her husband, she looked away and then she looked at me and said, "Married for life, my name means married for life".**

Twelve years later the marriage is strong as they are building upon the foundation of Jesus.

Isaiah 44:24-26

[24] Thus says the Lord, your Redeemer, and the one who formed
you from the womb,

"I, the Lord, am the maker of all things,
stretching out the heavens by Myself
and spreading out the earth all alone,
causing the omens of boasters to fail,
making fools out of diviners,
causing wise men [and women] to draw back
and turning their knowledge into foolishness,
confirming the word of His servant
and performing the purpose of His messengers...".

ANGIE AND THE CELLPHONE

For several years I volunteered at a local food shelf on Wednesdays. Late Wednesday night the food shelf would end and generally the volunteers were so tired that we would all head home and reassemble to clean the next day. As I was cleaning one Thursday morning I sensed that the LORD was teaching me to trust in Him only, I was reminded of the passage in Scripture **"ask no person for anything"**, and the LORD was calling me to ask Him for all things. As I was considering this I felt God prompting me to a life of radical faith. Angie had come to the food shelf from work as she was still wearing her Perkins restaurant uniform; as we were cleaning Angie asked me if she could use my cellphone. I gave her the cellphone and she made her call. As time passed we continued to clean, Angie had finished her conversation on my phone and I did not see my cellphone with her, I was concerned about my phone though I knew that this was a test from the LORD. I wanted to use the phone and I found myself distracted by the thought of it. I thought of asking Angie for my phone and then I was reminded in a still small voice **"ask no person for anything"** so I asked the LORD to remind Angie of my phone and I waited. As the day progressed I did not ask Angie for the phone though I thought of it more often than I care to admit. I kept thinking of the "worst case scenario" and of how inconvenient it would be if she left for home and forgot that she was carrying my cellphone. While we were finishing packing up Angie was looking like she was headed out to her van to go home and I helped her carry her things. As we walked to her van I was crying out to the LORD regarding the cellphone issue as I was concerned that she would drive away without returning my cellphone (certainly not on purpose). As we got to the van we loaded her things into the van and I was asking the LORD what to do-and I heard nothing. I placed my concern into God's hand and said goodbye to Angie as she climbed into the driver's seat of her van. I closed Angie's van door, I waved to Angie and I walked away praying, and at that very moment, at what seemed the last possible second, Angie said, "do you mind if I use your cellphone one more time before I leave?" and I said "no, no problem" while I was rejoicing in the LORD on the inside on the outside I just stood there looking at Angie as though I were waiting for her to use the cellphone, as I stood there looking at her she sat in the van looking at me, we were both looking at each other as if one were waiting for the other to make the first move (Angie thought that I had the phone). I eventually said to Angie "I think that you have the cellphone", and she checked her pockets and found it. After she used the cellphone she returned it to me, and I walked back to Angie to explain what had happened in great detail. Angie was smiling as it was clear that she saw the test from the LORD and we appreciated our experience together.

1 John 3:11, 17-24

For this is the message which you have heard from the beginning, that we should love one another…

But whoever has the world's goods, and sees his brother in need and closes his heart against him, how does the love of God abide in him? Little children, let us not love with word or with tongue, but indeed and truth. We will know by this that we are of the truth, and will assure our heart before Him in whatever our heart condemns us; for God is greater than our heart and knows all things. Beloved, if our heart does not condemn us, we have confidence before God; and whatever we ask we receive from Him, because we keep His commandments and do the things that are pleasing in His sight. This is His commandment that we believe in the name of His Son Jesus Christ, and love one another, just as He commanded us. The one who keeps His commandments abides in Him, and He in him. We know by this that He abides in us, by the Spirit whom He has given us.

ANNA, THE KIDS, AND GOD'S
STRONG SUPPORT

After being in jail for 8 months I began to assimilate back into society, while looking for employment I was overlooked hundreds of times. I can see that it was God's will for me to be humbled as He chiseled away the things that the world had defined me by. God needed to humble me and reestablish my identity-I was made to glorify God and make disciples, and, I had become distracted by the world, my career... After about eight months of looking for employment I was given a job in a plastics factory for what began as a fill-in position "for a few months" and later I was offered a full time position. While in the temporary status I had heard a local Christian radio station's appeal to listeners on behalf of needy children. KTIS radio station was hosting an annual fund raiser for Compassion International whose work in third-world-countries provides children with: food, clothing, medical care and a Christian education. At that time I felt a strong burden to support a child but I had no financial wiggle-room. I presented my burden to support a child to the LORD, to my daughter Hannah and to my mother, and I explained that God could provide beyond what we now had and I asked that we pray for the amount that we need and I asked that if that extra money came in could it be used to support a child. I was given the green-light by my mother who was in charge of the household finances, she agreed that if extra money "somehow" came in it could be used to sponsor a needy child. Hannah and I agreed that we felt the LORD leading us to support a girl Hannah's age, we did the math and calculated what was needed per month and divided that by 160 (hours/month at my job) calculating roughly what I would need for an hourly wage increase, as I recall it was about 30-35 cents/hour with taxes considered. I can remember praying faithfully for about a month and then praying less consistently as time went by.

Several months later I was approached by the plant manager

who told me that they would like offer me a full-time position. He told me that at that time he could only offer me a 30-35 cents/hour raise. I smiled on the outside though I was leaping on the inside; I explained the situation to him and how this was God's answer to prayer as that was the exact amount that we had asked for to support a needy child. We all rejoiced. Hannah and I began to sponsor Ana Maria Ramos Palacios born August 26th, 1995, she was born 4 day prior to my daughter Hannah. We now have a bowl on our entry way table where people put offerings for Anna and for the additional children that we sponsor. In all, since that time God has provided for the monthly support of five children for more than 10 years-praise God!

2 Chronicles 16

9"For the eyes of the LORD move to and fro throughout the earth that He may strongly support those whose heart is completely His..."

AXEL! WHO IS AXEL?

To write of only one or even a few of these situations feels as though to belittle the thousands of times that the LORD has done a thing like this in my life. However, this example stands out to me and I suspect for no other reason than that the LORD Himself would like me to write of it. As this incident was unfolding I was so caught off guard that it was probably funny watching my reaction as I bounced about like a wave on the spectrum of reactions, bewilderment, and amazement.

We were sitting in Perkins restaurant getting ready for our weekly Greek lesson. I was flipping through some old notes and I read the name "Axel" that I had hand written on the top of a page weeks before. I remembered writing the name "Axel" so as not to forget this man's name, I sense the LORD working in Axel's life and he seems like a kind soul. As I read the name Axel at the meeting I was thinking to myself "Axel, who is Axel?" this question was bothering me, and I then said out loud "Axel, who's Axel?" As I said his name out loud I looked up and the man "Axel" who I had met before and I made note of for future reference walked in and was standing a few feet away as though the LORD was answering my question "who is Axel?" the LORD said here you go Todd, this is Axel!

2 Kings 8

¹Now Elisha spoke to the woman whose son he had restored to life, saying, "Arise and go with your household, and sojourn wherever you can sojourn; for the LORD has called for a famine, and it will even come on the land for seven years." ²**So the woman arose and did according to the word of the man of God, and she went with her household and sojourned in the land of the Philistines seven years.** ³**At the end of seven years, the woman returned from the land of the Philistines; and she went out to appeal to the king for her house and for her field.**

[4]Now the king was talking with Gehazi [Elisha's servant], the servant of the man of God [Elisha], saying, "Please relate to me all the great things that Elisha [the prophet of YHWH, LORD God] has done." [5]As he was relating to the king how he had restored to life the one who was dead, behold, the woman whose son he had restored to life appealed to the king for her house and for her field. And Gehazi said, "My lord, O king, this is the woman and this is her son, whom Elisha restored to life."

BE ON GUARD AGAINST DISSIPATION

We spend God's resources on our pets while the starving children die at a rate of one every 3 seconds. We splurge on: "better" cable T.V., faster internet service, whiter teeth, better looking legs, nails, hair... We are so fixed on the shiny things of life, things that the enemy is waving under our noses that we fail to see that we are approaching the end of our lives. Though perhaps moral and quite possibly "well intended" yet we walk toward the end of the peer and the end of our lives. This is quite likely the very "dissipation" that the LORD warned against. In the words of Jesus "be on guard against dissipation [things that will amuse us, entertain us, and literally spread us thin, and consume our: time, energy, resources...]" see Luke 21:34, Ephesians 5:18, Titus 1:6, 1ˢᵗ Peter 4:1-4. Let us instead recall, regard, heed and practice the instruction of Solomon in Ecclesiastes 12:1 "Remember also your Creator in the days of your youth, before the evil days come and the years draw near when you will say, 'I have no delight in them'".

Ecclesiastes 1

The Futility of All Endeavor

¹**The words of the Preacher [Solomon], the son of David, king in Jerusalem.**
²"Vanity of vanities," says the Preacher,
"Vanity of vanities! All is vanity."
³**What advantage does man have in all his work**
Which he does under the sun?
⁴**A generation goes and a generation comes,**
But the earth remains forever.
⁵**Also, the sun rises and the sun sets;**
And hastening to its place it rises there again.

34 "[Jesus said]Be on guard, so that your hearts will not be weighted down with dissipation [spreading yourself thin] and drunkenness and the worries of life, and that day will not come on you suddenly like a trap; 35 for it will come upon all those who dwell on the face of all the earth. 36 But keep on the alert at all times, praying that you may have strength to escape all these things that are about to take place, and to stand before the Son of Man."

BEHOLD, WATER CAME

I was lying on my bed with the window open and I was reading the account of the prophet Elisha, Jehoshaphat king of Judah and the king of Edom and the building of the trenches in the valley in 2nd Kings Chapter 3. When I got to the point of the LORD's promise **"You shall not see wind nor shall you see rain; yet the valley shall be filled with water…and it happened in the morning about the time of offering the sacrifice, that behold, water came by the way of Edom, and the country was filled with water" (2nd Kings 3:17-20).** I pondered the statement **"behold water came"**, though I know that the LORD can do all things I was having a hard time imagining water just showing up. My question to the LORD at that very moment was, "how do you do that LORD?" How does water just show up? How is it that "behold water came"? It was while I was asking those questions, at that very moment, at that very second that I heard a pulsating spraying sound followed by blasts of water just a few feet away with the sound of whhhtitititi. The sprinklers had just popped up and began to spray water at the moment that I pondered the words "behold water came". And then I laughed, shook my head and I understood that "behold water came", and it still does. I love when the LORD does this kind of thing as it helps me to realize and appreciate that He is truly near to us-and He is very funny.

2 Kings 3

[11]But Jehoshaphat said, "Is there not a prophet of the LORD here that we may inquire of the LORD by him?" And one of the king of Israel's servants answered and said, "Elisha the son of Shaphat is here, who used to pour water on the hands of Elijah."[12]Jehoshaphat said, "The word of the LORD is with him." So the king of Israel and Jehoshaphat and the king of Edom went down to him. [13]Now Elisha said to the king of Israel, "What do I have to do with you? Go to the

prophets of your father and to the prophets of your mother." And the king of Israel said to him, "No, for the LORD has called these three kings together to give them into the hand of Moab." ¹⁴Elisha said, "As the LORD of hosts lives, before whom I stand, were it not that I regard the presence of Jehoshaphat the king of Judah, I would not look at you nor see you. ¹⁵"But now bring me a minstrel "And it came about, when the minstrel played, that the hand of the LORD came upon him. ¹⁶**He said, "Thus says the LORD, 'Make this valley full of trenches.' ¹⁷"For thus says the LORD, 'You shall not see wind nor shall you see rain; yet that valley shall be filled with water, so that you shall drink, both you and your cattle and your beasts. ¹⁸'This is but a slight thing in the sight of the LORD; He will also give the Moabites into your hand. ¹⁹'**Then you shall strike every fortified city and every choice city, and fell every good tree and stop all springs of water, and mar every good piece of land with stones.'" ²⁰**It happened in the morning about the time of offering the sacrifice that behold, water came by the way of Edom, and the country was filled with water.**

BILL AND HIS "HANG-UPS"

Bill is a friend, a brother in the LORD and he was recently baptized. I have been spending time with Bill and I recognize some encouraging signs. Bill is able to recognize the things of the Spirit regarding God's timing and ability to do the miraculous. Bill is putting effort into the study of the Scriptures and he asks good questions about the Scripture that he is reading. Bill seems serious about the things and the people of the LORD, he is a person much like me who formerly had regard for the things of the world, and is now putting effort into the "doing" side of his new faith in Jesus. Prior to Bill's baptism Bill invited me into his apartment "to meet his cats and to see his apartment". Bill gave me a tour of his apartment and I was impressed by the stark contrast of the things hanging on Bill's walls; there were some paintings of things of the LORD: the Last Supper, poems and prayers, and a painting of Jesus-there were also several pornographic pictures hanging on the walls. Here were two extremes, the things the LORD-and pornography. The pictures were very representative of the conflict that existed within Bill, the conflict between the Spirit and the flesh. My response was to silently pray, I said nothing to Bill, and I was asking the LORD to please "remove" these pornographic pictures and I envisioned these pornographic pictures falling to the floor. Over the next few weeks Bill and the pictures came into my mind and I prayed. Bill then asked me if I wanted to come up again and see his cats, and I went up and sat down in his living room chair. **I glanced up at the wall that had had one of the large pornographic pictures hanging on it and I was surprised to see that the pornography was replaced with a picture of Jesus while He was in the garden of Gethsemane. I asked Bill about his decision to exchange one picture for the other and he said "that he just felt that he needed to do that". Thank you LORD!**

[17]**Therefore if anyone is in Christ, he [or she] is a new creature; the old things passed away; behold, new things have come.**

"BIG GIRLS DON'T WHINE"

My then 14 y/o daughter Hannah was in church on Sunday and she was holding 6 week old Angelina. Angelina is a cute little girl with a lot of dark hair, she seems mild mannered and has a quiet cry-Angelina is the Granddaughter of Angie. While in church I overheard Hannah making plans to babysit and later she got around to asking me if it was ok with me if she could watch Angelina sometime. I said that we would talk about it later and she asked "what is there to talk about?" The week passed and I had heard nothing more about the babysitting plan. When I picked up Hannah from school on Friday afternoon she got into the car and brought up the subject of babysitting Angelina. We decided that an overnight would work best as Angie and the girls live across town; we made plans to babysit for the following afternoon-Saturday through Sunday morning. Hannah seemed a bit concerned about how things would go, she was anxious and she even became teary so we prayed together. I did my best to comfort Hannah, I thought that she was tired and that she would feel better in the morning. After a good night sleep we got up and met with my son Philip and his friends. During our meeting, coffee and time of study Hannah expressed her concern about whether or not she was ready for an overnight babysitting job. **It was clear that she had some very real concerns and quite frankly she looked scared, so again we prayed together.** After our meeting we wandered over to Half Priced Books. I took a very quick peek at the Bible section and the kids were standing behind me talking. After about a minute I turned and began to walk back toward the door and I looked at Hannah. Hannah was looking past me and was smiling as though she was receiving something very comforting. I stood quietly watching her. **Hannah with a look of excitement on her face said that she had just received a "sign from God". She explained that God had showed her a book titled "It's not about me", with the following books next to it: "Believe", "I [God] will carry [or I will be with] you" and "Big girls don't cry". Hannah received this as a sign** from the LORD and she said "I will be fine now, it's going to be ok". **From that moment on Hannah seemed as though a load had been lifted from her shoulders.** It was exciting for me to be an observer in this process. Hannah received the message from God, she received it in faith, and was confident in the outcome as God was in it-and it went just fine.

Hebrews 11

[6]**And without faith it is impossible to please Him [God], for he who comes to God must believe that He is and that He is a rewarder of those who seek Him.**

BROCK LESNER

My son Philip was living in the lower level of my parents' home for about 2 years, on one occasion he was watching T.V. and I went and sat down with him. Philip was watching a fight between two men who were in a cage, they were boxing, and kicking each other, it was very violent and upsetting to watch. One of the men was named Brock Lesner and he had his opponent pined on the ground-he was literally beating this man to death. I felt very bad for the man being beaten and I was angry with the man beating him. I felt the Spirit of the LORD prompt me to prayer and to proclaim out loud that "the man being beaten would win the match". **I prayed to myself "LORD let this man who is being beaten win the match"** I did not speak out loud as I was timid, doubtful and disobedient. At that very moment (and it still amazes me) the man on the bottom who was being beaten somehow, flipped around and grabbed the leg of the man that was beating him and he twisted his leg in such a way that he conceded the fight in great pain- and it all happened in a matter of seconds. O how I wish that I had that opportunity back, how I wish that I had been bold for the LORD at that moment and proclaimed it out loud as I was prompted to do.

1 Samuel 17

Goliath's Challenge

⁴⁰He took his stick in his hand and chose for himself five smooth stones from the brook, and put them in the shepherd's bag which he had, even in his pouch, and his sling was in his hand; and he approached the Philistine. ⁴¹Then the Philistine came on and approached David, with the shield-bearer in front of him. ⁴²**When the Philistine looked and saw David, he disdained him; for he was but a youth, and ruddy, with a handsome appearance. ⁴³The Philistine said to David, "Am I**

a dog that you come to me with sticks?" And the Philistine cursed David by his gods. [44]The Philistine also said to David, "Come to me, and I will give your flesh to the birds of the sky and the beasts of the field." [45]Then David said to the Philistine, "You come to me with a sword, a spear, and a javelin, but I come to you in the name of the LORD of hosts, the God of the armies of Israel, whom you have taunted. [46]"This day the LORD will deliver you up into my hands, and I will strike you down and remove your head from you. And I will give the dead bodies of the army of the Philistines this day to the birds of the sky and the wild beasts of the earth, that all the earth may know that there is a God in Israel, [47]and that all this assembly may know that the LORD does not deliver by sword or by spear; for the battle is the LORD'S and He will give you into our hands." [48]Then it happened when the Philistine rose and came and drew near to meet David, that David ran quickly toward the battle line to meet the Philistine.

BUT NEVER A VISION LIKE THIS

The visions that I typically receive are within my minds-eye, they are generally like pictures-and I have had many, but never before or since received a vision like this. I was meeting with my mentor early one morning for prayer and he invited me to a gathering to hear from a lady that claimed to have received revelation from the LORD regarding "the Joshua generation". The term "the Joshua generation" referred to the generation below her that would include my kids and grandkids and their strategic purpose during the return of Jesus. At the time I was wrestling with some doctrinal issues and I was not sure if I was going to attend the meeting or not. I explained to my mentor the dilemma that I felt as I was interested in going but was unsure if it was the LORD's will for me. We prayed and asked that the LORD would reveal to me if it was His will for me to attend and as I recall I asked the LORD to please let me know soon and then I left for work.

About mid-day, around first break or lunchtime I had what felt like a vivid and **clear memory** of a recent meeting in the park where our home church frequently met. In this **"memory"** the group was sitting on picnic tables and there was a middle aged lady with very short white hair holding handouts; the lady was preparing to pass out the handouts and then address the group. **Let me say this again, this felt just like I was recalling a memory.** My first response to this **"memory"** was **"oh yes, I remember that"**. I then became a bit confused as I scanned my memory as to when that memory was - it did not seem to make sense, my question was "when did this happen?" As I scanned my recent past I realized that this did not happen.

The timing of the vision was perfect, right before my break, and I was able to call my Pastor and I told him of my memory dilemma; my questions to him were, **"Did this happen?"**, and **"When did this happen?"**, **"I can't remember this happening though I seem to be**

27

remembering every detail of this event". My Pastor laughed out loud and said no that did not happen however, he said that he had just gotten off of the phone with Leslie, the lady that was planning to present "the Joshua generation" to the group. He said that my description match her description as she was indeed middle aged and had short whitish hair, and that they had just discussed her bringing handouts to the group.

I received this as conformation for me to go to the meeting. We had requested from the LORD a sign and the LORD quickly responded with what I received as a "YES, YOU CAN GO".

Isaiah 7

[10]**Then the LORD spoke [through the prophet Isaiah] again to Ahaz, saying,** [11]**"Ask a sign for yourself from the LORD your God; make it deep as Sheol or high as heaven."** [12]But Ahaz said, "I will not ask, nor will I test the LORD!" [13]Then he said, "Listen now, O house of David! Is it too slight a thing for you to try the patience of men, that you will try the patience of my God as well? [14]**"Therefore the Lord Himself will give you a sign: Behold, a virgin will be with child and bear a son, and she will call His name Immanuel.** [15]"He will eat curds and honey at the time He knows enough to refuse evil and choose good. [16]"For before the boy will know enough to refuse evil and choose good, the land whose two kings you dread will be forsaken.

CHECK THE TIME AND RUN THE RACE

Several days ago, as I was driving and I saw a man running along the side of the road. I noted that he had just rounded a corner and he looked at his watch and checked his time while he ran. I was reminded of the days some thirty years ago that I too was a runner. I could appreciate his looking at his watch to check the time and compare it to his goal for the pace that he was running. He seemed mindful of the goal and perhaps he was in pursuit of excelling beyond what he had thought possible. This man was thin and svelte; he was built like a greyhound and looked as though he was well prepared and disciplined for this event. Though I admired this man's apparent willingness to take so seriously this albeit temporal race, I felt a sense of pity for this man who was investing so much in this his temporary body. The LORD spoke to me regarding this man's preparation and his seemingly high regard and efforts as it pertained to this earthly body and race. **God also spoke to me regarding our need to focus on His goal for us, to prepare, to train and live in such a way as to win the race that He has set before us-our eternal race, not the temporal.** The LORD God has commanded us to **"run in such a way as to win" (1ˢᵗ Corinthians 9:24),** as He has referred to our pursuit of Him and the advancement of His Kingdom. Be wise, as the writer of the Proverbs says **"he [or she] who is wise wins souls" (Proverbs 11:30)**. Though our race will look entirely different from that of the world, ours will be a race to serve the LORD through: our service to others, to give generously, to share and live out the Gospel of the LORD, to be willing to do as we are called to do at a moment's notice... Our race will be a race of endurance in the LORD, and in His discipline, and, it will be nothing like that of the race of the world and of those serving in the world system-it will be a different pursuit in every way.

[16] For if I [Paul] preach the gospel, I have nothing to boast of, for I am under compulsion; for woe is me if I do not preach the gospel. [17] For if I do this voluntarily, I have a reward; but if against my will, I have a stewardship entrusted to me…[19] For though I am free from all *men*, I have made myself a slave to all, so that I may win more… [22] To the weak I became weak, that I might win the weak; I have become all things to all men, so that I may by all means save some. [23] **I do all things for the sake of the gospel, so that I may become a fellow partaker of it. [24] Do you not know that those who run in a race all run, but *only* one receives the prize? Run in such a way that you may win. [25] Everyone who competes in the games exercises self-control in all things. They then *do it* to receive a perishable wreath, but we [who are persuaded into the Kingdom of God through the LORD Jesus] an imperishable. [26] Therefore I run in such a way, as not without aim; I box in such a way, as not beating the air; [27] but I discipline my body and make it my slave, so that, after I have preached to others, I myself will not be disqualified.**

CHI-CHI'S MURMUR

Our family dog Chi-Chi had developed a heart murmur and it was so pronounced that we could hear her coming down the hall and from across the room-seriously. There were times that during a storm while she was hiding under the bed for security and safety I could literally hear her heart murmur whooshing and whooshing and I knew she was there without even looking under the bed. The murmur was very loud. We began to ask the LORD to heal Chi-Chi's heart as we were very concerned for her health. Time passed, perhaps months and one day my Mom mentioned that she did not hear Chi Chi's heart murmur anymore and she asked if I was able to hear it. I said "no Mom, I do not hear Chi's-Chi's murmur". I was amazed that I had completely forgotten about Chi-Chi's murmur and we were immediately reminded that we had been in prayer for Chi-Chi's healing. What a great demonstration of the LORD's power, love and concern for us and for the animals.

JONAH 4:11

"And should I [YHWH, LORD God] not have compassion on Nineveh, the great city in which there are more than 120,000 persons who do not know the difference between their right and left hand, as well as many animals?"

CRAIG AND "THE SIGN"

As I was driving near my home in Brooklyn Park, MN I frequently saw a man walking along 85th Ave. a very busy boulevard. He looked to be in his 50's, he walked bent over and his long hair draped over his face. His hair was messy, his clothes looked worn and dirty, he marched along very deliberately walking fast with his head down watching the road out in front of him and he carried a backpack of some kind with him. **He looked like the kind of man that the world disregards and makes fun of.** My heart went out to this man, he looked like he has had a difficult life and an interesting story, and I was hoping to meet him someday but was not sure how that would happen. I recall pointing this man out to my daughter Hannah on a number of occasions telling her that I felt drawn to this man and that "I would bet that he has an interesting life story". **On one occasion I asked Hannah if we could pray for this man, and we did pray "that he would be a believer in Jesus-that he would be drawn to and saved by the LORD".** As I recall, the next time that I saw this man walking I recognized him from a distance and everything about him looked the same: his hair, his walk, his cloths all looked as it always did, with the exception of two things but they were hard to figure out from a distance. As I got closer to him I saw that there was a full-page signs on his front and back with a message that I could not quite make-out. As I drove closer I read the words clearly and boldly printed on signs on his front and back **"I Love Jesus of Nazareth"**. I rejoiced and shared with my daughter Hannah that the Lord had answered our prayers. On another occasion I was able to stop and talk to this man, he was timid, and he seemed reluctant to talk to me at first, as though he had been hurt in the past, he seemed meek, kind, friendly and loving; his name is Craig and he knows the Lord.

Hebrews 13

[1]Let love of the brethren continue. [2]Do not neglect to show hospitality to strangers, for by this some have entertained angels without knowing it.

"DADDY I'M COLD!!"

Years ago I would pick up my daughter Hannah after school on Thursday afternoons to spend time together. We would typically go to a park and sit on a blanket, I would pack snack foods, sandwiches and drinks and we ate, chatted, read...

On this particular occasion, Hannah did homework, and I was studying through some ministry material; Hannah was interested in the material so I read it to her and we talked about it as we read. We were on a hill, Hannah was laying on a blanket that was spread out; she was laying all the way over to one side of the blanket and I was sitting up the hill about 5 feet from Hannah. It was an early fall day, on the cool side when the clouds shielded the sun. As I was reading and asking Hannah questions about the reading **Hannah stated emphatically 'Daddy! I'm cold!'** I immediately started in motion to cover her, I set the material down and I moved to stand-up, **at that very second a significant gust of wind blew and it caught the blanket and draped the blanket over Hannah covering her perfectly.** From the moment that Hannah said "Daddy I'm cold" to her being covered was no more than a few seconds. We looked at each other and knew without any question that God, Hannah's Father had heard her and met her request with a loving gust of wind. It was wonderful-and still is.

JOEL Chapter 2

[28]"It will come about after this
that I [YHWH, LORD God] will pour out My Spirit on all
mankind;
and your sons and daughters will prophesy,
your old men will dream dreams,
your young men will see visions.
[29]"Even on the male and female servants
I will pour out My Spirit in those days.

DAVID AND THE SEMINARIAN

On this particular occasion as I watched God demonstrate His timing, I could hardly believe my eyes and ears.

Several years ago my good friends David and Shannon were having problems in their marriage, we all agreed that getting together to go through a previously recorded relationship seminar would be a good idea. It was my assignment to get together with David and Shannon in their lower level apartment at 5th and Fry Street in St. Paul to facilitate the group. My daughter Hannah frequently joined us for these meetings on Friday evening, typically we would eat a meal, watch the message, discuss the session and pray. It was clear to see the involvement of the enemy on those Friday evening meetings. At that particular time David was dealing with some issues related to drugs and alcohol abuse. This Friday evening we got together and assembled in the living room, all but David were in attendance and we decided to begin on time. David later arrived intoxicated and there was immediate conflict between David and Shannon. **David and Shannon argued in the back bedroom about David's drinking, the discussion became heated as the recorded seminars teacher began discussing the topic of a drinking husband and the effects on the family; this was not staged, they were not listening as they were in the back bedroom arguing and we were in the living room. As David and Shannon would argue about something the teacher would deal with that topic, or the teacher would discuss a topic and then David and Shannon would argue about that very thing.** This was not planned and this was a very small part of this marriage seminar, as I recall of the many sessions this was the only segment dealing with this subject of "the drinking husband". **As David stumbled out of the bedroom and into the living room near the front door, the teacher of the recorded marriage seminar switched modes and began to describe the drinking husband preparing to leave his home and family while he was intoxicated.**

37

I was seeing and hearing the teacher describing on the T.V. what I was seeing unfold in the house around me to the smallest detail as though the teacher was commenting on David and Shannon's situation. I recognized that the LORD was declaring His presence and I pointed it out to the others, as we continued to watch and hear the conflict we listened to the commentator as he was describing exactly what was unfolding as though it were a live performance. I watched in amazement as the teacher described the drunken husband's behavior and the effects on the family, his disrupting the family, and then his leaving the family and "walking out of the door and leaving his family". This all took place with precision timing as David was disrupting the household and walked out the door leaving his family behind. **David literally was walking out of the door intoxicated as this recorded commentator was saying the words "the drunken husband opens the door and walks out of the door, closing the door, leaving his family behind". As the commentator said the words "…he closes the door leaving his family behind" David closed the door, leaving his family behind. It was amazing-still is. .**

Psalm 139

[1]O LORD, You have searched me and known me. [2]You know when I sit down and when I rise up; You understand my thought from afar. [3]You scrutinize my path and my lying down, and are intimately acquainted with all my ways.
[4]Even before there is a word on my tongue, behold, O LORD, You know it all. [5]You have enclosed me behind and before, and laid Your hand upon me. [6]Such knowledge is too wonderful for me; it is too high, I cannot attain to it. [7]Where can I go from Your Spirit? Or where can I flee from Your presence? [8]If I ascend to heaven, You are there; If I make my bed in Sheol [the place of the dead], behold, You are there. [9]If I take the wings of the dawn, if I dwell in the remotest part of the sea, [10]Even there Your hand will lead me, and Your right hand will lay hold of me. [11]If I say, "Surely the darkness will overwhelm me, and the light around me will be night," [12]even the darkness is not dark to You, and the night is as bright as the day. Darkness and light are alike to You [LORD God]. [13]For You formed my inward parts; You wove me in my mother's womb.

DAY 10

I recall that it was early into my fast, and based upon the dreams that I received on days 20 and 30 it is quite likely that this dream may have fallen on day number ten, though I am not certain. In this dream I was standing looking at my wife Linda, as we were standing together I noted three other ladies that were all the same person, there were a total of 4 Linda's, they all looked essentially the same, they were all smoking, though they were dressed differently standing side by side. Though they looked the same they were all four wearing different sets and styles of clothing. I was not sure of the meaning though I felt that they were an indication of or representations of different identities, different adaptations of the same person. Later I was told that Linda was struggling with several things that were "taking the place of God in her life", and she asked others for prayer. Linda seems to be doing very well now.

Amos 3

All the Tribes Are Guilty
[1]Hear this word which the LORD has spoken against you, sons of Israel, against the entire family which He brought up from the land of Egypt:
[2]"You only have I chosen among all the families of the earth;
Therefore I will punish you for all your iniquities."
[3]Do two men walk together unless they have made an appointment?
[4]Does a lion roar in the forest when he has no prey?
Does a young lion growl from his den unless he has captured something?
[5]Does a bird fall into a trap on the ground when there is no bait in it?
Does a trap spring up from the earth when it captures nothing at all?

[6]If a trumpet is blown in a city will not the people tremble?
If a calamity occurs in a city has not the LORD done it?
[7]Surely the Lord GOD does nothing
Unless He reveals His secret counsel
To His servants the prophets.
[8]A lion has roared! Who will not fear?
The Lord GOD has spoken! Who can but prophesy?

DAY 20-THE MAN THAT EXPLAINED MY LIFE TO ME

I believe that the enemy is unable to read our minds, though he does speak into our minds, and he listens to us speak to others. He reads what we write, he takes meticulous notes regarding the details of our lives and conversations. The enemy will tune-in to our conversations, our gossip, our arguments and even our prayers as he will glean information that he will try to exploit, to tempt us or even lie to us about others and God. Therefore, I am reluctant to speak at times in conversation and even out loud in prayer as vital information is being passed. The LORD God on the other hand knows our hearts and our thoughts.

This is information about me that I am quite sure that the enemy knows all too well. I struggle with fasting; fasting is very difficult for me and I have tried over and over in the flesh to fast, and I have often failed. I realize that the flesh is weak, the Spirit is willing and in Him all things are possible. I have been seeking the LORD regarding my past and the long term consequence of my sins. As I seek the Lord on this matter I continue to hear His "still-small" voice prompting me to "fast". God does not want to torture me but he wants me/us to resist and deny the strong desires (Greek, "epithumia" often translated "lusts") of the flesh to serve Him-God wants us to be disciplined. Twenty days into this partial fast I had a very interesting dream.

In the dream I was greeted by a small group of people who quietly met with me and delivered me to "a man of wisdom and discernment". We were meeting outdoors at what seemed to be a farm or a ranch of some kind, it was a very relaxed atmosphere and there were people quietly standing around and listening intently. The man that looked to be in his early thirties began to tell me about my life, I do not recall saying anything as I listened. **The man explained that my losing my medical license, and being incarcerated was a result of my sin and** of "God's grace"; he attached my sin and my so called "difficult life experiences" to the grace of God. He was explaining to me that God had graciously removed me from a career that was not healthy for me. This wise man went on to describe how the LORD was using my history, redeeming it and making it fruitful.

Joel 2

[12]"Yet even now," declares the LORD, 'return to Me with all your heart,
and with fasting, weeping and mourning; [13]and rend your heart and not your garments '
now return to the LORD your God, for He is gracious and compassionate,
slow to anger, abounding in lovingkindness and relenting of evil.
[14]Who knows whether He [LORD God] will not turn and relent and leave a blessing behind Him... Consecrate a fast, proclaim a solemn assembly... [21]Do not fear, O land, rejoice and be glad,
For the LORD has done great things. [22]Do not fear, beasts of the field...
[23]So rejoice, O sons of Zion, and be glad in the LORD your God;
For He has given you the early rain for your vindication and He has poured down for you the rain,
the early and latter rain as before. [24]The threshing floors will be full of grain,
and the vats will overflow with the new wine and oil.
[25]"Then I [YHWH, LORD GOD] will make up to you for the years That the swarming locust has eaten...
[26]"You will have plenty to eat and be satisfied and praise the name of the LORD your God,
Who has dealt wondrously with you; then My people will never be put to shame.
[27]"Thus you will know that I am in the midst of Israel, and that I am the LORD your God,
and there is no other; and My people will never be put to shame.

DAY 30

On day thirty of my partial fast I had a dream that I was sitting across from my wife at a table; it seemed to be in an office though I could see nothing but my wife as she was: nicely dressed, pleasant looking and pretty. We were talking nicely together. As we were sitting I realized that she looked younger, perhaps in her late 20s to her early 30s, she is now about 45 years old. The last time that we had had a nice talk like this would have been in about 1997, some 21 years prior to this dream. At that time Hannah would have been about 1 year old and Philip 9 years old and that would have been about or shortly before our breakup in 1998. *In this dream as we were talking and I was able to say things to my wife that I have not been able to communicate to her (telling her that I love her and that I am sorry for not treating her better…) as she has since "remarried"- it would not be appropriate for me to do so, though I have wanted to tell her these things many times.* It is interesting that the LORD has confirmed Himself on these pivotal days, that is, on day 10, day 20, and now day 30. It is as though He were giving signs of encouragement. As you may recall day 20 I was blessed to have been given a dream of a man in his early to mid-thirties explained my life's events and disappointments as He related to me that it was all related to my sin and God's grace. It made perfect sense at the time; and does now; though with my limited vocabulary it seems difficult to articulate. It seems that during this fast the LORD is helping me to work through the difficult times and questions I have had about my life. God is kind, and the kindness of the LORD leads men to repentance, (Greek metanoia), literally a change of perspective (See Romans 2:4).

Genesis 41

[1] **Now it happened at the end of two full years that Pharaoh had a dream,** and behold, he was standing by the Nile. [2] And lo, from the

Nile there came up seven cows, sleek and fat; and they grazed in the marsh grass. ³ Then behold, seven other cows came up after them from the Nile, ugly and gaunt, and they stood by the *other* cows on the bank of the Nile. ⁴ The ugly and gaunt cows ate up the seven sleek and fat cows. Then Pharaoh awoke. ⁵ He fell asleep and dreamed a second time; and behold, seven ears of grain came up on a single stalk, plump and good. ⁶ Then behold, seven ears, thin and scorched by the east wind, sprouted up after them. ⁷ The thin ears swallowed up the seven plump and full ears. Then Pharaoh awoke, and behold, *it was* a dream. ⁸ Now in the morning his spirit was troubled, so he sent and called for all the magicians of Egypt, and all its wise men. **And Pharaoh told them his dreams, but there was no one who could interpret them to Pharaoh.** ⁹ Then the chief cupbearer spoke to Pharaoh, saying, "I would make mention today of my *own* offences. ¹⁰ Pharaoh was furious with his servants, and he put me in confinement in the house of the captain of the bodyguard, *both* me and the chief baker. ¹¹ **We had a dream on the same night, he and I; each of us dreamed according to the interpretation of his *own* dream. ¹² Now a Hebrew youth *was* with us there, a servant of the captain of the bodyguard, and we related *them* to him, and he interpreted our dreams for us.** To each one he interpreted according to his *own* dream. ¹³ And just as he interpreted for us, so it happened; he restored me in my office, but he hanged him."

¹⁴ Then Pharaoh sent and called for Joseph, and they hurriedly brought him out of the dungeon; and when he had shaved himself and changed his clothes, he came to Pharaoh. ¹⁵ **Pharaoh said to Joseph, "I have had a dream, but no one can interpret it; and I have heard it said about you, that when you hear a dream you can interpret it."** ¹⁶ **Joseph then answered Pharaoh, saying, "It is not in me; God will give Pharaoh a favorable answer."** ¹⁷ So Pharaoh spoke to Joseph, "In my dream, behold, I was standing on the bank of the Nile; ¹⁸ and behold, seven cows, fat and sleek came up out of the Nile, and they grazed in the marsh grass. ¹⁹ Lo, seven other cows came up after them, poor and very ugly and gaunt, such as I had never seen for ugliness in all the land of Egypt; ²⁰ and the lean and ugly cows ate up the first seven fat cows. ²¹ Yet when they had devoured them, it could not be detected that they had devoured them, for they were just as ugly as before. Then I awoke. ²² I saw also in my dream, and behold, seven ears, full and good, came up on a single stalk; ²³ and lo, seven ears, withered, thin, *and* scorched by the east wind, sprouted up after them; ²⁴ and the thin ears swallowed the seven good ears. Then I told it to the

magicians, but there was no one who could explain it to me."

²⁵ Now Joseph said to Pharaoh, **"Pharaoh's dreams are one *and the same*; God has told to Pharaoh what He is about to do**. ²⁶ The seven good cows are seven years; and the seven good ears are seven years; the dreams are one *and the same*. ²⁷ The seven lean and ugly cows that came up after them are seven years, and the seven thin ears scorched by the east wind will be seven years of famine. ²⁸ It is as I have spoken to Pharaoh: God has shown to Pharaoh what He is about to do. ²⁹ Behold, seven years of great abundance are coming in all the land of Egypt; ³⁰ and after them seven years of famine will come, and all the abundance will be forgotten in the land of Egypt, and the famine will ravage the land. ³¹ So the abundance will be unknown in the land because of that subsequent famine; for it *will be* very severe. ³² **Now as for the repeating of the dream to Pharaoh twice, *it means* that the matter is determined by God, and God will quickly bring it about.**

DEAD FISH ON THE BEACH

It seems that the LORD will use all of nature to declare His glory and to reach out to mankind. With me God has used: dogs, birds, trees, deer…and just about everything else to get my attention; and on this occasion He used a dead fish. I was traveling to Florida with my wife, our son Philip, and our newborn daughter Hannah, it must have been about 1997 as Hannah is now 22 years old. We were going down to visit my wife's parents who had moved from Saint Paul, MN to Destin, FL. We were traveling to Florida from Des Moines, IA where I was attending Medical School. While en route I struck up a conversation with a group of people sitting near us on the plane and someone suggested that "while on the beach I should look for one of those fish bones that looks like Christ on the Cross". When they made the comment I suspected that it may be some vague resemblance of a cross if you look at it from the right angle and with enough imagination. As I recall they were adamant about this remarkable fish decomposing at sea and leaving behind a bone that looked "just like a cross with an image of Jesus on it".

One morning while I was running on the beach in Destin, FL. the sun was peeking over the horizon and I enjoyed seeing the great stuff that had washed up the previous night. **While scanning the area, my eyes locked onto a small (perhaps a 3"x5") white fragment on the beach, I picked it up I realized that it was a bony remnant. This bony fragment was the perfect image of the Christ on the cross just as our appointed travel companions had described.**

47

Romans 1

[18]For the wrath of God is revealed from heaven against all ungodliness and unrighteousness of men who suppress the truth in unrighteousness, **[19]because that which is known about God is evident within them; for God made it evident to them. [20]For since the creation of the world His invisible attributes, His eternal power and divine nature, have been clearly seen, being understood through what has been made, so that they [mankind] are without excuse.**

DEODORANT, SHAMPOO, BOOTS AND BELTS...

It never ceases to amaze me how the Lord has provided in great ways for the so-called "small and insignificant" things of life. There have been countless times that I have run out of things like: deodorant, shampoo, belts, underwear, clothing...and then it shows up. **For instance, the day that I ran out of deodorant I was walking past Shannon who was unloading a box at the food shelf where we were volunteering, she was not aware of my need for deodorant and as I walked past her she handed me a stick of deodorant and said "do you need this?", as far as I know it was the only stick of deodorant. Thank you LORD!**

On another occasion I had just run out of shampoo and I was wondering how the LORD would provide for this need. As I drove up to the food shelf I saw that there was a very large bottle of shampoo sitting all alone on the back steps as though it were waiting for me; it looked to have been discarded. I went in and inquired about the shampoo and nobody had any idea of where it came from or where it was going; though the top was cracked the rest of the large bottle was fine so I thanked the LORD for His gift.

I was in need of boots and I was in prayer for a pair. As I drove past a park bench in the light of day in the busy suburb of Saint Paul, MN I saw a pair of boots sitting all alone and I began to pull the car over. My daughter Hannah said "Dad! You can't take those boots" and I explained that I had been in prayer for boots. I agreed with Hannah that if the boots remained there "until tomorrow" that I was then to take them, she agreed and they were there the next day, in clear daylight right there on the bus bench in a busy St. Paul suburb.
Thank you LORD!

On one occasion as I was walking and I was praying for jeans. I looked over and lying in the road was a very nice pair of fine fitting jeans. Thank you LORD!

My belt was cracked, broken and "on its last leg". I was wondering how the LORD would be providing for this need. My dad who was unaware of this need asked if I could use a few new belts that he had bought and would not fit him, they were new and fit perfect. I passed one belt on to my Pastor/mentor who said that he was in need of a belt and he did not want to spend the LORD's resources on one as there were so many needs in the body. Thank you LORD!

Isaiah 45

¹**Thus says the LORD to Cyrus His anointed, Whom I have taken by the right hand,**
To subdue nations before him and to loose the loins of kings;
To open doors before him so that gates will not be shut:
²**"I will go before you and make the rough places smooth;**
I will shatter the doors of bronze and cut through their iron bars.
³"I will give you the treasures of darkness
And hidden wealth of secret places,
So that you may know that it is I,
The LORD, the God of Israel, who calls you by your name.
⁴**"For the sake of Jacob My servant,**
And Israel My chosen one,
I have also called you by your name;
I have given you a title of honor
Though you have not known Me.
⁵"I [YHWH, God] am the LORD, and there is no other;
Besides Me there is no God
I will gird you, though you have not known Me;
⁶That men may know from the rising to the setting of the sun
That there is no one besides Me [YHWH, LORD God].
I am the LORD, and there is no other,
⁷**The One forming light and creating darkness; causing well-being**
and creating calamity;
I am the LORD who does all these.

DO WE FIGHT THE ENEMY BY DAY
AND PLAY WITH HIM BY NIGHT?

A good question; do we seek the LORD by day and play with the enemy by night? Are we to sing the songs of the world system with our best, and sing to the LORD with our least? Are we to bow low to the things of the world, that is the: DOW, sports, entertainment, careers, our 401k and retirement portfolio, education, or even religious activities apart from the LORD with the best of our: time, energy, efforts, resources… and fane or fake our reverence for God. And then as if to throw the LORD a bone will we sit in church on Sunday only to rush home in time for the "the big game"? Are we to love and serve by day and in the dark of night to hoard and covet while we disregard the needs of others? In light of the Scriptures speaking more frequently and clearly about our storing up money for ourselves than issues of: homosexuality, drunkenness and murder, yet and in the same vein, are we to sow into the flesh and into our own security with the best years (or days) of our lives even if "well intended" with the intention of stockpiling enough wealth for ourselves that we will "later give to the LORD in ministry" while we never really get around to that. This is the religious myth far too often regarded, it is destructive to those sewing into it, and this hypocritical practice is destructive to the church as it is perpetuated from generation to generation. I believe that such service to self and disobedience to the teaching of the LORD demonstrates greater faith in the world system than in God. Without faith in God it is impossible to please Him (Hebrews 11:6) and the myth that it is ok or "normal" to serve the world system and then seek the LORD as if to placate or pacify Him is a counterproductive lie from hell. I have come to realize that though this is far too often the case and though I too was walking this path with "good intention" with the desire of "having my cake and eating it too", this is vanity and as Solomon describes "chasing after the wind" (see the Book of Ecclesiastes) and dead works. In a universe of black and white with no gray area, where there are only two potential recipients of our: praise, service and honor, that is the LORD YHWH, and the enemy. In a universe of two places, that being first-place and last-place; we will decide who will be placed in the only first place of honor and who will receive the "second" or "last-place"; that being the place of dishonor, and disregard.

Second (last) place is no place for God.

It is my sincere concern that as Scripture has told us "without faith [in and for all things, not simply trust in God for salvation] it is impossible to please God" therefore if our efforts are given to the collection of money even with the "intent" of doing good when we have "enough" (and we never will), then by definition we have given our greatest respect and regard to the money. Thus we have regarded greater the "money and the world system" than the LORD God. In this case it seems that we have replaced LORD God with our god (money); we have indeed set our hearts toward the very place from where we were delivered, we have in our hearts "returned to Egypt". (See Numbers chapter 11)

Matthew 7

[13] "Enter through the narrow gate; for the gate is wide and the way is broad that leads to destruction, and there are many who enter through it. [14] For the gate is small and the way is narrow that leads to life, and there are few who find it. [15] "Beware of the false prophets, who come to you in sheep's clothing, but inwardly are ravenous wolves. [16] You will know them by their fruits. Grapes are not gathered from thorn *bushes* nor figs from thistles, are they? [17] So every good tree bears good fruit, but the bad tree bears bad fruit. [18] A good tree cannot produce bad fruit, nor can a bad tree produce good fruit. [19] Every tree that does not bear good fruit is cut down and thrown into the fire. [20] So then, you will know them by their fruits.

[21] **"Not everyone who says to Me, 'Lord, Lord,' will enter the kingdom of heaven, but he who does the will of My Father who is in heaven *will enter*. [22] Many will say to Me on that day, 'Lord [master], Lord [master], did we not prophesy in Your name, and in Your name cast out demons, and in Your name perform many miracles?' [23] And then I will declare to them, 'I never knew you; DEPART FROM ME, YOU WHO PRACTICE LAWLESSNESS."**
[24] **"Therefore everyone who hears these words of Mine and acts on them, may be compared to a wise man who built his house on the**

52

rock. **²⁵ And the rain fell, and the floods came, and the winds blew and slammed against that house; and *yet* it did not fall, for it had been founded on the rock. ²⁶ Everyone who hears these words of Mine and does not act on them, will be like a foolish man who built his house on the sand. ²⁷ The rain fell, and the floods came, and the winds blew and slammed against that house; and it fell—and great was its fall."**

²⁸ When Jesus had finished these words, the crowds were amazed at His teaching; ²⁹ for He was teaching them as *one* having authority, and not as their scribes.

EDDIE AND THE DUNGEON

Sarah is a dear sister in the LORD, she has two sons, Eddie is about 7 and Joshua is about 4 y/o. Eddie and Joshua are very special young men. Eddie was recently put on a trial of an ADHD medication; this was a decision that was difficult for Sarah. Eddie came to church on the medication several weeks ago and he was very well behaved and he sat still. On my way home, as I recall, **I had a vision of Eddie locked in a stone dungeon with a wooden arched door, there was hay on the floor and Eddie was crouched over and looking in despair.** I resisted telling Sarah of the vision as I could imagine that it may be difficult and it may even sound judgmental, so I held it for a time. In a conversation with Sarah a few days later, the topic of Eddie and the medication came up, I was reminded of the vision and it seemed an appropriate time to share "the vision of the dungeon" with Sarah and she was receptive. A few days after our talk I received a text from Sarah **"[I] Asked Eddie how he felt about the meds. This boy confirmed your dream [vision]. [Eddie] Said he felt trapped inside something and couldn't get out."** **And in her next message she states, "It's heartbreaking".** Sarah is a fine mother of these two young men, and the enemy would like to destroy them.

Isaiah 44

[21]"Remember these things, O Jacob, and Israel, for you are My servant;
I have formed you, you are My servant,
O Israel, you will not be forgotten by Me [LORD God]. [22]"I have wiped out your transgressions like a thick cloud, and your sins like a heavy mist, return to Me, for I have redeemed you." [23]**Shout for joy, O heavens, for the LORD has done it! Shout joyfully, you lower parts of the earth; break forth into a shout of joy, you mountains,** O forest, and every tree in it; for the LORD has redeemed Jacob

and in Israel He shows forth His glory. [24]Thus says the LORD, your Redeemer, and the one who formed you from the womb, **"I, the LORD, am the maker of all things, stretching out the heavens by Myself and spreading out the earth all alone, [25]Causing the omens of boasters to fail, making fools out of diviners, causing wise men to draw back and turning their knowledge into foolishness, [26]Confirming the word of His servant and performing the purpose of His messengers.**

ELEMENTARY MY DEAR WATSON...
ELEMENTARY

Today as I was driving down the freeway I looked to my left and I saw a woman driving her four-wheel drive vehicle. Her hair and clothes looked stylish, as she pulled forward I looked at some stickers on the back of her vehicles tailgate. The stickers on the back of her vehicle included one about: fishing, hunting, and some other outdoor events, and at the bottom of the right tailgate was an ichthus, otherwise known as "a Jesus fish". As I evaluated "the big picture" I saw what appeared to be a woman who was nicely dressed with a stylish hair-cut, driving an expensive vehicle, she shared her love for: the outdoors, fishing, hunting and Jesus. At face value this picture looked nice and very "American"-a little bit of everything nice on her bumper. However as I looked I felt like I was looking at a picture of a divided heart, a heart in love with many things that were nicely displayed for all to see. I was reminded that God does not want nor does He deserve to be one of our many loves, God deserves to be our exclusive love. In the same way that a spouse does not want nor deserve to be first on a list of many lovers; the LORD God desires and deserves our exclusive devotion. Do we worship the created, aught not we worship the Creator and Him alone? It seems quite elementary, my dear Watson.

Psalm 39
[4] **"LORD, make me to know my end and what the extent of my days is;**
let me know how transient I am.
[5] **"Behold, You have made my days *as* handbreadths, and my lifetime as nothing in Your sight;**
Surely every man at his best is a mere breath... [6] **"Surely every man walks about as a phantom;**
surely they make an uproar for nothing; he amasses *riches* and does not know who will gather them...

[11] "With reproofs You chasten a man for iniquity; You consume as a moth what is precious to him;
Surely every man is a mere breath... [12] "Hear my prayer, O LORD, and give ear to my cry;
do not be silent at my tears; for I am a stranger with You, a sojourner like all my fathers.
[13] "Turn Your gaze away from me that I may smile *again* before I depart and am no more."

"FATHER KNOWS BEST"

This story reminded me of the T.V. series that began in the mid 1950's, **Father Knows Best.** Recall the characters: Jim Anderson, his wife Margaret and their three children: Betty, Bud and Kathy. It seemed that whatever situation the family may have found themselves in, Jim Anderson, the father, led the way through rocky terrain and into clear pastures.

A few weeks ago I was called by a friend in Shakopee, he asked if I could help a young Native American lady, Melda and her family; Melda and her 4 month old son were staying with a friend in Southwestern MN. Melda was in need of a ride to town 17 miles from where she was staying and would be en route to Bismarck, ND where she planned to reunite with her older son. My initial internal response was "why are you asking me to drive 110 plus miles to transport someone 17 miles and then return home, why are you asking me?" It seemed like a ridicules way to spend God's resources not to mention that I strongly dislike taking "road-trips". My response to his request was, "I will pray about it". As I prayed about the mission I felt the LORD clearly say "**I [God] want you to go and show the love of Jesus to this family**". The timing was perfect, it was a day that had I no other plans, I "happened" to have resources for the trip as well as a travel companion willing to go, with all of this in place yet still it made no sense to me, and I resisted. A short time later the cellphone rang and it was none other than Melda who said something to the effect of "I'm Melda, I need a ride to Mankato, I am with a friend and my baby is out of milk, **will you help us?**" As soon as she asked "will you help" I was reminded of Jesus' command **"and whoever shall force you to go one mile, go with him [or her] two. Give to him [or her] who asks of you, and do not turn away from him [or her] who wants to borrow from you." (Matthew 5:41-42)** yet I resisted still and said that I would call her right back. As I prayed it was very quiet, I was getting nothing from the LORD, nothing more than what He had already said to me, **"I [God] want you to go and show the love of Jesus to this family"** God had no reason to tell me again what He had already said once. God was clear in His communication to me and I was resistant to His will. This was inconvenient, expensive and was not my idea of a fun-time, yet the "still small" voice of God said "go", so I reluctantly went.

I picked up my ministry partner at about 5:50 A.M. and we set out. When we got to Melda and her son at about 10:00 A.M. she got right into the car as though we had known her for years, as though it was not unusual for her to take what she could get in the way of help for her and her two small boys. She seemed quiet, resilient, and adaptable, like a seasoned soldier-a leader. When Melda got settled into the car she said that she needed help getting to a bus, that she was in need of help getting a ticket and "could we stop and get something to eat?" There were plenty of impulses driving me to say "Hey! Enough is enough here, I didn't sign up for this!!" but the LORD was testing us while He was showing love to Melda through us, there was no denying that God's hand was at work here, so I remained quiet. We went in search of a bus and a ticket and some lunch. While getting her ticket we were informed that she would not be boarding for about 8 hours, we opted to spend the day with them and drive 110 miles north to Minneapolis and send them out of Minneapolis to Bismarck, ND some 11 hours later. This would prove to be time well spent. We spent the entire day with Melda, a young lady who had heard of the love of Jesus in the past and was now seeing the love of Jesus as He was providing for her and her sons through us, His people. Melda was eager to talk about the things of the LORD and asked early in our journey "So do you guys go to church?" Over the course of the day we heard her story of being raped by her dad at 14 years old, (her dad is currently in prison for that offense) and her being raised by her alcoholic mother. She also shared that she has had Christians around her from the time of her childhood. On the way to Minneapolis we had the opportunity to take her to visit with people from her past that we "just happened" to be good friends with and "just happened" to be near at the time, these were people that Melda identified with and trusted. We had a chance to see walls come down; stereotypes dealt with, relationships mended and reestablished on what seemed to be a healthy and Godly foundation. We also had the opportunity to share the Gospel of Jesus with Melda and she was eager to take the next step praying for the LORD to save her-Melda asked the LORD to come into her life that day.

60

What was presented as a 15-20 minute trip with Melda ended up being an 11 hour opportunity to bear fruit. We were given the opportunity to demonstrate the love of Christ not only to Melda but to an entire culture. It was expensive, time consuming, inconvenient and even illogical at face value. But this is exactly how the LORD often works. Ministry for the LORD, advancing the Kingdom of God certainly comes at a price, and that is exactly how it is supposed to be, and, how it should be as it tests our willingness and regard for God. After a short stop at the Mall of America, "something that I [Melda] always wanted to do" we traveled up 35W from the south, approaching Minneapolis, Melda was snapping pictures of the city skyline as she loved the city, I was happy to be getting close to home as it had been a long 17 hour day. Melda and her son boarded the bus with only a few small glitches and we got home about 10:00 P.M. feeling "spent", but in a good way. When I got home and slipped into bed I said "thank you LORD for the day, truly this was a good and fruitful day", God's response was, "get some sleep, and we will have another good and fruitful day tomorrow-if you are willing".

Proverbs 11:25-31

[25] The generous man will be prosperous, and he who waters will himself be watered. [26] He who withholds grain, the people will curse him, but blessing will be on the head of him who sells *it*. [27] He who diligently seeks good seeks favor, but he who seeks evil, evil will come to him. **[28] He who trusts in his riches will fall, but the righteous will flourish like the *green* leaf. [29] He who troubles his own house will inherit wind,**
And the foolish will be servant to the wisehearted. [30] The fruit of the righteous is a tree of life, and he who is wise wins souls. [31] If the righteous will be rewarded in the earth, how much more the wicked and the sinner!

FIREWORKS IN THE RAIN!!!!

My daughter Hannah is 14y/o, her birthday is August 15th; my son Philip is 22y/o, and his birthday is August 30th. Several years ago I was telling Hannah of how God had given Philip so many birthday gifts on his birthday-Hannah became very quiet and she began to cry. I asked Hannah why she was crying and she said through her tears "God didn't do anything for me on my birthday". **This opened a door for us to talk about the importance of our positioning ourselves so as to receive from the LORD.** We reviewed what Hannah had done on her birthday, she had gone to the mall and shopped, bought earrings and as I recall gone to a movie, she said that she did not see the LORD in it. Philip on the other hand had gone to church, invited friends and family for corporate worship and God's miracles that day were too numerous to recount. For example, on Philip's birthday the Pastor preached on Philip's favorite passage, they played his favorite song twice; God even showed Himself in the midst of an equipment malfunction (VK) and He told me in the presence of Philip "it's ok, you [Todd] can sit down now" as I went to assist in the problem (Philip will know exactly what I am talking about). I took the opportunity to explain to Hannah that we are told "do not love the world nor the things in the world [i.e. the system of the world] if anyone loves the world the love of the Father is not in him [or her]" see 1st John 2:15-17. I tried to explain that there is nothing inherently wrong with what she did, but it may point to what it is that she thinks will bring her happiness and fulfillment. Well she seemed to have gotten the point. The next year Hannah's birthday landed on a Saturday and as was true to form we had the "little-girls-ministry", and Hannah decided to go to church. She said that she felt that it was important for her and the other girls to be there. That afternoon we went and picked up the girls and brought them to church which included the youth-group for the girls and the Spanish speaking worship service for me. As you can imaging, all eyes were on the LORD wondering what He would do for Hannah's birthday. I do not recall many of the details

63

of the night though I do remember the group singing to Hannah and Hannah reporting how special and personal the message was to her, she also said that she saw the LORD in the midst of her very special birthday.

There is one detail that I do remember, and this is great. As we were driving back from church to Stillwater to drop off Megan and the other girls it was raining cats-and-dogs; the rain was "coming down in sheets". We were headed eastbound on 694 it was pouring rain to the point that it was hard for the windshield wipers to keep up. **As we looked over to the left and out in the distance there was an impressive fireworks display in the rain. I said to Hannah "you know that is for you don't you?" Hannah smiled and said "yes" and then Megan chimed-in and said "Hey! I got fireworks on my birthday too". As we talked we recalled fireworks on Megan's birthday as well heading home from church on the same 694 at about the same general area. A birthday gift from the LORD; who can beat that? Fireworks in the rain.**

Proverbs 8

[17]"I [YHWH, LORD God] love those who love me; and those who diligently seek me will find me.

FLYING WHILE TALKING WITH
STAN-THE DREAM WITH THE POLICE

Stan is a good friend and brother in the Lord, he has some very interesting spiritual gifts, and we have been friends for over 30 years. I had a dream that I was alone out in a field, it looked like it could have been an urban field as there seem to be trash lying around on the ground, the field was enclosed by roads on three sides and it looked like a freeway to the east. I recall that the dream was so real that even in the dream I questioned whether this was really happening. **While standing out in the open a gust of wind moved across the field, I lifted my arms perpendicular to my body, I held my hands out to the side as if to grab the gust and fly away. Much to my surprise I was lifted up and began to fly around in a circle using my arms to direct me.** I was very reluctant to go high or far at first as I spent time getting acquainted with my new skill. I was having great fun simply flying in a tight circle close to the ground landing and taking off again; I gradually become more confident and flew higher and expanded my circles-I was thrilled. I called Stan on my cell-phone while flying in a circle and with excitement I was trying to convince him that I was really flying saying "Stan I'm flying right now!"

On another occasion, in a time that Stan and I were praying over the phone on a regular basis and seeing God's great hand move. Again I dreamt that I was in a field at night, to the east was a large field and to the west was a residential area divided by a street. I was feeling uncomfortable, much like a kid skipping school, I felt timid and concerned that we were vulnerable. Stan was in front of me and he encouraged me to follow him and he said that "we would be ok" as though this was something that he did frequently and was well accustomed to doing though this was new to me. Stan and I walked for a short time on the edge of the field. To the west were cars in the middle of the road; the cars were either police cars, an accident or cars pulled over. There were six or so "police" together in the middle of the road and they were talking amongst themselves. It was clear that the police were in opposition to us, and it is likely that they were imposters. They were meeting several hundred yards away and were looking at Stan and me and talking amongst themselves. They then yelled at us "STOP LISTENING IN ON US!" Stan and I kept moving and seemed to laugh together. **I woke and knew that we were doing something very right. It was clear that the police in this dream represented the enemy, Stan and I were operating a covert operation for the LORD and we were frustrating the plan of the enemy.**

Joel 2

[28]**"It will come about after this that I will pour out My Spirit on all mankind; and your sons and daughters will prophesy, your old men will dream dreams, your young men will see visions.** [29]**"Even on the male and female servants I will pour out My Spirit in those days.**

"FOR SIGNS AND FOR SEASONS"

Oh that people would read their Bible's. Our mission to follow the LORD Jesus goes much farther than simply reading our Bibles; however, reading our Bibles is an important discipline-in my opinion. The Bible records lessons of others as they walked with God, and the Bible records the teachings of the Lord. The Bible, this Book that the LORD has written to us He has set before us with no neon lights, bells or whistles attached to it. The Bible is our manual for life. The Bible far too often sits unread while we bask in our own selfishness and languish in a world of entertainment. I have learned to cherish my Bible, as the years go by the inside of my Bible is looking more "war-torn" than the outside of it. If only people would begin to read this great book and request of the LORD that He might open their eyes to this chest of treasures. **I am reminded of sitting across from my Grandma a few days prior to her death, my Bible was between us and she commented "I wish that I had taken the time to read this".**

In the opening pages of the Scriptures we are told "**Then God said, 'Let there be light in the expanse of the heavens** to separate the day from the night, **and let them [stars] be for signs and for seasons...**" (Genesis 1:14). **In the New Testament Jesus referred to Himself as living water, "whoever drinks of the water that I [Jesus of Nazareth] shall give him [or her] shall never thirst; but the water that I shall give him shall become in him [or her] a well of water springing up to eternal life" (John 4:14)**. And again Jesus said, "If any man [or woman] is thirsty, let him [or her] come to Me and drink. He who believes [is persuaded] in Me, as the Scripture said, from his innermost being shall flow rivers of living water" **(John 7:37, 38)**.

Is anyone thirsty? Come to the Water, come to the Well, come all who are thirsty, hurting and broken, come and be healed. Consider the signs and the seasons, the stars in the sky. **What more do you require** oh man, for the LORD Himself to write it in the sky? Well He has, but it seems only a few care to follow to drink and partake. **Consider The Big Dipper in the sky and be persuaded by Him to come and drink deep of the Water.**

It is interesting that the LORD has created the sign of The Big Dipper in the heavens beckoning us to come and drink of Him- please drink.

Joshua 1

[8]**"This book of the law shall not depart from your mouth, but you shall meditate on it day and night, so that you may be careful to do according to all that is written in it; for then you will make your way prosperous, and then you will have success.**

GOD MET WITH PHILIP

I was sitting in the Saturday evening church service and the little girls (Hannah and her group of friends) were in their youth group meeting. I was in prayer and listening to the Pastor address the church group. As I recall Philip was not involved yet and though we were talking about the deeper things of the LORD there seemed to be a disconnect-at least that was my perception. As I was sitting and praying the LORD began to speak to me and it was as though all and everything around me was still and silent. The LORD was speaking to me about **"the God of your fathers"**, more specifically He was explaining to me how it is one thing to hear about God from our relatives or friends, however it is quite another to meet with the LORD personally. This made great sense to me and seemed to be addressing my son Philip. The LORD directed me to the passages in Scripture regarding the Patriarchs: Abraham, Isaac and Jacob; I flipped to Genesis chapter 12 and the LORD had me read Abraham's reaction of faith and his building of an altar after meeting with the LORD, "And the LORD appeared to Abram [later named Abraham] and said 'to your descendants I will give this land'. So he built an altar there to the LORD". **(Genesis 12:7)** God then led me to the life of Isaac, the son of Abraham in Genesis chapter 22 and we read of Isaac who was hearing of the LORD but in chapter 26 we read of God meeting with Isaac personally, and then he seemed a radically changed man "And the LORD appeared to him [Isaac] the same night and said, 'I am the God of your father Abraham; do not fear, for I am with you. I will bless you and multiply your descendants...so he [Isaac] built an altar there..." **(Genesis 26:24)** God then led me to the life of Jacob who was later renamed Israel. Jacob was a deceitful young man who had heard of the God of his father, and like his father Isaac and his grandfather Abram (renamed Abraham) the LORD met personally with Jacob in Genesis chapter 28 and again in Genesis chapter 32, and he too seemed to be a changed man.

I received in faith that the LORD was communicating to me that He wanted to meet with Philip, and in faith I asked Philip if we could meet so as for me to share with him from the LORD, and he agreed. As I recall Philip made an effort, in faith, to meet as we did and I explained to him what I had received from the LORD regarding the LORD wanting to meet with Philip, and I presented the information in faith. Philip seemed to receive the word from the LORD in faith. I encouraged Philip to open his heart and prepare for such a meeting with the LORD. As I recall it was at that time that I began to write Bible study lessons and present them to Philip daily and he did the work. Soon thereafter the LORD indeed began to reveal Himself to Philip, Philip began to testify of the signs and wonders of the LORD and Philip had personal encounters with the LORD. I have watched Philip and I am excited to report that in the process Philip has become a changed man as well.

Isaiah 44
²Thus says the LORD who made you
and formed you from the womb, who will help you,
'Do not fear, O Jacob My servant…whom I have chosen.
³**"For I [YHWH, LORD God] will pour out water on the thirsty land**
and streams on the dry ground; I will pour out My Spirit on your offspring and My blessing on your descendants;
⁴**and they will spring up among the grass like poplars by streams of water.'** ⁵**"This one will say, 'I am the LORD'S'; and that one will call on the name of Jacob; and another will write on his hand, 'Belonging to the LORD,'**
And will name Israel's name with honor. ⁶"Thus says the LORD, the King of Israel and his Redeemer, the LORD of hosts: 'I [LORD God, YHWH] am the first and I am the last, and there is no God besides Me.
⁷"Who is like Me [the creator, LORD God]? Let him proclaim and declare it; yes, let him recount it to Me in order,
from the time that I established the ancient nation.
And let them declare to them the things that are coming and the events that are going to take place.
⁸"Do not tremble and do not be afraid; have I not long since announced it to you and declared it?
And **you are My [YHWH, LORD God's] witnesses, is there any God besides Me,**
or is there any other Rock?
I know of none.'"

GOD SAYING "PLEASE"

There have been times that I have been in prayer and I have heard my words echoed back to me as if the LORD was communicating to me the same message that I was communicating to Him. This happened when I was saying "please" to the LORD and it has happened when I was saying "thank you" to the LORD as well.

On this particular occasion I was alone with the LORD and in prayer, I was saying "please" to the LORD, while in my mind I was filling in the blanks with silent thoughts. I would say "please" then in the silence of my mind I thought "please help me with…", I was repeatedly saying out loud "please" then again silently saying "provide…". Again for the sake of clarity my only audible word was "please" as I recall, with a silent moment of pause. **This time of prayer was unusual for me as I at times did not even know what I was saying "please" for as it seemed most of all an acknowledgement that I was needy and that He is the Provider, that I was in need of receiving and that He is the Giver (James 1:17). This was a simple and humble acknowledgement that He is the Potter and I am the clay (Isaiah 64:8, Romans 9:21).** It was in a moment of time that I seemed to be receiving insight into the reality that we really are just dust and apart from Him we are without hope, this is not just some religious cliché. As I was in prayer and saying the word "please" over and over I heard the word "please" return to me, I said the word "please" and then heard the word "please" as if it were an echo. **Upon hearing the word "please" I was given insight as to what the LORD was communicating to me. I believe that the LORD was saying "please" step out in faith, "please" try Me, "please" be willing to test the limits of faith, "please" stop limiting Me by a life of relative faithlessness. Please live a life walking in radical faith, trusting Me for everything as everything but Me is fake, and phony-a mirage.**

[1]"I [Jesus of Nazareth] am the true vine, and My Father is the vinedresser. [2]"Every branch in Me that does not bear fruit, He takes away; and every branch that bears fruit, He prunes it so that it may bear more fruit. [3]"You are already clean because of the word which I have spoken to you. [4]"Abide in Me, and I in you. As the branch cannot bear fruit of itself unless it abides in the vine, so neither can you unless you abide in Me.[5]"I [Jesus] am the vine, you are the branches; he who abides in Me and I in him, he bears much fruit, for apart from Me you can do nothing. [6]"If anyone does not abide in Me, he is thrown away as a branch and dries up; and they gather them, and cast them into the fire and they are burned. [7]"If you abide in Me, and My words abide in you, ask whatever you wish, and it will be done for you. [8]"My Father is glorified by this, that you bear much fruit, and so prove to be My disciples. [9]"Just as the Father has loved Me, I have also loved you; abide in My love. [10]"If you keep My commandments, you will abide in My love; just as I have kept My Father's commandments and abide in His love. [11]"These things I have spoken to you so that My joy may be in you, and that your joy may be made full. [12]"[Jesus of Nazareth said] This is My commandment, that you love one another, just as I have loved you. [13]"Greater love has no one than this that one lay down his life for his friends.

[14]"You are My [Jesus'] friends if you do what I command you.

GOD SAYING "THANK YOU"

There have been two times that I have been in prayer and I have heard my words echoed back to me as if the LORD Himself was communicating to me the same message that I was communicating to Him. This happened when I was saying "thank you" to the LORD and it has happened when I was saying "please" to the LORD.

On this occasion I was thanking the LORD as I had been working with Ricardo, a young man from Mexico, and I was thankful for this opportunity. Ricardo is the son of an evangelist, Pastor-teacher ministering in a poor Mexican city. Ricardo seemed to be running from the God of his father when I had first met him, Ricardo has great gifts and potential for the LORD and I loved him like a son from almost the first time that I met him. On this particular occasion Ricardo was sharing a recent breakthrough in his faith-a manifestation of the Spirit working in his life. Upon hearing the news and seeing the joy of the LORD in Ricardo face I was feeling intense joy as well as great affirmation of my efforts with Ricardo-I was thanking God for working with Ricardo. **I recall simply saying "thank You LORD, thank You, thank You" and as I was saying "thank You to the LORD for working with Ricardo" I was hearing it echo back to me, as if the LORD Himself was saying "thank you for working with Ricardo" to me. I believe that God was thanking me for my working with Ricardo as well.**

JOHN 15

¹²"[Jesus of Nazareth said] This is My commandment, that you love one another, just as I have loved you. ¹³"Greater love has no one than this, that one lay down his life for his friends. ¹⁴"**You are My [Jesus'] friends if you do what I command you.** ¹⁵"No longer do I call you slaves, for the slave does not know what his master is doing; but I have

73

called you friends, for all things that I have heard from My Father I have made known to you. **¹⁶"You did not choose Me but I chose you, and appointed you that you would go and bear fruit, and that your fruit would remain, so that whatever you ask of the Father in My name He may give to you. ¹⁷"This I command you, that you love one another. ¹⁸"If the world hates you, you know that it has hated Me before it hated you. ¹⁹"If you were of the world, the world would love its own; but because you are not of the world, but I chose you out of the world, because of this the world hates you.**

²⁰"Remember the word that I said to you, 'A slave is not greater than his master ' If they persecuted Me, they will also persecute you; if they kept My word, they will keep yours also. ²¹"But all these things they will do to you for My name's sake, because they do not know the One who sent Me. ²²"If I had not come and spoken to them, they would not have sin, but now they have no excuse for their sin.

²³"He who hates [disregards] Me hates [disregards] My Father also. ²⁴"If I had not done among them the works which no one else did, they would not have sin; but now they have both seen and hated [disregarded] Me and My Father as well. ²⁵"But they have done this to fulfill the word that is written in their Law, 'THEY HATED [disregarded] ME WITHOUT A CAUSE.' **²⁶"When the Helper [Greek, "parakleos" one called alongside as an advocate, a legal representative] comes, whom I will send to you from the Father, that is the Spirit of truth who proceeds from the Father, He will testify about Me,** ²⁷and you will testify also, because you have been with Me from the beginning.

GOD WILL BRING US BACK
FROM WHENCE WE CAME

In our little home-church we have been studying Acts chapter 9, the conversion of "Saul of Tarsus". Saul was traveling on the road to Damascus to; round up, persecute, incarcerate and perhaps kill Christians; he was then met by the LORD, converted and later referred to as Paul. Paul became the human author of much of the New Testament. **After being filled with the Spirit, Saul/Paul testified of Jesus in Damascus, and he witnessed in Jerusalem. As a result of his bold testimony there arose a plot to kill Paul. From there Paul was sent to Tarsus, the very Tarsus from where he came. Paul was sent to the very place that he had lived prior to his conversion that he might bear witness to the truth and show evidence of the life changing work of the LORD.** As we were talking about Paul in church we began to shared stories of how the LORD has taken us back to the very cities, blocks, buildings, rooms and to the people that we interacted with prior to our knowing the Lord. I recalled one of the many examples of this in my own life. On one occasion I was in an evangelistic Bible study on the very plot of land that I had earlier been involved in organized "book making" (gambling)... In another example of doing ministry 5 feet from the place that I did frequent street-drug "deals" as a teen; and the most impressive to me, I live and I am disciplining my mom in this home that I once misbehaved horribly in-I recently baptized my mom in this very home. Interesting that I was just reminded today that quite possibly the greatest miracle that the LORD ever did was to change the hearts of people from their hardened condition and turn them to follow after Him. **God will indeed return us to these very plots of soil and to the same people from our past as an opportunity for us to bear witness to the changing power of the LORD through Jesus, the anointed King.**

The Conversion of Saul

[1] Now Saul [prior to his conversion], still breathing threats and murder against the disciples of the Lord [Jesus], went to the high priest, [2] and asked for letters from him to the synagogues at Damascus, so that if he found any belonging to the Way [that is, followers of the LORD Jesus], both men and women, he might bring them bound to Jerusalem. [3] As he was traveling, it happened that he was approaching Damascus, and suddenly a light from heaven flashed around him; [4] and he fell to the ground and heard a voice saying to him, **"Saul, Saul, why are you persecuting Me?"** [5] **And he said, "Who are You, Lord?" And He** *said,* **"I am Jesus whom you are persecuting,** [6] but get up and enter the city, and it will be told you what you must do." [7] The men who traveled with him stood speechless, hearing the voice but seeing no one. [8] Saul got up from the ground, and though his eyes were open, he could see nothing; and leading him by the hand, they brought him into Damascus. [9] And he was three days without sight, and neither ate nor drank…

Saul [later renamed the Apostle, Paul] Begins to Preach Christ

Now for several days he [Saul, later named Paul] was with the disciples who were at Damascus, [20] and immediately he began to proclaim Jesus in the synagogues, saying, **"He is the Son of God."** [21] **All those hearing him [Saul, later named Paul] continued to be amazed, and were saying, "Is this not he who in Jerusalem destroyed those who called on this name, and who had come here for the purpose of bringing them bound before the chief priests?"** [22] **But Saul kept increasing in strength and confounding the Jews who lived at Damascus by proving that this Jesus is the Christ.** [23] When many days had elapsed, the Jews plotted together to do away with him, [24] but their plot became known to Saul They were also watching the gates day and night so that they might put him to death; [25] but his disciples took him by night and let him down through an opening in the wall, lowering him in a large basket. [26] **When he came to Jerusalem, he was trying to associate with the disciples; but they were all afraid of him, not believing that he was a disciple.** [27] But Barnabas took hold of him and brought him to the apostles and described to them how he had seen the Lord on the road, and that He had talked to him, and how at Damascus he had spoken out boldly in the name of Jesus. [28] And he was with them, moving about freely in Jerusalem, speaking out boldly in the name of the Lord. [29] And he was talking and arguing with the Hellenistic Jews; but they were attempting to put him to death. **³⁰But when the brethren learned of it, they brought him [Saul of Tarsus] down to Caesarea and sent him away to Tarsus [the very place from whence he came].** ³¹So the church throughout all Judea and Galilee and Samaria enjoyed peace, being built up; and going on in the fear of the Lord and in the comfort of the Holy Spirit, it continued to increase.

GREG'S EXTENSION OF (VOICE) BENEFITS

I have a very good and longtime friend Greg, Greg is about 5 years my senior and he has known the LORD for about 3-5 years longer than I have. In our younger years we sought God together, our families shared our meals together, we ran together, and we would host foreign and local ministers in our homes... Throughout our ministry time together it was clear to see that Greg has had a gift of evangelism-persuasion. Greg and his wife Karen eventually took their family to the Philippines to work as missionaries in a support and teaching role; they sought to serve the LORD. I, on the other hand went off to Medical School to pursue "my dream"; I sought to serve myself. Many years have passed, Greg and his family have returned from the mission field and Greg has put his gift of evangelism and his persuasive vocal cords into selling gold and other "precious metals" of all things. Several years ago Greg called me in what seemed to be a bit of a panic, he said that he was having a hard time talking and that the doctors were concerned that he was losing his voice and that he would be permanently disabled. **My response to Greg was that this was a wake-up call from the LORD, that we all are given a finite number of words with which to speak and the LORD is tracking our every word, and our every thought**. God so wills us to be used and literally used to the point of our wearing out for His great purpose. I appealed to my friend to stop spending his limited time and energy making much of the world and the things that the world values (gold...) and to use his every breath for the purpose of which he was made. It seemed to me, that Greg was giving his best effort and time to the sale of gold for the purpose of financial gain, security..., while he was giving the LORD what was left over, therefore deferring the LORD to a lesser place in his heart-this is nothing less than idolatry. **As I prayed through this with my Pastor/mentor we both had a similar cry in our heart "LORD how is it that your evangelists are selling gold?"**

As it turned out Greg's voice was restored (for now), Greg (and his gifted vocal cords) has resumed his career in sales (in convincing man of their need for "precious metals"), and I am reminded of the parable of the two sons.

Matthew 21

Parable of Two Sons

28 "[JESUs said] But what do you think? A man had two sons, and he came to the first and said, 'Son, go work today in the vineyard.' 29 And he answered, 'I will not'; but afterward he regretted it and went. 30 The man came to the second and said the same thing; and he answered, 'I *will*, sir'; but he did not go. 31 Which of the two did the will of his father?" They *said, "The first." Jesus *said to them, "Truly I say to you that the tax collectors and prostitutes will get into the kingdom of God before you. 32 For John came to you in the way of righteousness and you did not believe him; but the tax collectors and prostitutes did believe him; and you, seeing *this*, did not even feel remorse afterward so as to believe him.

HANNAH AND THE BILLBOARD

It was January/8/2008, Hannah and I were driving South on I-94 E, we were approaching the Camden area north of the Lowery Street Tunnel. It was Sunday morning and we were headed to Saint Paul en route to our home church meeting at Angie's house. As we drove we were having a serious conversation about the LORD; I think that I was stressing the importance of daily reading of the Scriptures, service to others... At that moment (driving 65 miles/hour) we looked up at a local vendor's billboard advertisement to the right side of the freeway and it had a Scripture reference verse posted on it, Hannah opened the Bible and read Psalm 45:10 **"Lister O daughter, give attention and incline your ear"**. We both received that timely sign as the LORD's strong support of what I was trying to impress upon Hannah. Hannah and I were both impressed by the LORD's timing and strong support and just like a good Father the LORD was telling Hannah to listen and pay close attention.

Psalm 45

[10] **"Listen, O daughter, give attention and incline your ear: Forget your people and your father's house"**

HOLDING HANNAH'S HAND

There have been many times that I have picked up my daughter Hannah and she seems distant. I tended to take it very personal and quite frankly it felt hurtful to me. Over time I realized that there was demonic oppression going on, spirits were trying to cause division between us and they were lying to her and to me. I have learned to address the issue quietly with prayer and patience-though I have failed many times. On one occasion I picked up Hannah from school one Friday afternoon. Hannah looked at me and we talked a bit about her week and I asked how she was. After a few minutes we sat somewhat quietly and I began to ask the LORD to soften Hannah's heart, I asked the LORD if while I held Hannah's hand He would move through her and that His Spirit would touch her in such a personal way that He would move her to tears as a demonstration of His love. I reached over and with my right hand and I held Hannah's left hand. We drove silently for maybe a minute, and I was silently praying that the LORD would move and fall onto Hannah. As we drove Hannah's eyes welled up with tears and she began to cry and soften. This was such a tender moment that we shared-it was truly a gift from Almighty God.

Isaiah 44

³'For I [LORD God] will pour out water on the thirsty land
and streams on the dry ground;
I will pour out My Spirit on your offspring
and My blessing on your descendants;
⁴and they will spring up among the grass
Like poplars by streams of water.'

HANNAH AND THE DREAM OF THE WHITE TIGER-"WITH BLACK STRIPES!"

My daughter Hannah had a dream, she woke up scared and made the long walk from the family room where she was staying to my room where I was sleeping. As she was walking toward my room she was facing a mirror that stands over the dresser in my room. Hannah later described seeing reflections of dark demonic images darting to and fro around her, by the time she had gotten to my bedside she was notably shaken and scared. Hannah spoke with a shaky voice and told me that she had a very bad dream and asked if we could talk. As we talked she became calm and she wanted to share her dream with me. Hannah said that in her dream she was in her bedroom at her Mom's house and that she was being led by the Spirit of the LORD praying over things that the LORD indicated needed prayer. Hannah said that she was pointing to and rebuking things in the name of the LORD Jesus. **She said that in her dream she approached a stuffed white tiger with black stripes and she began to pray over it rebuking it in the name of the Lord Jesus. While she was praying the tiger "morphed" into a demon and it leapt at her and knocking her to the ground onto her back-she described the demon as having fiery red eyes.** Hannah then awoke and made her way to my room seeing images in the mirror as she walked.

The next morning we went to church and Hannah shared her dream in detail with the entire congregation, I was very proud and we prayed for her. Following our church service we were called to go to a ladies home to help with something and to visit; this lady was a girlfriend of one of the men in our group and she seemed drawn to Hannah. We pulled into her driveway; Hannah went to the door and was greeted by the lady who asked Hannah to come in as she "had a gift for her". As Hannah later walked out to the car and I could see a look of confirmation, affirmation and concern on her face. **Hannah returned** to the car with a box of small stuffed animals. Hannah told me that the lady had handed her a box and Hannah's question to her was "is there a white tiger with black stripes in there?" The lady said "yes there is", Hannah's response to her was "I [Hannah] won't be taking that one [the white tiger with black stripes] with me".

Amos 3

[7]Surely the Lord GOD does nothing
unless He reveals His secret counsel
to His servants the prophets.
[8]A lion has roared! Who will not fear?
The Lord GOD has spoken! Who can but prophesy?

HOLDING THE HAND OF THE POOR
AND NAKED CHILDREN

This is tough for me write as it is so vivid in my memory, and it may be difficult to articulate. I was in prayer regarding our flippant, careless attitude and downright disregard for those in need as we value our comfort and entertainment above the needs of the poor. What troubles me with regard to this issue is the "out-of-sight-out-of-mind" attitude of most people; we seem to care little, that is, we may well say "oh that's too bad for them" but we are unwilling to give sacrificially to meet their needs.

While in prayer the LORD gave me a vision of every person walking around in our day-to-day business much as it is, we were shopping, eating and going about the day-and the vision was in vivid color. Everything was as it is and in color, with one exception, everyone was holding the hand of a poor, dirty, emaciated, naked, despondent child with a bloated belly due to malnutrition. In the vision everything was in color except for the child-the child was in black-and-white. This was a very troubling image to say the least. **As we were walking and holding the hand of this poor child we would be thought to be criminals if we would dare to order food for ourselves and neglect to provide food for the child that we were holding hands with. In fact some in this vision were doing just that as they were ordering food, eating and some were even throwing away the leftover food while the child that they were connected with starved to death. In the vision, upon the death of their assigned child they were given a new child to care for. In this vision people seem to be stepping over the poor, the starving and the dying in our effort to get to their favorite buffet line.**

During this time the LORD was explaining that mere distance from the poor does not negate our responsibility to meet their needs;

again, whether a child or poor person is holding our hand or is 5 thousand miles from us, that distance does not negate our responsibility to our God to meet their needs. We are all assigned children and our response or lack thereof is being meticulously recorded to the smallest detail.

Matthew 25

The Judgment
[35]**'For I [Jesus of Nazareth, the King] was hungry, and you gave Me something to eat; I was thirsty, and you gave Me something to drink; I was a stranger, and you invited Me in;** [36]**naked, and you clothed Me; I was sick, and you visited Me; I was in prison, and you came to Me.'** [37]**'Then the righteous will answer Him, 'Lord, when did we see You hungry, and feed You, or thirsty, and give You something to drink?** [38]**'And when did we see You a stranger, and invite You in, or naked, and clothe You?** [39]**'When did we see You sick, or in prison, and come to You?'** [40]**'The King will answer and say to them, 'Truly I say to you, to the extent that you did it to one of these brothers of Mine, even the least of them, you did it to Me.'**

[41]"Then He will also say to those on His left, 'Depart from Me, accursed ones, into the eternal fire which has been prepared for the devil and his angels; [42]for I was hungry, and you gave Me nothing to eat; I was thirsty, and you gave Me nothing to drink; [43]I was a stranger, and you did not invite Me in; naked, and you did not clothe Me; sick, and in prison, and you did not visit Me.' [44]"Then they themselves also will answer, 'Lord, when did we see You hungry, or thirsty, or a stranger, or naked, or sick, or in prison, and did not take care of You?' [45]**'Then He will answer them, 'Truly I say to you, to the extent that you did not do it to one of the least of these, you did not do it to Me.'** [46]**'These will go away into eternal punishment, but the righteous into eternal life."**

HONORING THE DEAD WITH RESOURSE FOR THE LIVING

Consider our treatment of the dead; we put resources into declaring their death (obituaries), we spend resources preparing their dead bodies (embalming and preparation) and we place expensive monuments as their head pieces while the poor starve at a rate of one every three seconds. And yes I will say it, you ought to be ashamed of yourself for doing so. It has become common-place for us in this country to spend thousands of dollars on the preparation of dead bodies, on a place for their bodies to rot and we even employ people to maintain gravesites; and all of this while the poor are starving and dying at a rate of 1 every three seconds. Though we may have material wealth in this nation I perceive that we experience poverty of the Spirit of God, we suffer spiritually for our apathy-we will be judged.

Proverbs 14

31He who oppresses the poor taunts his Maker, but he who is gracious to the needy honors Him [LORD God].

1 John 3

17But whoever has the world's goods, and sees his brother in need and closes his heart against him, how does the love of God abide in him? 18Little children, let us not love with word or with tongue, but in deed and truth.

Jeremiah 22

16"He [Jehoiakim, the son of king Josiah] pled the cause of the afflicted and needy; then it was well

Is not that what it means to know Me?" Declares the LORD.

Micah 6

[8]He has told you, O man, what is good;
And what does the LORD require of you
But to do justice, to love kindness,
And to walk humbly with your God?

Luke 14

[13]"[Jesus said] But when you give a reception, invite the poor, the crippled, the lame, the blind, [14]and you will be blessed, since they do not have the means to repay you; for you will be repaid at the resurrection of the righteous."

HUMBLED BY MY WORDS

There have been many times that the LORD gave me living examples of my own hypocrisy. For example, I have been judging someone and the LORD has pointed out to me that at that very moment I was/am guilty of the very thing that I am judging the others for. This has happened many times. There have also been times that I have been humbled publically in a moment of pride if even in jest. On one occasion I was leading a Bible study at a local coffee shop. I was quizzing the group with Bible verses and I boldly commented that "asking these questions gave me a sense of power" and as I recall as I was saying the words "a sense of power" I began to stammer my words and I was unable to speak as my mouth twisted and contorted. On another occasion I was at the dinner table and Hannah was asking if she could do something that was very reasonable and I was kidding her regarding "my absolute power" in this matter. As I was saying the words "my absolute power" I began to stammer and I was unable to produce a fluent word. As I was stammering in my speech my tongue and mouth literally felt unresponsive to my attempts to form words. Hannah and Philip and I picked up on what the LORD seemed to be doing and we all erupted in laughter.

Matthew 23

¹Then Jesus spoke to the crowds and to His disciples, ²saying:
"The scribes and the Pharisees have seated themselves in the chair of Moses; ³therefore all that they tell you, do and observe, but do not do according to their deeds; for they say things and do not do them. ⁴"They tie up heavy burdens and lay them on men's shoulders, but they themselves are unwilling to move them with so much as a finger. ⁵"But they do all their deeds to be noticed by men; for they broaden their phylacteries and lengthen the tassels of their garments. ⁶"They love

the place of honor at banquets and the chief seats in the synagogues, [7]and respectful greetings in the market places, and being called Rabbi by men. [8]"But do not be called Rabbi; for One is your Teacher, and you are all brothers. [9]"Do not call anyone on earth your father; for One is your Father, He who is in heaven. [10]"Do not be called leaders; for One is your Leader, that is, Christ.[11]"But the greatest among you shall be your servant. [12]**"Whoever exalts himself shall be humbled; and whoever humbles himself shall be exalted.**

I AM A WORM

As I walked down the driveway to deliver the newspapers I saw the remnants of an overnight thunderstorm. On the ground there were worms laid out in lines like solders in marching-order. There were thousands of scattered worms that had abandoned their flooded homes and headed for higher ground; it was hard to imagine that the earth could contain so many of these slimy little creatures. I was reminded of a similar time that I saw the dried remnants of worms on the black-tar road hours after a storm, the worms had died, dried, and were little more than a spot or stain, and then **the LORD spoke to me and reminded me that we are like the worm.** I could see the silhouette of the worms and a darkened area where they had died and dried and yet they became all but a stain on the ground then washed away unnoticed by most. The worm had yielded the water and elements from its body, returned it into the ground-and once again it was dust. **I said to the LORD "Wow LORD" and He replied "you [mankind] are not much more than these".**

Psalm 103:13-19

Just as a father has compassion on his children, so the LORD has compassion on those who fear Him.
For He Himself knows our frame; he is mindful that we are but dust.
As for man, his days are like grass; as a flower of the field, so he flourishes.
When the wind has passed over it, it is no more, and its place acknowledges it no longer.
But the lovingkindness of the LORD is from everlasting to

everlasting on those who fear Him, and His righteousness to children's children, to those who keep His covenant and remember His precepts to do them.
The LORD has established His throne in the heavens, and His sovereignty rules over all.

"I HAVE A MESSAGE FROM GOD FOR YOU"

There have been times that the LORD has prompted me to say and do things that seemed odd, offended people, and may have tested social boundaries at times. I have come to understand that "here lies the test". In these situations the LORD has confronted me with the question "do you love Me more than these?", and "these" being people, reputation... The question asked in these cases "are you willing to risk fitting-in for your obedience to Me?" This was very fitting for the Prophets of the Bible as they seemed to be "misfits" in this world, people who were called to a higher calling, people called to speak and act in ways that may seem odd to the world. On one occasion the LORD had me fix my eyes on a lady that was walking past me and He said to tell her that **"what they once had the LORD wants to have again"**, she walked past me and she went outside, I felt very uncomfortable as I did not know her. **I said to the LORD "LORD please if this is really You I will tell her that message if you have her walk up to me", as I finished I looked and the lady was walking right up to me and she stood in front of me as though I had called her to that place. I then gave her the message from the LORD "the LORD told me to tell you 'what you once had with Him the LORD wants to have again'".** At first she looked at me and smiled as though I was kidding, I then explained that the LORD had told me to tell her the message and that I asked Him to send her back my way as a conformation, she then looked very serious, she thanked me and walked away looking concerned and thoughtful. After I had shared this message with the lady her friend shared with me that she had had a past with the LORD and perhaps pulled away-soon after she received this word calamity struck her.

Malachi 3

[7]"From the days of your fathers you have turned aside from My [LORD God's] statutes and have not kept them. Return to Me, and I will return to you," says the LORD of hosts.

John 21:15-17

So when they had finished breakfast, Jesus said to Simon Peter, "Simon, son of John, do you love Me more than these?" He said to Him, "Yes, Lord; You know that I love You." He said to him, "Tend My lambs." He said to him again a second time, "Simon, son of John, do you love Me?" He said to Him, "Yes, Lord; You know that I love You." He said to him, "Shepherd My sheep." He said to him the third time, "Simon, son of John, do you love Me?" Peter was grieved because He said to him the third time, "Do you love Me?" And he said to Him, "Lord, You know all things; You know that I love You." Jesus said to him, "Tend My sheep.

I HAVE BEEN PACKING FOR ALMOST 40 YEARS

While in my early twenties, prior to my getting married, I did a bit of traveling, I was trying to fill a void, seeking pleasure, adventure and fulfillment through travel-though it never seemed to last. To a point my travel experiences were good if for no other reason than to expose the lie that traveling in-and-of-itself will bring fulfillment-it did not. As is always the case, while in the world and seeking fulfillment in the things of the world it looked better and more fulfilling than it turned out to be. For the most part I was thinking about returning home almost as soon as I left, and I was never really able to escape the "rat race" of life even while "on vacation" things never really turned out the way that the travel brochure had described. This is the way of the world and of the enemy; the enemy will promise us a "cookie" so-to-speak, he will promise us a reward of some kind for our labors. Some reward for our service-to-self and to our vanity, or so it seems-though the reality is while we seek to serve ourselves we are literally serving the devil. When we seek to serve our own desires apart from the LORD we serve the enemy. We walk in the light in Christ or we walk in the darkness of Satan. Regarding my travels, in most cases the most enjoyable time was planning and packing in anticipation of leaving for "the perfect trip". The problem for me was that I knew that all too soon the trip would be ending and I would be back to the proverbial "grind", back to the "salt mine", and as I was away I was consumed by the brevity of the time, I began counting the days remaining in "paradise" as they seemed to tick by like "nobody's business". This is quite contrary to our service to the LORD as He calls us to hard service and He seems to feed us ice cream along the way; He promises His great rewards to us and He always delivers in abundance and right on time. As though we may set out to serve the LORD and so we should, yet in the process we see Him serving and providing for us along the way. However, with regard to our time to come with the LORD, and as great as it is even now to be His child, the thought of everlasting paradise with the LORD I am thankful for. I look forward to my new home and my new body with great anticipation, knowing that it could be at any moment only adds to the anticipation. **I liken this anticipation of my new body and my new home with the LORD to packing for my great and everlasting vacation. I look forward to my great departure from this world and away from this world system, in my thoughts and in my heart I seem to be in the "packing mode". I am packing my bags for this great departure, and I have been packing for almost forty years now.**

Philippians 1

To Live Is Christ

21 For to me [the Apostle Paul, formerly Saul prior to his conversion], to live is Christ and to die is gain. 22 But if I am to live on in the flesh, this will mean fruitful labor for me; and I do not know which to choose. 23 But I am hard-pressed from both directions, having the desire to depart and be with Christ, for that is very much better; 24 yet to remain on in the flesh is more necessary for your sake. 25 Convinced of this, I know that I will remain and continue with you all for your progress and joy in the faith, 26 so that your proud confidence in me may abound in Christ Jesus through my coming to you again.

27 Only conduct yourselves in a manner worthy of the gospel of Christ, so that whether I come and see you or remain absent, I will hear of you that you are standing firm in one spirit, with one mind striving together for the faith of the gospel; 28 in no way alarmed by *your* opponents—which is a sign of destruction for them, but of salvation for you, and that *too*, from God. 29 For to you it has been granted for Christ's sake, not only to believe in Him, but also to suffer for His sake, 30 experiencing the same conflict which you saw in me [Paul], and now hear *to be* in me.

I HAVE SINNED

Prior to my: working in a plastics factory, being incarcerated and the seven years that I was very ill - I was a medical doctor. Shortly after my wife and I split in 1998 I fell into a deep and dark depression and I agreed to take antidepressant medication, soon after that I became disinhibited. For the next seven years I experienced: disinhibition, grandiosity, paranoia, dilutions and eventually florid psychosis with hallucinations of all kinds. I realize that the terms: "delusion", "mania", "psychosis" and other "mental illnesses" is the world systems way of defining what the world system do not, and cannot understand. I believe that I was attacked persistently by demonic forces. Toward the end of the seven years of attack or "illnesses" I was literally building large fires on my property in order that I may see what I perceived was attacking me (and my children) by night. I was hearing voices, seeing visual manifestations of demonic forces in the woods, and in my home, and, I was feeling physical manifestations on and in my body. After seven years the proverbial bottom fell out of my life. I began drinking alcohol and toward the end of the seven years in an effort to find joy, peace, stability and balance I began to use prescription and street drugs. What was interesting was that I abused drugs while I was in the midst of helping others be freed from their addictions and in the final analysis I likely contributed to their addictions and suffering. In my life I have sinned to a great extent, and I have many regrets, but not in the LORD. I have no misconceptions regarding my need for a savior, I have no misconception regarding my unrighteousness apart from Christ. I have no misconceptions regarding the sinful nature of my flesh, and, I have absolutely no hope for salvation apart from the LORD Jesus Christ.

In William Barkley's <u>THE PARABLES OF JESUS</u>, and referring to the Book of Luke 7:36-50, THE PARABLE OF THE TWO DEBITORS, Barkley states that this parable teaches that the one who has been forgiven greater sins will likely feel the greatest love and appreciation for the One paying the price for their redemption-Jesus and His redemptive work on the Cross. Barkley referrers to John Oxenham's imaginary reconstruction of the life of Barabbas after the crowd chose him to be released and set free and thus, sending Jesus to the Cross in Barabbas' place. According to this imaginary account and after the verdict Barabbas followed Jesus to Calvary, the place of Jesus' crucifixion. When the nails were driven through Jesus' hands one thought was on the mind of Barabbas "These nails should have been driven through my hands, not His [Jesus']-He [Jesus] saved me." When he [Barabbas] saw Jesus finely hanging on the Cross the feeling was on Barabbas' heart, "I should have been hanging there, not He- He [Jesus] saved me [Barabbas, and me as well]."

Luke 7

36 Now one of the Pharisees was requesting Him [Jesus] to dine with him, and He entered the Pharisee's house and reclined *at the table.* 37 And there was a woman in the city who was a sinner; and when she learned that He was reclining *at the table* in the Pharisee's house, she brought an alabaster vial of perfume, 38 and standing behind *Him* at His feet, weeping, she began to wet His feet with her tears, and kept wiping them with the hair of her head, and kissing His feet and anointing them with the perfume. 39 **Now when the Pharisee who had invited Him saw this, he said to himself, "If this man were a prophet He would know who and what sort of person this woman is who is touching Him, that she is a sinner."**

40 **And Jesus answered him, "Simon, I have something to say to you." And he replied, "Say it, Teacher." 41 "A moneylender had two debtors: one owed five hundred denarii [a coin representing a typical day laborers wage. The KJV translates it "a penny"], and the other fifty. 42 When they were unable to repay, he graciously forgave them both. So which of them will love him more?" 43 Simon answered and said, "I suppose the one whom he forgave more." And He [Jesus] said to him, "You have judged correctly."**

44 Turning toward the woman, He said to Simon, "Do you see this woman? I entered your house; you gave Me no water for My feet, but she has wet My feet with her tears and wiped them with her hair. 45 You gave Me no kiss; but she, since the time I came in, has not ceased to kiss My feet. 46 You did not anoint My head with oil, but she anointed My feet with perfume. 47 For this reason I say to you, her sins, which are many, have been forgiven, for she loved much; but he who

100

is forgiven little, loves little." ⁴⁸ Then He said to her, "Your sins have been forgiven." ⁴⁹ Those who were reclining *at the table* with Him began to say to themselves, "Who is this *man* who even forgives sins?" ⁵⁰ And He said to the woman, "Your faith has saved you; go in peace."

IF YOU SEE A PIN ON MY SHIRT

Several years ago while I was thinking of the things of the LORD and reading through the Scriptures. I was thinking about a passage that talked of the wonders of the LORD and God's desire that we share His deeds with others-to the next generation. I thought about my daughter Hannah and I wondered how we could somehow keep track of the many signs, miracles and wonders of the LORD, and then share them with others. At that moment a vivid picture of an exercise using safety pins came to mind-this vision was detailed. In the vision Hannah and I were to carry a handful of safety pins in our pocket or purse. When the LORD would do a great sign and wonder we would check with the LORD and if He prompted us we would then attach a safety pin to our: shirt, garment, book bag or backpack. The pin would serve as an opportunity for people to inquire as to why we had pins on our garments and or book bag, or backpack. If anyone was to inquire we would testify regarding God's miracles, signs and wonders. Most people did not ask, though it was interesting as to those who did. At the end of the shift usually the days end (or the school day in Hannah's case) I would kneel at the bed, thank the LORD for His great miracles and ask that **"the miracles continue and increase"** and then I would attach the days pins to a blanket that I have draped over a small piece of furniture, as an alter unto the LORD. The blanket is host to thousands of pins at this time, and I recall hearing from the LORD as we began this effort "you [Todd] are going to need a bigger blanket"

1 Chronicles 16

⁸"Oh give thanks to the LORD, call upon His name; make known His deeds among the peoples.
⁹Sing to Him, sing praises to Him; speak of all His wonders.
¹⁰Glory in His holy name; let the heart of those who seek the LORD be glad.
¹¹Seek the LORD and His strength; seek His face continually.

103

¹²Remember His wonderful deeds which He has done, His marvels and the judgments from His mouth,

¹³O seed of Israel His servant…His chosen ones…

²²"Do not touch My anointed ones, and do My prophets no harm."

²³Sing to the LORD, all the earth; proclaim good tidings of His salvation from day to day.

²⁴Tell of His glory among the nations, His wonderful deeds among all the peoples.

²⁵For great is the LORD, and greatly to be praised; He also is to be feared above all gods.

²⁶For all the gods of the peoples are idols, but the LORD [YHWH] made the heavens.

²⁷Splendor and majesty are before Him, strength and joy are in His place.

²⁸Ascribe to the LORD, O families of the peoples, ascribe to the LORD glory and strength.

²⁹Ascribe to the LORD the glory due His name; bring an offering, and come before Him; worship the LORD in holy array.

³⁰Tremble before Him, all the earth; indeed, the world is firmly established, it will not be moved.

³¹Let the heavens be glad, and let the earth rejoice; and let them say among the nations, "The LORD reigns."

³²Let the sea roar, and all it contains; let the field exult, and all that is in it…"

IS THIS YOUR DAD'S?

My kids and I attended a local church on Saturday nights for a while, the services was delivered in Spanish though the message was translated into English, the music was wonderful and brought us to tears on many occasions. Philip was with me while Hannah and her friends were part of the youth group-I was blessed to be in that setting together with my kids. On one occasion I was sitting with Philip to my right, I was holding onto a piece of paper with a message that I wanted to share with Philip-it was important to me and I made this note as my reminder of something that I felt lead to share with Phillip. As I looked over at Philip I saw that his eyes were closed, I recall seeing that he looked to be deep in prayer. I recall that as I looked at Philip I was faced with the question of **"do I interrupt the LORD and Philip's conversation for a conversation with me?"** and my answer to that was an easy **"no way will I interrupt my son's time with God"**. Though I felt that it was the LORD's will that I share the information on the paper I could see a test from the LORD in this; I felt the LORD leading me to faith. I said to the LORD **"LORD I thought that You wanted Philip to read what I am holding and I do not feel comfortable interrupting Your time with him for my time with him, so, I will drop this message in the offering plate and let you work out the details."** I dropped the message in the offering plate of this very large Spanish speaking church and went and sat down again. At the end of the service Philip and I talked, hugged and we said goodbye and walked out into the crowded church corridor. Philip was walking quite a distance in front of me, he then turned completely around and walked back to me and he was holding a folded piece of paper in his hand and smiling. As he approached me Philip handed me the paper and said that someone had given it to him and asked **"is this your Dad's?"** though it did not have my name on it or any form of identification. **My response to Philip was "it's ok with the LORD for you read that now"**.

"[Jesus said] The kingdom of heaven is like a treasure hidden in the field, which a man found and hid again; and from joy over it he goes and sells all that he has and buys that field. Again, the kingdom of heaven is like a merchant seeking fine pearls, and upon finding one pearl of great value, he went and sold all that he had and bought it. Again, the kingdom of heaven is like a dragnet cast into the sea, and gathering fish of every kind; and when it was filled, they drew it up on the beach; and they sat down and gathered the good fish into containers, but the bad they threw away. "So it will be at the end of the age; the angels will come forth and take out the wicked from among the righteous, and will throw them into the furnace of fire; in that place there will be weeping and gnashing of teeth. "Have you understood all these things?" They said to Him, "Yes." And Jesus said to them, "Therefore every scribe who has become a disciple of the kingdom of heaven is like a head of a household, who brings out of his treasure things new and old."

IT LOOKS GOOD TODAY BUT NOT TOMORROW; IT LOOKS BAD TODAY BUT NOT TOMORROW

The Kingdom of the LORD and the kingdom of the world system (Greek "kosmos") are in direct opposition. It has been my observation that while serving God, today seems fine. That is, I always have enough: money, time, gas, energy, joy, and peace…to do what God is calling me to do today, while tomorrow looks tough. Though tomorrow may look bleak, tomorrow never seems to get here-and all is well. I can see that this is the LORD's way of keeping us dependent upon Him as He is our day-by-day source. In the case where there may be excess: money, gas, leisure…those excess amounts may become an idol. That is, if we pray for a truckload of money and God should grant it, we tend to horde the money and place our faith in it as our security-we trust it. Our hope for the future too often becomes the money; a false hope fixed on a false sense of security, the money literally becomes an idol as we forget the LORD, or, we may regard the LORD but we regard Him less than we do the money. In a world of only two places we tend to give money the 1st place while perhaps God takes second. Recall that the children of Israel were told to take only the manna needed for the day and no more, except on the Sabbath (Exodus 16:4-5). In the New Testament, Jesus prays, "[Father] give us this day our daily bread" (Matthew 6:11), Jesus also teaches "do not [a command] worry about tomorrow; for tomorrow will care for itself…" (Matthew 6:34).

In the Lord's work there is always enough for today, though tomorrow may look bleak, however, tomorrow never seems to get here and all is well.

By contrast the enemy's lie goes something like this; "today there may not be enough: money, time, gas, energy, joy, peace…but if you continue to serve hard in the "rat race" of the world system, then tomorrow will be great, comfortable and fulfilling". In other words the enemy promises to give us a reward of sorts, a cookie for our efforts, yet he never pays up. We serve hard in the world "chasing our tail" with the promise that tomorrow will be better and brighter than today, however, tomorrow never ever seems to get here.

In the world system, as we serve the enemy, ourselves…though today is bleak, exhausting, empty and unfulfilling but the promise for tomorrow is good. However, tomorrow never seems to get here and nothing is well.

Matthew 6

[25]"For this reason I [Jesus of Nazareth] say to you, do not be worried about your life, as to what you will eat or what you will drink; nor for your body, as to what you will put on. Is not life more than food, and the body more than clothing? [26]"Look at the birds of the air, that they do not sow, nor reap nor gather into barns, and yet your heavenly Father feeds them. Are you not worth much more than they? [27]"And who of you by being worried can add a single hour to his life? [28]"And why are you worried about clothing? Observe how the lilies of the field grow; they do not toil nor do they spin, [29]yet I say to you that not even Solomon in all his glory clothed himself like one of these. [30]"But if God so clothes the grass of the field, which is alive today and tomorrow is thrown into the furnace, will He not much more clothe you? You of little faith! [31]"Do not worry then, saying, 'What will we eat?' or 'What will we drink?' or 'What will we wear for clothing?' [32]"For the Gentiles eagerly seek all these things; for your heavenly Father knows that you need all these things. [33]"But seek first His kingdom and His righteousness, and all these things will be added to you. [34]**"So do not worry about tomorrow; for tomorrow will care for itself. Each day has enough trouble of its own.**

108

JERUSALEM, JUDEA AND THE REMOTEST PART OF THE EARTH

Following His resurrection Jesus remained in Jerusalem for forty days, He then appeared to more than 500 witnesses as a testimony to His claim to be the risen Son of God (see 1st Corinthians 15:6). Recall Jesus' statement **"and you shall be My [Jesus'] witnesses both in Jerusalem, and in all Judea and Samaria, and even to the remotest part of the earth" (Acts 1:8).** It is interesting that Jesus' directive seemed to resemble a target with "Jerusalem" representing the center signifying "His home base". As we move out "Judea" representing the next ring of the target, Judea was near to Jerusalem, its neighbor. The next ring of the target "the remotest parts of the earth" represents all of the area beyond our neighboring region to include the entire world. Therefore Jerusalem or home-base first, Judea our geographic neighbors and then everybody else. "Our Jerusalem" seems to be represented by our home, our families…, this is our primary mission field. Unfortunately our homes too often are the place that we are the least on guard, the place that we are the most hypocritical... Recall Jesus' statement regarding the Pharisees "do as they say and not as they do" **(Matt 23:3).** We far too often will go into the world, our Judea and the outer most regions and will "look the look" and "talk the talk" after leaving our homes and our families where we have been a poor example. This seems contrary to the teachings of the LORD, as our primary place of effective discipleship, is our homes, the very place where we will be most transparent and vulnerable. **The notion "if we can do it [true Biblical discipleship] there [in our homes] then we can do it anywhere" implies that if we can be loving when we are tired, if we can be forgiving when hurt by those closest to us, if we can deny the flesh consistently where we are watched the closest and we can demonstrate service to God in our homes and make disciples of our: children, spouses, mom and dad's, brothers and sisters, roommates…then we will be well equipped for ministry in all other places. That is, if we effectively**

109

walk with Jesus and disciple in our homes then all other places will take care of themselves. As in the case of shooting at a target, we aim at the center, so we ought to focus on our center, our "Jerusalem" and in doing so we are training for our "Judea" and for the "remotest parts of the earth" as well. Jesus' life exemplified non hypocritical household discipleship, recall Jesus' mother Mary was an active follower of the LORD, as were His brothers James and Jude. It comes as little surprise that both James and Jude wrote powerful New Testament books and both deal with the topics of serious service and devotion to the LORD.

We are to: teach, train, and be living examples of "agape [God's unconditional love]", being patient, being kind, not jealous, not bragging, and not arrogant, not acting unbecomingly, not seeking our own, not provoking and not taking into account wrongs suffered at the hands of others, not rejoicing in unrighteousness but in truth, bearing all things, believing all things in our homes as this is where discipleship is to take place first, though not exclusively. I believe that the LORD was instructing us as to His strategic desire for His people to live in such a way that we might shine the brightest for Him in our homes as "if we can do it [true Biblical discipleship] in our homes then we can do it anywhere".

Acts 1:8

[Jesus said] but you will receive power when the Holy Spirit has come upon you; and you shall be My [Jesus'] witnesses both in Jerusalem, and in all Judea and Samaria, and even to the remotest part of the earth."

110

"JUST GIVE ME ONE EXAMPLE"

I was talking on the phone with my friend Greg about all the ways that the LORD had been opening my eyes with: revelation, signs, wonders... I was thinking that I may be coming across boastful and I was feeling uneasy, but, I trusted that it was a conversation that God was using. As we chatted Greg began to ask me for some details of how the LORD was speaking to me, and quite frankly there had been so many examples that to mention one felt as if to discredit all of the others. Greg was persistent and said "give me one example, just one!", so I scanned my memory and said with some reluctance, **"Ok but this may seem a little odd. A bird (trapped in the factory that I was working) chirped and got my attention, I tried to help the bird and in the process the LORD conveyed a message (using the chirping bird) regarding man's discomfort with letting go of 'the seen world and then trusting in Him in the unseen world'"**. In the midst of my sharing the bird story my dear friend Greg began laughing quietly and as I continued he laugh more noticeably and louder. As Greg was laughing I finished my story and I was feeling that he was laughing at me; finally I realized that this was not malicious laughter and that it seemed quite out of character even for this character Greg, and I asked him "what are you laughing about? What is so funny"?! **Greg stopped laughing and said "I have had a bird sitting in front of me looking at me and chirping as you were telling me your story about the chirping bird".** And that was great confirmation LORD!

2 Chronicles 16
⁹"For the eyes of the LORD move to and fro throughout the earth that He may strongly support those whose heart is completely His.

111

LIKE A MAN'S HAND

I was looking into the sky and the LORD had me fix my gaze on a clear blue cloudless area. There was a wisp of white in the sky of what looked to be no larger than a feather; the wisp was almost no wisp at all as it looked more like a thread of white silk in the sky. It was a cloud that was beginning to form-it was almost nonexistent. I watched as this tiny white thread-sized wisp in the sky rolled and began to increase in size. **A cloud was forming before my very eyes as I starred I marveled at this wonderful sight.** As the cloud was forming it took the shape of a man's fist and after the tiny fist-shaped cloud was formed an appendage formed that extended outward to form the shape of an index finger. In my excitement I called my Pastor/mentor Daniel Trygg and I recounted the details of the cloud forming from seemingly nothing and I described it to look much like a man's hand. At that Dan began to laugh and he reminded me of Elijah's servant description of a cloud was "small as a man's hand" that had formed in the sky.

1 Kings 18

Elijah's Prayer

³⁶ At the time of the offering of the *evening* sacrifice, Elijah the prophet came near and said, "O LORD, the God of Abraham, Isaac and Israel, today let it be known that You are God in Israel and that I am Your servant and I have done all these things at Your word. ³⁷ **Answer me, O LORD, answer me, that this people may know that You, O LORD, are God, and *that* You have turned their heart back again."** ³⁸ Then the fire of the LORD fell and consumed the burnt offering and the wood and the stones and the dust, and licked up the water that was in the trench. ³⁹ When all the people saw it, they fell on their faces; and they said, "The LORD, He is God; the LORD, He is God." ⁴⁰ Then Elijah said to them, "Seize the prophets of Baal; do not let one of them escape." So they seized them; and Elijah brought them

down to the brook Kishon, and slew them there.

41 Now Elijah [the prophet of the Most High God] said to Ahab [the wicked king of Israel], "Go up, eat and drink; for there is the sound of the roar of a *heavy* shower." 42 So Ahab went up to eat and drink. But Elijah went up to the top of [Mount] Carmel; and he crouched down on the earth and put his face between his knees. 43 He said to his servant, "Go up now, look toward the sea." So he went up and looked and said, "There is nothing." And he said, "Go back" seven times. **44 It came about at the seventh *time*, that he said, "Behold, a cloud as small as a man's hand is coming up from the sea."** And he said, "Go up, say to Ahab, 'Prepare *your chariot* and go down, so that the *heavy* shower does not stop you.'" 45 In a little while the sky grew black with clouds and wind, and there was a heavy shower. And Ahab rode and went to Jezreel. 46 Then the hand of the LORD was on Elijah, and he girded up his loins and outran Ahab to Jezreel.

LISA AND THE BABY BABIES

The LORD gives manifestations of the Spirit to His people. In our home-church congregation we were led to have a prayer time. During our prayer times we would lay hands on a member of the congregation while they were sitting in the so called "hot seat", then we would pray and ask the LORD to reveal things to us through: visions, words, insights... On one particular occasion we had Angie's daughter Lisa in the "hot seat" and we were praying for her. **While we were sharing our words and visions with the group I received a word in what sounded like my own voice and the word was simply "baby".** At that time Lisa was not interested in a male relationship and the likelihood of pregnancy seemed slim. When I received the word "baby" I felt that it may offend Lisa as I did not know if the word was referring to her having a baby, her acting like a baby or anything else related to a baby. I kept the information to myself and shared it in private with my Pastor/ mentor Danniel and we were soon told that **Lisa was indeed pregnant**.

Fast forward about two years and I was preparing for Sunday's teaching at our new home-church, I felt led to devote our meeting to prayer as we had done in the past. I sensed that we were stuck in a rut and that the LORD wanted to manifest His Spirit to us during prayer. We had not had this type of service with this particular group in this tailor park, and I was a bit anxious. As I was trying to find some supporting passages for this type of meeting things were not coming together so I supposed that the LORD was not in support of what I was preparing and I prepared for another lesson. When I got to the lesson time at our meeting things seemed to fall into place for prayer and we asked the Holy Spirit to reveal Himself to us through words, visions... We had only a few people in the "hot-seat" and one of them was Lisa. This was two years after our previous prayer time with Lisa when God revealed her first pregnancy. **While praying for Lisa I received the word "babies" and I shared it with Lisa, Lisa received the word in** faith; and she felt compelled to check. Lisa texted two days later to tell me that she is indeed pregnant again and acknowledged the LORD for reveling it to her again through His wonderful Spirit.

1 Corinthians 12

[3]Therefore I make known to you that no one speaking by the Spirit of God says, "Jesus is accursed"; and no one can say, "Jesus is Lord," except by the Holy Spirit. [4]Now there are varieties of gifts, but the same Spirit. [5]And there are varieties of ministries, and the same Lord. [6]There are varieties of effects, but the same God who works all things in all persons. **[7]But to each one is given the manifestation of the Spirit for the common good. [8]For to one is given the word of wisdom through the Spirit, and to another the word of knowledge according to the same Spirit; [9]to another faith by the same Spirit, and to another gifts of healing by the one Spirit, [10]and to another the effecting of miracles, and to another prophecy, and to another the distinguishing of spirits, to another various kinds of tongues, and to another the interpretation of tongues. [11]But one and the same Spirit works all these things, distributing to each one individually just as He wills.**

LOOKING INTO THE PERFECT
WIND INSTRUMENT

Prior to my: working in a plastics factory, being incarcerated, learning to drive a "semi-truck" and during the seven years that I was ill (by the worlds definition), prior to all of this I was a medical doctor. After my wife and I split in 1998, I became acutely depressed and I began taking antidepressant medication, shortly thereafter I became disinhibited and for the next seven years I decompensated from mild disinhibition to delusions of grandeur, mania and florid psychosis. I was full-blown psychotic. I realize that what the world defines as "delusion", "mania", "psychosis"… is their way of describing what they cannot and do not understand. I believe that I was persistently attacked by demonic forces. I understand that my decisions and behaviors opened the door to demonic forces-it was a consequence us my sin. Toward the end of the seven years of attacks or "illness" I was literally building large fires on my property that I may see what was attacking me by night. I was: hearing voices, seeing manifestations of demonic trolls in the woods and in my home and I was feeling them on my body. It was interesting that I began using "street drugs" as I was attempting to help others with their addictions-I likely added to their suffering. After seven years of decompensation the proverbial bottom fell out of my life.

Prior to all of this I went to medical school and while in a medical school cadaver lab in first year medical school, "gross anatomy" as a first year medical student we literally dissected and were tested on what seemed to be every fiber of the human body. Everything about the human body was so detailed and organized, the body looked like a machine with compartmentalized systems. The cadaver lab looked like a large factory of human body machines displayed and prepared for viewing. During our gross study of the head and neck we dissected the larynx otherwise known as "the voice-box". **While looking into the human voice-box I was amazed to be looking into a perfect wind-**

instrument of such perfect precision and detail. I recognize now this was indeed the handiwork of the LORD, His creation of the perfect wind instrument. I'm sure that this "perfect wind instrument" was created that we may speak and sing praise to God and to speak: encouragement, psalms, hymns, and spiritual songs to the brethren. While I studied this complexed amazing structure I was in awe, I knew that this was no random act-we were created in God's image.

Psalm 139:7-16

Where can I go from Your Spirit? Or where can I flee from Your presence [LORD God]?
If I ascend to heaven, You are there; if I make my bed in Sheol [the abode of the dead], behold, You are there. If I take the wings of the dawn, if I dwell in the remotest part of the sea, even there Your hand will lead me, and Your right hand will lay hold of me. If I say, "Surely the darkness will overwhelm me, and the light around me will be night," even the darkness is not dark to You, and the night is as bright as the day. **Darkness and light are alike *to You*. for You formed my inward parts; You wove me in my mother's womb. I will give thanks to You, for I am fearfully and wonderfully made; wonderful are Your works, and my soul knows it very well. My frame was not hidden from You, when I was made in secret, *and* skillfully wrought in the depths of the earth; Your eyes have seen my unformed substance; and in Your book were all written the days that were ordained *for me*, when as yet there was not one of them.**

MODERN-DAY APOSTLES, PROPHETS AND CROSSES

In or around 2007 I met Dennis, a man that claimed to be an Apostle; he claimed that he had been commissioned by Jesus Himself. At the time of his claim regarding Apostleship I had no reason to disbelieve him as it is quite possible for Jesus to appear to people today. I had only known Dennis for a short time and he seemed credible to me, beyond that I had no reason to believe him either. I recall thinking that the truth would be made known; God would certainly validate or invalidate these claims in time. As time passed I observed and listened, things were happening that were validating Dennis' claim; God seemed to be getting behind Dennis with His strong support. As a few years passed I and others were convinced of Dennis' claim of Apostleship and this Apostle had become a dear friend to me. Dennis is not a refined scholar, quite frankly Dennis a bit rough-around-the-edges, we joke together about him being a bit "peculiar" and not fitting into the world, this is a complement to him-this describes me as well. Dennis was an over-the-road truck driver and it is in that context that Dennis came face-to-face with Jesus. It was interesting that Dennis (though with no car at that time) just seemed to show-up at times as though out of nowhere and in ways that still make me laugh. I am part of a house-church group, we do not meet in a designated church building on a regular basis-we typically meet in homes. We sometimes meet together in a park in the summer for our Sunday service and share a meal together. On one unusual Sunday morning Dennis showed up at the park that we were meeting. Newell Park in St. Paul, MN is a very nice and wooded park with houses on three sides and in the north eastern corner has a wooded patch at the base of wooded hill. I was happy to see Dennis show up early for the meeting, I greeted him and hugged him, he returned the gestures and as usual he said few words which most certainly included an emphatic "Praise the LORD!" As we were sharing and talking of the things of the LORD I looked to my left and saw over in the wooded area three very

119

distinct and proportionate crosses standing with what looked like the middle cross either slightly larger than the others or slightly closer to us than the others. The crosses looked to be about nine feet tall and five to six feet across; they were so perfect that no imagination was required to see them and they were so pronounced that it was difficult for me to see anything else. I pointed to the wooded area as Dennis was facing me; Dennis turned to his left and acknowledged seeing the crosses in spite of a problem with his vision. **We were not like two men looking at some obscure image while using our imaginations. We were overcome and fixed on what we were looking at, there were three very distinct large proportionate crosses standing in front of us a few hundred yards away on the outskirts of the park.** As I recall Dennis and I were silently staring at the crosses until we were interrupted by the activity around us, I went toward the woods and Dennis stayed behind. As I approached the crosses it became clear to me that the three vertical posts of the crosses were in fact trees, perfect, tall and straight. Behind them and up the hill a tree or trees had fallen into perfect position laterally instead of obeying the laws of physics they or it had fallen sideways to make up a perfect horizontal beam for the three crosses. As I got closer, and then closer still, I lost the ability to appreciate the crosses as everything began to blend together. Sometime later in the morning I could see Dennis wandering over to the wooded area to get a closer look at the crosses as I had done earlier. **From where I was standing at a distance I could see Dennis standing at the foot of the crosses. What a great memory, the image of my friend, this unusual man-of-God standing at the foot of the three crosses looking up in reverence.** It was obvious that what we had both seen had imprinted upon us in a powerful way; Dennis and I shared this great gift from the LORD. Today I called my friend the Apostle of Jesus and after he had given me a word from the LORD, and after our reflecting on the crosses he reminded me that it is all the LORD and that "he is just Dennis". Dennis has since passed on-I'll see you soon dear friend.

1 Corinthians 12:28-30

And God has appointed in the church, first apostles, second prophets, third teachers, then miracles, then gifts of healings, helps, administrations, various kinds of tongues. All are not apostles, are they? All are not prophets, are they? All are not teachers, are they? All are not workers of miracles, are they? All do not have gifts of healings, do they? All do not speak with tongues, do they? All do not interpret, do they? [31]But earnestly desire the greater gifts. And I show you a still more excellent way.

120

MOM AND THE INSURANCE

I was facing a situation. I was in need of a very costly treatment that was to take a year and a half to two years and involved 4 treatments per month, and I had no medical insurance. My Mother was getting worried about how the LORD would provide, and I had no idea of how the LORD would provide-so we prayed. About this time we received a letter in the mail that described a government program that was initiated to follow people with "mental-health diagnoses". They were accepting applications for a study that dealt with "people like me". The applicants would be pooled and selected "by lottery"; not all applicants would be selected. Those selected would receive very good medical insurance for $10/month. All recipients were to meet with interviewers during the application process; those who were selected would be required to meet on a monthly basis with a case manager in order to review their progress. As I moved through the process I found that these interviews seemed little more than the LORD's opportunity for me to testify of His greatness-and so I did. As I reached the "lottery" I was given the opportunity for the medical insurance and I was assigned a case manager who asked me standard questions regarding my life: my goals and my general mission in life. As you can imagine I told him all about the LORD over and over, month after month, and he had to listen as it was his job to do so, and so it went month after month, year after year; his name was Victor King (Note his initials "VK" for future reference) and he testified toward the end of our mandatory meetings that he was closer to the LORD at the end than when we had begun to meet. During the two years of the essentially free medical insurance I was able to completely fulfill my treatment requirements and testify of the LORD many times. As I completed the required program my need for insurance ended and then my insurance ended. Note as well that none of this was solicited, I had not asked anyone for this insurance-it just came when I needed it and discontinued when I did not.

This was an amazing experience.

As we wondered how to cover this insurance need an unsolicited invitation came in the mail for essentially free insurance. The only catch was that I tell "my story", that is my testimony of the LORD, over and over again to people that had to listen to me, over and over.

Psalm 26

[1]Vindicate me, O LORD, for I have walked in my integrity, and I have trusted in the LORD without wavering.
[2]Examine me, O LORD, and try me;
Test my mind and my heart. [3]For Your lovingkindness is before my eyes, and I have walked in Your truth.
[4]I do not sit with deceitful men, nor will I go with pretenders.
[5]I hate the assembly of evildoers, and I will not sit with the wicked.
[6]I shall wash my hands in innocence, and I will go about Your altar, O LORD,
[7]That I may proclaim with the voice of thanksgiving and declare all Your wonders.
[8]O LORD, I love the habitation of Your house and the place where Your glory dwells.
[9]Do not take my soul away along with sinners, nor my life with men of bloodshed,
[10]In whose hands is a wicked scheme, and whose right hand is full of bribes.
[11]But as for me, I shall walk in my integrity; redeem me, and be gracious to me.
[12]My foot stands on a level place; in the congregations I shall bless the LORD.

"NOW, GO READ THE BOOK OF JUDE"

God has called me to do and say things that may seem unusual to most people-but maybe not to the children of the Kingdom. On one occasion the LORD asked me to take a printed Bible verse and "go sit down in a cafeteria", the Bible verse in my hand was calling us to serve God. I do not recall what the verse was though I have prayed about it many times; however it was one of the many verses in the Scripture calling us to serve God. As I headed to the cafeteria holding the Bible passage I was wondering what would happen next and I sat down and questioned whether I was truly hearing from the LORD and I recall saying "well here I am LORD, now what?" Within a minute of my sitting down, someone walked up to me and said "what is that in your hand?" my silent response was "ok LORD, here we go" and my verbal response to this man was "a verse about service to the LORD". The person that was questioning me became very defensive and said "you need to be careful with that verse as you will lead people into thinking that they need to serve God". When I heard this statement I about fell over and I said "we do need to serve God" as we parted ways the LORD said "now go read the book of Jude". On my drive home later that afternoon I recall crying out loud and repeatedly saying "LORD I am not the one who wrote it" (referring to the Scripture passage), at that very moment I heard the distinct words "I AM", and I realized that the LORD had just defended Himself with this great "I AM" declaration. I cried while driving. What an honor it was to hear the LORD say "I AM" as both the Father and Jesus had done in the Old and New Testaments. I soon arrived home and I was able to read the great Book of Jude, **"For certain persons have crept in unnoticed, those who were long beforehand marked out for this condemnation, ungodly persons who turn the grace of our God into licentiousness [a license to do as one pleases] and deny [disregard] our only Master and Lord, Jesus Christ." (Jude 4).** The Book of Jude clearly addressed people who use God's grace as an excuse to deny the LORD God the right to run our lives. These people use the grace of God as a license to do as they please while disregarding the LORD's call to serve. The Book of Jude goes on to describe these people as "autumn trees without fruit", "clouds without water", essentially fake and phony creatures that will look as though they will yield to their Master and give what they were created to give, however they simply will not give, and they will not submit and serve. These were later referred to as "doubly dead, uprooted".

Recall that the denial of the LORD and Master does not simply refer to the denial of the existence of God but to the refusal to do what He tells us to do. Refusal to obey is denial. Disobedience is denial of God's inherent right to use His creatures for the purpose that they were created. Denial is saying "no" to our Master-in my opinion.

Jude 5

For certain persons have crept in unnoticed, those who were long beforehand marked out for this condemnation, ungodly persons who turn the grace of our God into licentiousness and deny our only Master and Lord, Jesus Christ.

NOW THAT'S ENTERTAINMENT!!
THIS WAS SO COOL.

I spend most evenings away from: people, T.V. and other forms of entertainment as I opt for prayer and study. I have found that the LORD is capable of entertaining me through: visions, vivid dreams and words from Him. God communicates in ways that makes Hollywood look like child's play. On one particular occasion I was asking the LORD to "please show me something new and interesting regarding His Kingdom, even if for no other reason than to entertain me and reward me for turning away from the things of the world". That very night I had a dream; in the dream I was walking through the hallway of a huge marble building with impressive indoor marble pillars, it looked much like a museum to me; I was walking with a man who was introducing me to the building much like a tour guide. It was obvious that this person was a good character "one of the good guys". As we were walking through the hall we were coming up to a set of doors on the left leading to a lunchroom, cafeteria or breakroom. As we approached the breakroom the doors opened and two huge stone creatures walked out and they were approaching and passing close by us. These creatures were about 9-10 feet tall and almost as wide as they were tall, these guys were: big, broad, solid and made of rock-very intimidating. The two stone creatures were dressed like Roman soldiers with the breastplates, leather skirts and armor. The two soldiers had spears that were as thick as huge tree limbs and they walked right out in front of us and I jumped out of their way. **My concern was not that they were trying to hurt me; my concern was that one of these gigantic rock solid fellows would as much as brush against me and I would be broken to pieces. I recall the guy that was showing me around laughed and said "Oh don't worry, these are our guys"**

[16]**So he [Elisha] answered, "Do not fear, for those who are with us are more [greater] than those who are with them."** [17]Then Elisha prayed and said, "O LORD, I pray, open his eyes that he may see" And the LORD opened the servant's eyes and he saw; and behold, the mountain was full of horses and chariots of fire all around Elisha.

OIL AND WATER

OIL

This may sound arrogant at first glance however I do not for a minute take any credit for the understanding of this information; this was revealed to me by the LORD and it makes perfect sense to me. With regard to the revelation concerning oil this may be scoffed at by most, however, let me simply say "we shall see". The LORD revealed to me that this whole belief that the oil supply pumped from the ground being related to the old dinosaurs and rotten plants is simply not the case. He then explained that the oil is a byproduct of the high energy molten activity that is churning, bubbling and exploding below out feet. This is well supported, according to the physics law of the conservation of energy. Energy changes form but does not simply dissipate (known as energy transformation, or energy conversion). The energy in the form of heat is transformed into the chemical energy, the chemical energy of the fuel is released upon ignition. **It is like the LORD to store oceans of volatile fuel that react with fire in the same general area as oceans of molten lava.** The only reason that the world does not explode is that the LORD has not said to explode-not yet anyway.

1 Kings 10

The Queen of Sheba

¹Now when the queen of Sheba heard about the fame of Solomon concerning the name of the LORD, she came to test him with difficult questions. ²So she came to Jerusalem with a very large retinue, with camels carrying spices and very much gold and precious stones. When she came to Solomon, she spoke with him about all that was in her heart. **³Solomon answered all her questions; nothing was hidden [By LORD God] from the king which he did not explain to her.** ⁴When the queen of Sheba perceived all the wisdom of Solomon, the house that he had built, ⁵the food of his table, the seating of his servants, the attendance of his waiters and their attire, his cupbearers, and his stairway by which he went up to the house of the LORD, there was no more spirit in her.

ORIENTATION DAY

I had a dream that I was in a river of air that was flowing up into the sky and into the heavens; there was one other young lady in the river headed into heaven. The girl looked pleasant and was a person of few words, I did not recognize her as anyone that I had ever met. While headed to heaven I recall being surprised at the few in number that were actually headed for heaven; my question to the girl was "where is everybody?" I do not recall any reply from her. While en route we began talking and I said to her "Wow! Wasn't it great? Our journey with the LORD wasn't it great?" and I asked her to tell me about her walk with the LORD. When we arrived at our heavenly destination we were trained in a type of orientation; we were taken through a series of orientation exercises and we were coached by what seemed heavenly personal trainers. I recall being trained with our new bodies to ride bikes in the sky while flying and to walk through walls, and I distinctly remember getting stuck while walking through a wall.

1 Corinthians 2

³I [Paul] was with you in weakness and in fear and in much trembling, ⁴and my message and my preaching were not in persuasive words of wisdom, but in demonstration of the Spirit and of power, ⁵so that your faith would not rest on the wisdom of men, but on the power of God. ⁶Yet we do speak wisdom among those who are mature; a wisdom, however, not of this age nor of the rulers of this age, who are passing away; ⁷**but we speak God's wisdom in a mystery, the hidden wisdom which God predestined before the ages to our glory; ⁸the wisdom which none of the rulers of this age has understood; for if they had understood it they would not have crucified the Lord of glory;**

129

⁹but just as it is written,
"THINGS WHICH EYE HAS NOT SEEN AND EAR HAS NOT HEARD,
AND which HAVE NOT ENTERED THE HEART OF MAN,
ALL THAT GOD HAS PREPARED FOR THOSE WHO LOVE HIM."

¹⁰For to us God revealed them through the Spirit; for the Spirit searches all things, even the depths of God. ¹¹For who among men knows the thoughts of a man except the spirit of the man which is in him? Even so the thoughts of God no one knows except the Spirit of God.

OUR GOOD FORTUNE

I have my weaknesses. Coffee has been something that I have enjoyed for a long time, I enjoy the taste of coffee, I enjoy the lift that the caffeine delivers and I like the general feel surrounding sitting and sipping a hot cup of coffee. For some reason the LORD has had me on a very strict diet, I am reminded of John the Baptist who survived on a diet of "locust and wild honey" (Matthew 3:4, Mark 1:6). Though my diet may not be one of locust and wild honey the LORD has made it clear to me that I am not to eat chocolate or drink coffee, two things that I have enjoyed immensely. I get horrible headaches from both coffee and chocolate. God has been very patient through the years as I have caved-in to temptation, drank coffee and or ate chocolate on more than a few occasions, and, I have suffered the consequences of what is typically a three-day headache. For some reason this past week I caved-in to a tempting pot of coffee at the Perkins restaurant, I had a few sips and then a few more. These past few days I have indeed been paying the price with a horrible headache, and I have cried out to the LORD-Oh my aching head!.

This being the second day and night of headaches I went out to the local Chinese restaurant with my Mom and Dad, in my headache misery I opened my fortune cookie and I was pleasantly amazed to read the words. **"YOU HAVE TASTED THE BITTERNESS AS WELL AS THE SWEETNESS OF COFFEE".** I carry the laminated fortune in my wallet to this day

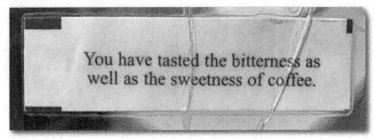

131

"Please hear my argument, and listen the contentions of my lips. Will you speak what is unjust for God, and speak what is deceitful for Him? Will you show partiality for Him? **Will you contend for God? Will it be well when He examines you? Or will you deceive Him as one deceives a man? ...Though He slay me, I will hope in Him [for where else would I hope?].** Nevertheless I will argue my ways before Him. This also will be my salvation, for the godless man may not come before His presence...**Only two things do not do to me, then I will not hide from Thy face: remove Thy hand from me, and let not the dread of Thee terrify me.**"

OUR HAIR AND NAILS

It may be true that the Lord created us with hair and fingernails with some functional purpose in mind I'm sure. But I believe that things like this are for the primary purpose of our testing. I would like to suggest that the LORD has given us these things so as to see what we will do with them. For example we are told in Scripture that **"if a brother or a sister is without clothing and in need of daily food, and one of you says to them, 'go in peace, be warmed and be filled', and yet you do not give them what is necessary for their body, what use is that? Even so faith with no works is dead, being by itself."** **(James 2:15-17)** I would suggest that we all know that there are people starving to death at this very moment, we are all aware of it, and yet we seem to turn a blind-eye. Consider hair and fingernails, God has given us hair, fingernails, eyebrows…and I would suggest that He uses them to test us, His question to us is, will you care for your hair and nails while you neglect the poor? Will you utilize the resources of the King on your hair and nails while you neglect the poor? Will you pamper yourself with haircuts and manicures while God's resources could have been used to feed people, as the poor starve to death at a rate of one every 3 seconds? Hair and nails are nothing but dead material that will be cut and swept into the garbage-as they become garbage. **Now, if we are willing to spend our time and resources on what we will soon throw away when it could be used for the poor, then we are placing greater value on our garbage than on the poor.**

And what of your time, will you pamper, primp and curl, color or spike your hair while you neglect or even minimize your time with the LORD in prayer and in the study of His Scriptures? Shampoo, nail polishes, endless hair and nail products, it is a slap in the face to the LORD to see His people live in vain while the poor die of starvation.

Proverbs 19:17

One who is gracious to a poor man [or woman] lends to the LORD, and He [the LORD] will repay him for his good deed.

Proverb 21:13

He who shuts his ear to the cry of the poor will also cry himself and not be answered.

Proverbs 28:27

He who gives to the poor will never want, but he who shuts his eyes will have many curses.

Proverbs 29:7

The righteous is concerned for the rights of the poor, the wicked does not understand such concern.

Ecclesiastes 12:8

"Vanity of vanities," says the Preacher, "all [of our striving for more] is vanity!"

James 2:15-16

If a brother or sister is without clothing and in need of daily food, and one of you says to them, 'Go in peace, be warmed and be filled,' and yet you do not give them what is necessary for their body, what use is that?

"OUR TIME"

And what of "our time"? We seem quite content with cheering for sports teams, being entertained day-in and day-out while the poor starve and the homeless remain in their condition. We bulldoze farmland where food could grow for the poor while we build: golf courses, shopping malls, movie theaters and even church buildings while the poor die at a rate of one every three seconds, all of this while we say that we are Christ's followers-and the world looks on. We demonstrate that: our personal pleasures, our entertainment and vanities are more important to us than the poor. Are we not more concerned with our: own future, our own plan for "retirement" and our comfort than we are for the poor and the hurting? Think about it! We honor the dead with: elaborate caskets, well-groomed grave sites, flowers…while the poor starve at a rate of one every 3 seconds. God is watching.

2 Corinthians 8

[13]For this is not for the ease of others and for your affliction, but by way of equality-- [14]at this present time your abundance being a supply for their need, so that their abundance also may become a supply for your need, that there may be equality;

Matthew 25

[44]"[Jesus said] Then they themselves also will answer, 'Lord, when did we see You hungry, or thirsty, or a stranger, or naked, or sick, or in prison, and did not take care of You [Lord]?' [45]"Then He will answer them, 'Truly I say to you, to the extent that you did not do it to one of the least of these, you did not do it to Me.' [46]"These will go away into eternal punishment, but the righteous into eternal life."

Proverbs 31

⁸Open your mouth for the mute, for the rights of all the unfortunate. ⁹Open your mouth, judge righteously, and defend the rights of the afflicted and needy.

Isaiah 1

¹⁶"Wash yourselves, make yourselves clean; remove the evil of your deeds from My sight. Cease to do evil, ¹⁷learn to do good; seek justice, reprove the ruthless, defend the orphan, plead for the widow.

Psalm 41

¹How blessed is he who considers the helpless; the LORD will deliver him in a day of trouble. ²The LORD will protect him and keep him alive, and he shall be called blessed upon the earth; and do not give him over to the desire of his enemies. ³The LORD will sustain him upon his sickbed; in his illness, You [LORD God] restore him to health.

Galatians 2

¹⁰They only asked us to remember the poor--the very thing I [Paul] also was eager to do.

OUT OF OR OUT-FROM

I have been studying Greek with my daughter Hannah and my son Philip, we meet Saturday mornings and we have been systematically working through the Book of 1ˢᵗ John for the past 6 months. We are working through 1ˢᵗ John as it seems to be one of the books of the New Testament with the most basic Greek. Both Hannah and Philip have been consistent regarding their studies and they both seem to have a genuine interest in and an aptitude for Greek. In our lesson today we studied 1ˢᵗ John 3:8-9, as we worked through the text together Philip read the Greek word "ek" from the words "ex" and "ek", meaning "out from" or "out of". **Philip read and translated the word "out from" or "out of" as he burped out of or out from his mouth and we all laughed as this was not intentional on his (Philip's) part. He then read the word again and he sneezed out of, or out from his mouth and we all laughed again.** God was making His great presence known to us all, it was clear to me that it was the LORD by the expression on Philips face. It was clearly a sign from the LORD and it was funny. Thank you LORD.

With regard to the Greek words "ek" and "ex" translated "out from" or "out of"; the Greek word "Ek-klesia" is from "Ek [out from]" plus "klesis" or "kaleo [a calling] and is therefore translated "a calling out from" or "ones called out from the world by God for a purpose". The Greek Ekklesia is often translated "assembly", "gathering", or "chuch".

Matthew 16

Pharisees Test Jesus
¹ The Pharisees and Sadducees came up, and testing Jesus, they asked Him to show them a sign from heaven. ² But He replied to

137

them, "When it is evening, you say, '*It will be* fair weather, for the sky is red.' ³ And in the morning, '*There will be* a storm today, for the sky is red and threatening.' Do you know how to discern the appearance of the sky, but cannot *discern* the signs of the times? ⁴ An evil and adulterous generation seeks after a sign; and a sign will not be given it, except the sign of Jonah." And He left them and went away.

⁵ And the disciples came to the other side *of the sea*, but they had forgotten to bring *any* bread. ⁶ And Jesus said to them, "Watch out and beware of the leaven of the Pharisees and Sadducees." ⁷ They began to discuss *this* among themselves, saying, "*He said that* because we did not bring *any* bread." ⁸ But Jesus, aware of this, said, "You men of little faith, why do you discuss among yourselves that you have no bread? ⁹ Do you not yet understand or remember the five loaves of the five thousand, and how many baskets *full* you picked up? ¹⁰ Or the seven loaves of the four thousand, and how many large baskets *full* you picked up? ¹¹ How is it that you do not understand that I did not speak to you concerning bread? But beware of the leaven of the Pharisees and Sadducees." ¹² Then they understood that He did not say to beware of the leaven of bread, but of the teaching of the Pharisees and Sadducees.

"PC" ON THE HIGH SCHOOL WALL

I was at Hannah's annual dance recital at Stillwater High School in Stillwater MN in about 2009. I need to be honest in saying that I do not like the idea of people watching young girls dressed in small outfits dancing on stage but I go to support my daughter. Halfway into the program I went outside to pray and I sat down on the grass looking in the direction of the north wall of a school building. As I was sitting on the ground I was praying and expressing my discontent in these people who were approving of young girls dancing on stage, I was praying and asking the LORD to please declare Himself to me there and then in that place. **As I was praying I was focused onto the brick wall of the school out in front of me and my vision focused on bricks that were darker in color than the others in the shape of the letters "PC", literally there was a clear and large "PC [Philip Crawford]" on the wall that I was facing.** These were not designed for this purpose, they were discolored and would be easily overlooked and it is likely that I was the only one to have ever seen them, they were perfect and from the LORD. I laughed as I saw the letters "PC" and I thought of my son Philip Crawford and I prayed that the LORD would give me an opportunity to share this great sign with Philip. **At about that moment Philip walked out of the building and he came over to sit with me. I then told Philip the story of my prayer and I asked him to look out across the grassy area and onto the wall. He looked and focused onto the wall and I saw his face light-up as he read his initials PC imprinted on the wall of his High School-just as the Lord has planned. Good times!**

"All your sons will be taught of the LORD; and the well-being of your sons will be great.

"In righteousness you will be established; you will be far from oppression, for you will not fear; and from terror, for it will not come near you. "If anyone fiercely assails *you* it will not be from Me [God]. Whoever assails you will fall because of you. "Behold, I [LORD God] Myself have created the smith who blows the fire of coals and brings out a weapon for its work; and I have created the destroyer to ruin.

"No weapon that is formed against you will prosper; and every tongue that accuses you in judgment you will condemn. This is the heritage of the servants of the LORD, and their vindication is from Me," declares the LORD.

PHILIP AND THE SHADOW

There was a Monday morning men's group that met at Perkins. There were six or so men on a typical Monday morning. We met to study various Biblical topics and have some time for sharing and prayer-it was good to bring the young man and the older men together. My son Philip was injured and had time off from his job and he was able to join us. We met in the North East corner table of Perkins and Angie almost always waited on us. That day I was sitting with my back to the window and Philip was across the table from me. As we ended our discussion we began to pray with our heads bowed and eyes closed. **As the group prayed to the LORD for me I saw what seemed to be a shadow, and things became darker.** Though my eyes were closed light was still passing through my eyelids and something came between me and the window behind me. I could tell that there was something blocking the light that was passing through the window as though there had been a shade lowered, it was pronounced. I continued to pray but I could appreciate the change-things looked darker. **As we finished our prayer time we began to talk more casually around the table. My son Philip looked across the table and said to me in the presence of the group "Dad when we were praying for you I saw Jesus standing behind you with His hand on your shoulder".** I looked at him and said something to the effect of "well that would explain the shadow that I saw". That was very cool-thank You Lord!

JOEL Chapter 2:28-29

It will come about after this that I will pour out My [YHWH, LORD God's] Spirit on all mankind;
and your sons and daughters will prophesy, your old men will dream dreams, your young men will see visions. Even on the male and female servants I will pour out My Spirit in those days.

PEOPLE IN TENTS

Prior to the "great recession" of late 2008, I recall that the LORD placed on my heart to pray for an economic collapse to occur in the United States to such an extent that people would be moving in together, many people in one household. I had such a clear vision, people were crowded in the halls to the point that people would be literally stepping over each other in the homes. Many homes were vacant and boarded up and few still had running water and heat therefore people lined the halls and rooms like sardines in a can. This was functional and strategic making the spiritual battlefield smaller for believers to achieve mass evangelism, sharing and ministry. This also lent itself well to testing of believers as we were confined to a very small area-close quarters. I recall that the LORD gave me two clear visions regarding this matter, in the first vision people were sneaking out of homes through boarded up windows, they were literally sneaking out onto the dark depressed looking streets like rats sneaking out in search of food. The streets looked like the streets of a ghost-town. This vision included the once wealthy people being humbled and seeking refuge with God's people. The second vision was one of homeless people living in tents and gathering in areas of the people of God, people were living in tents in the parking lots and in the sanctuaries of churches. **People were forced away from their homes and the people of the LORD were in charge of distribution of food and shelter. In other words there seemed to be a shift of resources away from the people of the world and into the hands of the people of the LORD.** People were living in tents on and in the properties of the God's people. I recall that I was so moved by this call to prayer by the LORD that I stopped what I was doing and called my Pastor/mentor Dan, I shared the burden with him-and we prayed. And so it has come to pass, and I suspect that it will become increasingly depressed; if the LORD tarries.

Psalm 23

A Psalm of David.

The LORD is my shepherd,
I shall not want.
He makes me lie down in green pastures;
He leads me beside quiet waters.
He restores my soul;
He guides me in the paths of righteousness for His name's sake.
Even though I walk through the valley of the shadow of death,
I fear no evil, for You are with me;
Your rod and Your staff, they comfort me.
You prepare a table before me in the presence of my enemies;
You have anointed my head with oil;
My cup overflows.
Surely goodness and lovingkindness will follow me all the days of
my life, and I will dwell in the house of the LORD forever.

PHILIP AND THE CAR

My son Philip had been looking for a car for some time, he was struggling financially and we were seeking the LORD together asking God to please provide a car. It has been my prayer that the LORD would be declaring His greatness to my kids and persuading them away from this world system and into the His Kingdom. Philip was planning to drive over to Toyota City, a local auto dealer to look into used cars with my dad as I walked out to the mailbox to check the mail. I was thinking that the timing of me checking the mail and Philip leaving to look for a car was interesting. As Philip and my dad began to drive away I opened the mail and saw that I had received what looked to be a check in the mail. The timing was perfect, Philip was still within ear shot and I yelled "Philip please call me before you sign anything", and Philip seem to pick up on the fact that the LORD was up to something, he smiled and yelled "ok". As I recall the check was for about $500, and my tithe (literally "a tenth") was therefore $50 leaving $450 for a car. Philip returned after finding nothing within his price range and he then received a call from a friend or associate that said that he had a car for sale and he was thinking of Philip's need for a car, and the price was $400, as I recall. Philip drove out to see his friend's $400 car, and as he **walked around the corner facing either the front or the back of the car, he was able to see the license plate of the car. Philip said that his eyes began to tear up as he read the license plate, VKJ... (God uses VKs as signs to us, but that's another story) he knew that this car (and the money to pay for it) was a gift from the LORD Himself.**

The enemy tries to convince us that he is the provider, and this is false, he [Satan] is the pseudo or false provider. The LORD God is our provider-and there is no other.

[Jesus the anointed King said] When you pray, you are not to be like the hypocrites; for they love to stand and pray in the synagogues and on the street corners so that they may be seen by men Truly I say to you, they have their reward in full. "But you, when you pray, go into your inner room, close your door and pray to your Father who is in secret, and your Father who sees what is done in secret will reward you. "And when you are praying, do not use meaningless repetition as the Gentiles do, for they suppose that they will be heard for their many words. "So do not be like them; for your Father knows what you need before you ask Him. "Pray, then, in this way:

'Our Father who is in heaven, Hallowed be Your name. 'Your kingdom come, Your will be done on earth as it is in heaven.[11]**'Give us this day our daily bread. 'And forgive us our debts, as we also have forgiven our debtors. 'And do not lead us into temptation, but deliver us from evil. [For Yours is the kingdom and the power and the glory forever. Amen.]'** "For if you forgive others for their transgressions, your heavenly Father will also forgive you. "But if you do not forgive others, then your Father will not forgive your transgressions.

PHILIP AND THE POTHOLE

Several years ago I had a dream. In this dream my son Philip and I were walking in a construction area where they were building large, expensive homes. The homes being built were nearing completion, the yards were dirt with no sod on them, the driveways and the road in front of them was unpaved-a lot of dirt and mud. Everything was wet as though there had just been a soaking rain, Philip and I walked on the road in front of the homes, there were dips and potholes filled with water. As we walked Philip stepped into what looked like a small shallow pothole and was completely submerged in an instant. I dropped to my knees reaching into the hole frantically grabbing for anything or any part of his body as I was trying to grab him and pull him to the surface. As I reached for Philip I was crying and screaming uncontrollably and I was unable grab hold of him. When I woke up I felt that that the dream addressed the dangers of the world's draw-the love of money, and the potential to be overcome by it.

Psalm 1

[1]How blessed is the man [or person] who does not walk in the counsel of the wicked,
nor stand in the path of sinners, nor sit in the seat of scoffers!
[2]But his [or her] delight is in the law of the LORD, and in His law he meditates day and night.
[3]He [or she] will be like a tree firmly planted by streams of water, which yields its fruit in its season
and its leaf does not wither and in whatever he does, he prospers.
[4]The wicked are not so, but they are like chaff [the worthless parts] which the wind drives away.
[5]Therefore the wicked will not stand in the judgment, nor sinners in the assembly of the righteous.

⁶For the LORD knows the way of the righteous,
but the way of the wicked [those that disregard the Lord] will perish.

₁ₛₜ Timothy 6:10

**"For the love [excessive regard] of money is a root of all of evil,
and some by longing for it have wandered away from the faith and
pierced themselves with many griefs."**

PHILIP AND THE TRACTOR

In a time of my son Philip's life that he seemed to be pulled by the world on one side and by the LORD on the other we had had a talk about what I perceived to be happening-and we agreed to pray together. As I recall we were asking the LORD to speak to Philip in a personal way regarding the matter in order to set the issue straight. Within a few days Philip had a dream. In his dream Philip was driving on a path or road between two ditches and he was driving a tractor that had a very interesting steering mechanism. The steering mechanism operated by way of two independent parallel levers, one on the right and one on the left. The premise of the steering mechanism was much like the steering of some "BOB-CAT's" or old military tanks that works as follows; when you want to turn left you push the left lever and let up on the right. When you want to turn right you push the right lever right and let up on the left. **The side that you choose to turn to requires that you let up or compromise on the other side; one side is chosen over the other and the other is compromised.** This was so clear to me that I thanked the LORD for the interpretation and literally laughed that it could be so clear a message to me. The LORD wanted Philip, me and everyone to understand that we can serve only one side. To serve one is to neglect the other; to regard one is to disregard the other; to honor one is to dishonor the other; to love one is to hate the other. Recall Jesus' statement **"No one can serve two masters; for either he will hate [Greek, disregard] the one and love [regard] the other, or he will be devoted to one and despise the other You cannot serve God and wealth." (Matthew 6:24)** There is no "middle ground" and "no gray area" the middle and the gray are lies from the devil.

Genesis 40:8

"Do not interpretations [of dreams] belong to God?"

149

Ecclesiastes 12

Remember God in Your Youth

¹Remember also your Creator in the days of your youth, before the evil days come and the years draw near when you will say, "I have no delight in them"...⁸"Vanity of vanities," says the Preacher, "all is vanity! "Purpose of the Preacher ⁹In addition to being a wise man, the Preacher also taught the people knowledge; and he pondered, searched out and arranged many proverbs. ¹⁰The Preacher sought to find delightful words and to write words of truth correctly. ¹¹The words of wise men are like goads, and masters of these collections are like well-driven nails; they are given by one Shepherd. **¹²But beyond this, my son, be warned: the writing of many books is endless, and excessive devotion to books is wearying to the body. ¹³The conclusion, when all has been heard, is: fear God and keep His commandments, because this applies to every person. ¹⁴For God will bring every act to judgment, everything which is hidden, whether it is good or evil.**

PRAYING FOR SUDAN, AND
THE VISION OF THE EGYPTIAN "god"

Several years ago our church group began to pray for Sudan during the humanitarian crisis in Darfur where there was reported to be persecution of poor Christians by wealthy Muslims in Northern Sudan. While praying with my eyes closed I saw a tall and muscular male creature taking three long strides toward me as if to introduce himself. This creature was wearing a loin-cloth, feet coverings with high-tops and he was shirtless stepped toward me walking on a solid level sandy floor; he was wearing a tall linear headpiece and I was not able to see his face. He walked up to me in a non-threatening way as his hands were to his side, non-the-less I literally jumped, my eyes were then wide open and my heart was pounding my chest. I could hardly talk though I said **"Wow LORD, what was that about? Why did you do that?"** I could sense that the LORD was chuckling, in fact I heard Him as he He said to me **"I [LORD God] wanted you to see what you were getting yourself into [while praying for Sudan]"**. Recall that the Republic of Sudan is bordered by Egypt to the north, the Red Sea to the northeast, the Nile divides the country between east and west sides. The people of Sudan have a long history extending from antiquity which is intertwined with the history of Egypt. **Eastern Sudan or Nubia was known to the Egyptians as Cush and had strong cultural and religious ties to Egypt.** The image that I saw looked very much like the **"Egyptian god" referred to as Anubis otherwise known as "the destroyer".** I believe that the LORD was revealing to me that there were strongholds in Sudan that remain as a result of the worship of these false gods dating to antiquity, and that we needed to be informed and pray accordingly. The LORD did not like the idea of scaring me but He seemed to be amused by my dramatic reaction as I nearly jumped out of my skin when I saw "that thing" walk right up to me. I can understand this amusement as I too am a dad, and I have enjoyed watching my kids jump a few times too.

151

¹²"Behold, let me tell you, you are not right in this, for God is greater than man. ¹³"Why do you complain against Him that He does not give an account of all His doings? ¹⁴"Indeed God speaks once, or twice, yet no one notices it. **¹⁵"In a dream, a vision of the night, when sound sleep falls on men, while they slumber in their beds, ¹⁶Then He opens the ears of men, and seals their instruction,**

¹⁷That He may turn man aside from his conduct, and keep man from pride; ¹⁸He keeps back his soul from the pit, and his life from passing over into Sheol [the abode of the dead]. ¹⁹"Man is also chastened with pain on his bed, and with unceasing complaint in his bones; ²⁰so that his life loathes bread, and his soul favorite food. ²¹"His flesh wastes away from sight, and his bones which were not seen stick out.

PROVERBS 21:1 DEMONSTRATED

There have been many times that the LORD has changed people's minds and turned their hearts right in front of me after I had requested of the LORD. There was one particular time that I was talking to a government official regarding a levee of my account or paycheck. I was calling with the hope of meeting a deadline that would prevent the levee of funds from my account. As I was on the phone the person stated that "it was too late for her do anything and that she was not going to get it done soon enough to effect the outcome for today. It's just not going to happen!" there were no if and or buts with regard to this matter. At that moment I could feel that the LORD was calling me to prayer. I thanked the lady on the phone and I called my Mom and I told her about the conversation sensing that the LORD wanted us to demonstrate faith and persevere in prayer. Together mom and I prayed and reminded the LORD of His promise in Proverbs 21:1 "The king's heart is like channels of water in the hand of the LORD; He [LORD God] turns it [the hearts of people] wherever He wishes." After a few minutes passed the phone rang. I answered the phone and the lady that I had recently talked to simply stated that she had taken care of the issue and that it was done in time to effect the outcome for today, and she said it as though that were the plan all along. Again I thanked her and, I testified to her and gave great praises to the LORD for turning her heart and turning the events of the day. So much for "It's just not going to happen!"

Proverbs 21:1-8

The king's heart is like channels of water in the hand of the LORD; He turns it wherever He wishes. Every man's way is right in his own eyes, but the LORD weighs the hearts. To do righteousness and justice is desired by the LORD more than sacrifice. Haughty eyes

153

and a proud heart, the lamp of the wicked, is sin.
The plans of the diligent lead surely to advantage, but everyone
who is hasty comes surely to poverty. The acquisition of treasures by
a lying tongue is a fleeting vapor, the pursuit of death. The violence
of the wicked will drag them away, because they refuse to act with
justice. The way of a guilty man is crooked,
but as for the pure, his conduct is upright.

RAISING THE DEAD IN THE CADAVER LAB-AND THE SCREAMING PEOPLE

Prior to my being incarcerated I was a medical doctor; I went to medical school in Des Moines Iowa and I graduated in 2000. One of the first classes that I took in medical school was gross anatomy. The term "gross" does not refer to the fact that it is "icky" or "yucky" to dissect human beings. The term "gross" in this context means "total" or "entire". In gross anatomy the total or entire human body is dissected and the bodies being dissected are referred to as "cadavers". The class runs about 6 months, I should know as I had to take it twice. In the class there are medical students in white coats all over the place, and there are lots of cadavers as well, though fewer in number than the white coated medical students, non-the-less there are a lot of partially dissected cadavers up on tables all around in the "cadaver lab".

I had a dream a few months ago. In my colorful dream I was standing in a large sterile looking laboratory with about 12-15 other people, we were all wearing lab coats, we were facing a cadaver that was laid out on a table and there was a man standing to the left of the cadaver. The cadaver was dried out and had most of its skin removed, it looked like dried muscle over bone in the shape of a human. We were all Dr.'s, with the exception of the cadaver of course; we were being instructed by the man next to the cadaver. For some reason I was singled out by the instructor and called on by him in what seemed to be in a sarcastic manner, almost as though he were mocking God he called me to the front. The instructor called me foreword in front of all of the other Dr.'s and I walked up next to the instructor and stood between him and the cadaver, the instructor mocked me for my love of God. I stood next to the cadaver for what seemed only a few seconds and I do not recall that I was told to do anything. As I stood over the cadaver I held out my hand over the cadaver's face or chest and feeling empowered I boldly and loudly said, **"In the name of Jesus of Nazareth, Rise!"**

155

At that very moment the cadaver began to sit up and all of the people screamed and ran to the opposite corner of the room. While the people were screaming in the far corner I remained next to the cadaver and simply said **"why do you marvel at this?"**, and my thought was that God made us from dust why is it so hard to believe that He can heal us and raise us from the dead?

Acts 3

[1]Now Peter and John were going up to the temple at the ninth hour, the hour of prayer. [2]And a man who had been lame from his mother's womb was being carried along, whom they used to set down every day at the gate of the temple which is called Beautiful, in order to beg alms of those who were entering the temple...[6]**But Peter said, "I do not possess silver and gold, but what I do have I give to you: In the name of Jesus Christ the Nazarene--walk!"** [7]And seizing him by the right hand, he raised him up; and immediately his feet and his ankles were strengthened. [8]With a leap he stood upright and began to walk; and he entered the temple with them, walking and leaping and praising God. [9]**And all the people saw him walking and praising God;** [10]and they were taking note of him as being the one who used to sit at the Beautiful Gate of the temple to beg alms, and they were filled with wonder and amazement at what had happened to him. [11]**While he was clinging to Peter and John, all the people ran together to them at the so-called portico of Solomon, full of amazement. [12]But when Peter saw this, he replied to the people, "Men of Israel, why are you amazed at this, or why do you gaze at us, as if by our own power or piety we had made him walk?**

RICARDO AT THE TABLE

When I began working in the plastics factory, I seemed to have a type of tunnel-vision as I did not see people other than the Hispanics. As a result, during our first break we all walked into the cafeteria and I looked around for a table to sit at, there were a lot of tables with a lot of people; however I seemed only to see one long table and it was all Hispanics. I went and sat down with all of these people that I did not know and I for the most part did not understand them, neither did they understand me. It is clear to me that it was the LORD that was leading me there as he was shielding my vision from any other options of people to bond with and minister to. Later I saw other people and I literally laughed to myself, I simply did not see any other options of people to interact with, it really was quite funny. As I sat down at the table all eyes seemed to be on me, all of the people were talking in their native language and I simply did not understand what they were saying, so I smiled and nodded. They seemed to include me, we shared food and I listened and nodded a lot, and so it continued, day after day. **As I recall, I began to** *question the LORD, "LORD I know that you brought me here and I believe that you wanted me to sit at this place, but, why am I here?" My question to the LORD "why am I here?" Was not a complaint as if to say "poor me, why am I here?" No, not at all, I was literally asking the LORD what His desire was for me, what do You LORD want me to do next, what is your purpose for me here? I repeated my request of the LORD a few more times as I politely, nodded and smiled to the others at the table.* **I felt very awkward as I sat at the table and I was praying to the LORD "Ok LORD why am I here?"** at that very moment, a voice from the far right end of the table said in broken English *"are you a Christian?"* When I heard the question posed from the far end of the table **"are you a Christian"** I snapped my head to the right and looked into the face of a Hispanic looking young man looking to be in his twenties, and he was looking at me-the young man's name is Ricardo. *At the moment that I looked at*

Ricardo, as I recall, I heard the LORD say "watch over him, because of the prayers of his parents." Ricardo told me that he "use to be a Christian" he went on to explain that he now was a boxer, and he liked to dance, he asked me "do you think it is ok for me to dance?" If so would you help me to find some dye for my black dance pants? I said yes and went on a mission from the LORD to find this young man some dye for his black dance pants. Ricardo went on to explain to me that he had left Mexico and he wanted to escape the rules, confines and essentially he wanted to escape from the God of his father. Little did he know that in his attempt to escape the God of his father he found himself surrounded by believers in the LORD and now he was in my life as well. Since that time Ricardo and I have developed and maintained a very close relationship, we began to study the Scriptures together, we began to see God's signs and wonders, as well we get together several times a week for lunch and I had the privilege of seeing Ricardo return to the LORD. One of my fond memories was to sit with Ricardo in church and to watch him break down before the LORD, to walk up to the altar and to weep before the LORD. Ricardo and I went on to develop a very close relationship, I feel love for him like a father for a son, in addition Ricardo and my son Philip have developed a relationship of brotherly love. My daughter Hannah and Ricardo's niece are the best of friends as well-we are family.

1 Samuel 18

Jonathan and David

¹Now it came about when he had finished speaking to Saul, that the soul of Jonathan was knit to the soul of David, and Jonathan loved him as himself. ²Saul took him that day and did not let him return to his father's house. *³Then Jonathan made a covenant with David because he loved him as himself. ⁴Jonathan stripped himself of the robe that was on him and gave it to David, with his armor, including his sword and his bow and his belt.* ⁵So David went out wherever Saul sent him, and prospered; and Saul set him over the men of war. And it was pleasing in the sight of all the people and also in the sight of Saul's servants. ⁶It happened as they were coming, when David returned from killing the Philistine, that the women came out of all the cities of Israel, singing and dancing, to meet King Saul, with tambourines, with joy and with musical instruments.

158

[7]The women sang as they played, and said,
"Saul has slain his thousands,
And David his ten thousands."

[8]Then Saul became very angry, for this saying displeased him; and he said, "They have ascribed to David ten thousands, but to me they have ascribed thousands. Now what more can he have but the kingdom?" *[9]Saul looked at David with suspicion from that day on.*

"RIGHT. NO! YOUR OTHER RIGHT"

In 2007 my daughter Hannah and I went to Emmanuel Christian Center's Saturday night service. I was led to go so as to find a good Latino speaking church for those who I was evangelizing and working with. Hannah realized that their kid's ministry was a blessing to her and she had a burden to bring some of her friends that they may come to know the LORD as well. We moved on the prompting-Hannah invited some friends and they came. Typically we would pack sandwiches, drinks, chips and treats for the group, drive out to Stillwater, get the kids and go to church and get the kids home. Round trip it was about 8 hours, it seemed very fruitful-a very good investment. Over the course of our time together about a half dozen kids committed themselves to the LORD including Hannah. One of the stars of this story is Megan. Megan is one of Hannah's very good friends and she became a fixture in our household along the way and it has been a blessing to get to know Megan and her family. One of the very first nights of "the little girl's ministry" was Megan's first night. I had not met Megan or her family and I wanted to present myself as responsible and in a manner worthy of her parents trust for these Saturday outings. I did not want to be late picking her up or dropping her off. It was no coincidence that for several months prior to this that the LORD had been teaching me to be led by His voice; it started in the seemingly small things. God would tell me to do something, I typically wrestled with whether I was responding to my own thought, **I would obey as to test-out this voice and God would affirm me. It was happening time and time again; I was being trained by the LORD, see Hebrews 5:14.** This particular day we were to pick up Megan by a predetermined time, we picked up Hannah's friend Mackenzie first and then we headed down the driveway with only a few minutes to get to Megan's house. Rural Stillwater and Hugo are "in the sticks", farmland and dirt roads are not uncommon. As we headed down the driveway toward the road I said to the girls "Ok, how do we get there [referring

161

to Megan's house]?" and the girls said "I don't know". I sat at the end of the driveway knowing that if the LORD wanted this to work out, He would need to make a way. I remember the girls saying "do you want us to go back to the house and call her or get her address?" I said no we don't have time for that. The girls were all talking loud in the back and I was praying to the LORD and reminded that the LORD had been training me to hear His voice. I said "LORD you have been training me for this purpose" and asked Him to please lead me to Megan's house on time. I put my hands on the wheel and said "Ok LORD which way?" I thought or heard "right" and I said in prayer "LORD I thought or heard 'right' so I'm turning right" and I turned right and drove for about a quarter of a mile and approached a turn and said "LORD I could go straight or turn right again, I thought or heard "right" and again I said "LORD I heard or thought 'right' so I'm going right unless you stop me" God didn't stop me, so, I went right. This time I drove for quite a while until I came to a stop and I needed to turn either right or left, I said "LORD I need to turn either right or left" and I thought or heard "left" so I turned left and again drove for what seemed like forever but was really only about a mile or two. Again I approached a stop and needed to either turn right or left. As I approached I said "LORD I will need to either turn right or left and I heard "right" and continued foreword moving toward the stop sign, starting to turn and heard "No, Right!" as if to correct me, when I heard "No, Right!" I realized that though I intended to turn right I was actually turning left and was stopped in the left lane beginning to turn left. I then said **"Oh, right, right!"** realizing that I was turning left I changed direction and turned right thinking of how funny it was yet still being nervous as we were running out of time and I still had no idea of where Megan lived. It was as we turned right that one of the girls from the back seat chimed-in and said **"Megan's house is right over there"** up to that point the girls were disengaged in what I and the LORD were up to. We pulled into Megan's driveway on-time and the rest is history or should I say "HIS-STORY" as Megan and several other girls involved in the "little girl's ministry" have committed to the LORD and have shown signs of life.

John 10:3-4

[Jesus, the Good Shepherd said] To him the doorkeeper opens, and the sheep hear his voice, and he calls his own sheep by name and leads them out. When he puts forth all his own, he goes ahead of them, and the sheep follow him because they know his voice.

162

ROBERT, THE TV, THE INTERRUPTED REBUKE, AND, THE GAMBLING INTERVENTION

I have a good friend and we have an interesting history together. Robert was a patient and I was a doctor, though at the time I may have been much worse off than Robert was. Robert and I "randomly" reunited at the church food shelf and we quickly became friends. Robert is a tall lanky fellow, he is: kind, generous, amusing, and very quirky-Robert is hard not to like. Recently Robert sold his TV and then immediately regretting it, he wanted a new TV. I told Robert that if the LORD wanted him to have a TV someone could walk up and offer him a TV-Robert agreed and we prayed for a TV. When I returned home from my visit with Robert my neighbor called and asked me if I knew anyone that needed a TV, and I replied "yes I do!" and then I shared the story about Robert's need with my neighbor.

Robert was thankful and he asked if I could drop off the TV, I told him that I would need to drop it off at about 10:45 A.M. as I had a discipleship meeting at 11:30 out his way. Robert explained that the timing of my dropping off his TV was perfect as "it kept me [Robert] from sinning". Robert explained to me that he was struggled with gambling, and that he was planning to go to a casino at that time and he recognized that this was God's intervention. When I heard this I became angry with Robert and though I felt that I needed to be quiet (clearly from the LORD) I told Robert that I did not approve and **"had I known that he was gambling I would not have been giving him money…" I was harsh, rebuking Robert when I should have been quietly listening and praying.** Though it was true that I was upset, I felt convicted that I had not been quiet as the LORD was telling me; as I was feeling convicted in my heart I said "Robert!, Robert!" thinking that we were still talking and that Robert's feelings may have been hurt. At that point I realized that Robert was not on the phone but that we

163

had been cut off and he was trying to call me on the other line. As I answered the call and I talked to Robert it was clear that the LORD had intervened on my behalf and terminated the call at the point that I was harshly rebuking Robert-the timing was perfect. Robert did not hear one word of my harsh rebuke as our call was dropped. When it was all-said-and-done Robert recognized the LORD for providing the TV, and for keeping him away from the casino that day. I stood in agreement with him and I silently thanked the LORD for His intervention and for His terminating the call the way that He did. Thank You for Your kindness and provisions LORD!

Ecclesiastes 5

¹Guard your steps as you go to the house of God and draw near to listen rather than to offer the sacrifice of fools; for they do not know they are doing evil. ²Do not be hasty in word or impulsive in thought to bring up a matter in the presence of God For God is in heaven and you are on the earth; therefore let your words be few. ³For the dream comes through much effort and the voice of a fool through many words. ⁴When you make a vow to God, do not be late in paying it; for He takes no delight in fools Pay what you vow! ⁵It is better that you should not vow than that you should vow and not pay. ⁶Do not let your speech cause you to sin and do not say in the presence of the messenger of God that it was a mistake. Why should God be angry on account of your voice and destroy the work of your hands? ⁷For in many dreams and in many words there is emptiness. Rather, fear God. **⁸If you see oppression of the poor and denial of justice and righteousness in the province, do not be shocked at the sight; for one official watches over another official, and there are higher officials over them.** ⁹After all, a king who cultivates the field is an advantage to the land.

SCREAMS OF TERROR OR HYMNS OF PRAISE

It was in 2006 that the LORD began to reveal Himself to me in powerful ways, though He did do some very cool stuff prior to that as well. Not surprisingly, that time of enlightenment was accompanied by waves of: attack and temptation from the enemy, and testing from the LORD. I recall going through intense night terrors at that time and I would wake the house with my screams in response to dreams and visions. I also had waves of illnesses of various kinds including: vomiting, headaches, infections... At that time I was living downstairs in my parent's home and on the weekends my daughter Hannah stayed in the family room. I would typically fall asleep long before Hannah and it was not uncommon for her to wake me up as I was: thrashing, screaming and crying out. During this time I recall sensing that if I persisted and remained faithful to the LORD that these attacks would end-and they did. On one occasion, and it may have been toward the end of these attacks, as though the LORD Himself was proclaiming His victory He gave me a dream; **in the dream I was standing on a cliff overlooking the ocean waves and I was raising my hands to the LORD and singing a hymn of praise. Hannah woke me as I was singing hymns in my sleep.** This was an end of these attacks, as I recall.

James 4:7

Submit therefore to God. Resist the devil and he [the devil] will flee from you.

Psalm 17

A Prayer of David.

¹Hear a just cause, O LORD, give heed to my cry;

165

Give ear to my prayer, which is not from deceitful lips.
²Let my judgment come forth from Your presence;
Let Your eyes look with equity.
³You have tried my heart;
You have visited me by night...
⁸Keep me as the apple of the eye;
Hide me in the shadow of Your wings
⁹From the wicked who despoil me,
My deadly enemies who surround me.
¹⁰They have closed their unfeeling heart,
with their mouth they speak proudly.
¹¹They have now surrounded us in our steps;
they set their eyes to cast us down to the ground.
¹²He [the enemy] is like a lion that is eager to tear,
And as a young lion lurking in hiding places.
¹³Arise, O LORD, confront him, bring him low;
Deliver my soul from the wicked with Your sword,
¹⁴From men with Your hand, O LORD,
From men of the world, whose portion is in this life,
And whose belly You fill with Your treasure;
They are satisfied with children,
And leave their abundance to their babes.
¹⁵As for me, I shall behold Your face in righteousness;
I will be satisfied with Your likeness when I awake.

SHANNON AND SO MANY WARNINGS...

Several years ago, while en route to a prayer meeting I was beginning to recognize that the LORD was communicating with me via license plates. On that day I was driving to meet with my Pastor/mentor and as I recall it was about 3:30 A.M. In these weekly meetings we would lay out a long list of the people that we were associated with in our home church group and we would pray for them. It was surprising how long the list had become in the short time that I had been involved with the group. As I was driving to the meeting I noted a few cars or trucks had driven past with "VKs" on the license plates, I acknowledged the "VK's", I thanked the LORD though I recall being distracted as I was thinking about Shannon. Shannon is a young lady that was then new to the group, she had come from a rough background and I had no real feel for her in the LORD, though at that moment I was thinking about her safety and her potential for God's Kingdom. At that time I did not connect the "VK's" that I was seeing with the thoughts of Shannon that I was having. I have since understood that the LORD seems to speak though my thoughts about a particular subject and He confirms Himself by way of "VK's" on license plates and other ways as well. God has also used license plates as He has directed me, corrected me, confirmed things and gotten my attention with a timely "VK". As I was driving I felt as though the LORD was trying to get my attention as the "VKs" were flying by though I did not know what the LORD was trying to communicate to me in connection with my thoughts of Shannon. Finally it was as though "the lights went on" and I connected the two events taking place: the "VKs" flying by and my thoughts and concerns for the welfare of Shannon and her family-they were connected. I recall saying "what is it LORD, what are you trying to communicate to me?" and I literally felt as though I were playing charades with the LORD; I would get a thought and I would say out loud "Shannon!, is this about Shannon?" and a "VK" would fly by. So after establishing that this message was about Shannon I again said "what LORD! What about

167

Shannon?" I then began to think about Shannon's protection and our need as a church to watch over her, as I thought of Shannon and our need to watch over her I recall saying "LORD is this about You wanting us to watch over Shannon?" and a "VK" flew by at that moment. After establishing that the LORD was calling me and those in the flock to "watch out for Shannon" I realized that this was my order from the LORD, and I took the word directly to my Pastor, in fact it was the first thing that I said to him, the first order of importance; as if I were currier of important military information, and all else seemed less important. As I walked into his house I said "God wants us to watch out for Shannon" and my Pastor/mentor asked immediately if I had talked with anyone that knew what was going on with Shannon, and especially with what had transpired the night before, and I replied "No I have not". My Pastor/mentor then explained the events of the night before with regard to Shannon and her family, how their housing had been lost and that one of the congregations was thinking of taking them into their home, though she was reluctant and was seeking the LORD on His will in the matter. This was great confirmation for the church and for me. Praise God for His willingness to communicate so personally with us.

Psalm 56

[3] **When I am afraid, I will put my trust in You. [4] In God, whose word I praise,**
In God I have put my trust; I shall not be afraid what can mere man do to me?

[9] **This I know, that God is for me...**

[13] **For You have delivered my soul from death, indeed my feet from stumbling, so that I may walk before God**
in the light of the living.

SHANNON GOT THE MESSAGE

I had not heard from Shannon in several years and I had a strong concern for her one morning-I felt that I had a word from God for her. I called Shannon's phone and there was no answer so I left a message. My message to Shannon was "Shannon I feel that I have a word from God for you. It's time for you to get serious about your relationship with the LORD, put Him first or God will get your attention through difficult times. "I felt timid and concerned that this message may sound judgmental, I didn't want to offend Shannon as I had no idea what she had been up these past two years, but I did and said what I was feeling led to do and say. A few hours later Shannon called and she explained that she had gotten my phone message, she said that she had been in the back of a police car when I called and that she had been detained by the police and that the timing was perfect-she had gotten the message loud and clear. God was calling Shannon back to Himself-thank You LORD! Great timing!

Hebrews 12:5-6

"and you have forgotten the exhortation which is addressed to you as sons, "My son [and daughter], do not regard lightly the discipline of the Lord, Nor faint when you are reproved by Him; for those whom the Lord loves He disciplines, and He scourges every son whom He receives ."

SISTER SUE AND THE CARDINALS

When I first became a believer I was zealous, well intended, argumentative, condemning and self righteous at times; I see that I stirred up many a dust storm while attempting to open the eyes of the lost. I now realize that opening the eyes of the lost is not my job-it is the LORD's job (See Jeremiah 24:7, John 6:65, and 2nd Timothy 2:25…). It seems that over the past years the dust has begun to settle, I have learned the value of being still, loving my neighbor as myself, serving and trusting that the LORD Himself will lead people to repentance through His kindness, and sometimes I even need to step out of God's way. My mom and I have been praying for my sister and her family for several years. A few days ago my sister Sue called to talk with mom, mom was not home so we chatted. Sue said that she wanted to talk to mom about our Grandma Eileen who had passed away several years ago; Sue related that while reflecting about Grandma, she sees Cardinals and receives it as "a sign" (I know that this is a sign from God, not a sign from my grandma-I quietly prayed). We both agreed about the sign and we talked about other times that we had seen cardinals at key spiritual moments, I also shared how the LORD uses deer and other animals in my life as signs. Sue agreed and said "O my gosh! You too?" she then said in a thoughtful and soft voice **"maybe you and I are not so different after all"**. I realize that it is not about us but that statement **"you and I are not so different after all"** touched my heart, and I suspect that it touched the LORD as well and it seemed somehow reverent toward the LORD. After a nice and serious talk we said goodbye and I returned to where I had my Bible open at the desk, I was already thankful and rejoicing as I looked to the Scripture where I had left off before our conversation; my eyes focused on **Psalm 46:5** *"God is in the midst of her, she will not be moved; God will help her when morning dawns."* I receive that too as a sign from God regarding my sister Sue-thank you LORD.

Isaiah 44

I will pour out My Spirit on your offspring
And My blessing on your descendants;
⁴And they will spring up among the grass
Like poplars by streams of water.'
⁵"This one will say, 'I am the LORD'S';
And that one will call on the name of Jacob;
And another will write on his hand, 'Belonging to the LORD,'
And will name Israel's name with honor.

SPYS LIKE US

I felt prompted to get a devotional book for my Daughter Hannah and my son Philip's then girlfriend Chin (Chin and Philip are now married); I felt that Hannah and Chin may benefit from this book as it deals with spiritual warfare and the battle field of our minds. I felt that Hannah may resist the idea if I presented it to her and I determined to remain quiet, be still and know that He is God.

This morning I was in bed reading and for some reason I began looking for my phone, I searched and I shifted and I searched and I shifted some more as I looked for my lost phone. I later realized that as I was searching for my phone I was actually holding my phone in my left hand the whole time. It was interesting that I even made a mental note to myself, **"I did not ever recall losing my phone only to find that I was holding it in my left hand"**.

A few hours later my daughter Hannah called from school, Hannah said that she was not feeling well and that she needed a ride home from school. **I arrived at Hannah's school, met her in the office and then I walked her to her locker, while walking to the locker she shared with me that that very morning she had lost her phone only to find that as she was looking for her phone she was holding it in her left hand the whole time.** We laughed as we shared our stories and we acknowledged that the LORD seemed to be up to something. For some reason we then began to discuss our being spies; as we drove home we got into a light discussion regarding our being "spies" and living incognito. This gentle banter lasted into the late afternoon.

I meet with my son Philip for dinner weekly; as we met for dinner **(the very evening that Hannah and I were joking about our being "spies")** I read to Philip an excerpt from the devotional book that I have been reading through with several other people. I explained that I felt prompted by the LORD to order a copy's of this book for

173

Hannah and Chin. Philip was quick to encourage me too give the books to Chin with the idea that Chin would approach Hannah with the idea that Hannah and Chin would together read these books while being accountable to each other. Philip and I agreed that Hannah would likely resist if I suggested the idea though she would likely engage with great enthusiasm if her good friend Chin suggested the idea. I explained to Philip that it was my original idea that Chin and Hannah would work through the books together, however I did not want to push the issue and I put the idea into the good hand of the LORD.

I explained to Philip about the joking with Hannah that very day regarding the topic of "spies like us" and I explained that this seemed a spy mission for the purpose of good. The LORD has a fabulous sense of humor and He is a warrior. Recall that **"the LORD will fight for you while you keep silent" (Exodus 14:14)**. As I pulled out of the restaurant parking lot Hannah sent me a text joking that she was a spy-cool timing LORD!

Exodus 15:3

"The LORD [YHWH] is a warrior; the LORD [YHWH] is His name."

Late entry, about a week after writing this article I went to dinner with Hannah, Chin and Philip. Hannah explained to me that she and Chin had been working through a book that she was "really enjoying", the books that I had given to Chin. :)

STEVE AT THE FOOD SHELF THEN DIED

The timing of the LORD is great. While working at the food shelf we have had countless opportunities for ministry, it seems that the LORD uses the food like a fisherman uses worms as bait. On one occasion a man in his early 40s was in the food line, his name was Steve. While in the food line I talked with Steve and I helped him to his car with his boxes of groceries, as we finished packing his car I noted a blank and lost look on Steve's face. **As he looked at me he said that "he had once had a relationship with the LORD", and that he missed the relationship that he once had had with God.** I affirmed his regard for the LORD and I understood his concern. I challenged Steve to not waste his time on earth as we do not know when our time in these bodies will come to an end. Steve was very receptive and we prayed together in the parking lot asking the LORD to come into Steve's life-Steve renewed his commitment to the LORD that day. I told Steve that I would like to help him and I asked him if he had a Bible to read, he said no but that he would like to have a Bible and that he would read the Bible if he had one. I told Steve that I would look for a good Bible for him. A few days later I found a very nice leather bound Bible at the book store and I knew that the LORD intended it for Steve. The next week I gave the Bible to Steve and his eyes welled up with tears; he was very thankful, he said that he was serious about his commitment to the LORD, that he planned to read and that he "planned to see me at church on Sunday". The next Sunday Steve was not in church and there was a massage on the church recorder from Steve's girlfriend, she said that Steve's body was found on his bed, that he had apparently died suddenly and that Steve had his Bible with him when he died. Steve's girlfriend testified that Steve's life had changed right before his death and that he had become serious about the LORD again. Praise God!

Psalm 3

[4]"LORD, make me to know my end
and what is the extent of my days;
let me know how transient I am.
[5]"Behold, You [LORD God] have made my days as handbreadths,
and my lifetime as nothing in Your sight;
surely every man [person] at his best is a mere breath. Selah.
[6]"Surely every man walks about as a phantom;
surely they make an uproar for nothing;
He [they] amasses riches and does not know who will gather them.
[7]"And now, Lord, for what do I wait?
My hope is in You [LORD my God].

THE LORD, STAN, ME AND TIM

I had given my life to the LORD a few years earlier, and for the most part all of my friends seemed to run the other way when they saw me coming. By some turn of events, Tim a high school friend of my sister called me, I had been a good friend of Tim's younger brother and this seemed an unusual call. Tim was looking for someone to partner with as he wanted to buy a fixer-upper home that "required very little work and we would easily make a bundle on"-famous last words. I listened to Tim, and we bought the house together-this was "a can't-miss deal". As part of our strategy for fixing up the home we brought in Stan (a taper) my good friend and outspoken brother in the LORD. Nothing of the project seem to work out as we had planned, that is, everything was much more time consuming, much more expensive, and there was one disaster after another. Through the process we spent a lot time together, and the three of us worked in very close proximity to one another. This seemed to be a perfectly planned evangelistic opportunity, as I see it now, what the enemy meant for evil, **"God meant it for good in order to bring about this present result, to preserve many people alive" (See Genesis 50:20).** At the time Stan and I were in our spiritual childhood and Tim showed no interest in the things of the LORD. Tim was respectfully flippant in his comments, we had numerous bouts of friendly banter, Stan and I continued to talk to Tim about our experience with the LORD-and so it continued. There were more than a few times that I felt that our debates were heated and unfruitful-but Stan and I continued to pray and do as we felt led. The entire house project must have lasted 4-6 months, and we spent extended periods of time together far beyond what was planned and we talked about the LORD, over and over. As the project ended we sold the house and as I recall we lost money or we were happy to break even. As we all parted ways Stan and I agreed to place Tim in the capable hand of the LORD, and as David did with his son Solomon so we did with our friend Tim-we encouraged him to trust in the LORD. "**[David said to his son Solomon] know the**

177

God of your father, and serve Him with a whole heart and a willing mind; for the LORD searches all hearts, and understands every intent of the thoughts. If you seek Him, He will let you find Him; but if you forsake Him, He will reject you forever." (1 Chronicles 28:9)** And so we parted ways both physically and spiritually on friendly and cordial terms.

Some 15 years later I got a call from Tim, at the time of Tim's call I was in an on-call room at Hennepin County Medical Center, I was consumed in my medical career and deeply entrenched in a miserable life style that must have looked good on the outside but was not on the inside. This time of my life was like running on a treadmill, chasing a promise but never catching up or even getting close to being fulfilled. Tim's life had not turn out the way he had planned either, the proverbial bottom fell out; his wife and he split, though all else in Tim's life was described as "a mess", he explained with great excitement that he was **"one of us now".** In the face of Tim's pursuit of: money, career, sex, entertainment, sports and vanity, nothing worked out as planned, nothing filled the God shaped void in his life. Tim commented that nothing brought him peace except for the seeds that were sown during that time that we talked of the LORD. At some point Tim opened his heart to the LORD and the LORD entered in as He had promised. Recall Jesus' statement **"20 Behold, I stand at the door and knock; if anyone hears My voice and opens the door, I will come in to him and will dine with him, and he with Me. 21 He who overcomes, I will grant to him to sit down with Me on My throne, as I also overcame and sat down with My Father on His throne. 22 He who has an ear, let him hear...."** (Revelations 3:19-20)** God used this time and He turned this into a different kind of investment, in spite of our motives, and pursuits at the time, only now some 25 years later can I see a glimpse of what God's plan for us was. What we did perhaps motivated by evil in pursuit of earthly gain the LORD did for eternal gain. Praise God!

Isaiah 55

1 "Ho! Every one who thirsts, come to the waters; and you who have no money come, buy and eat. come, buy wine and milk without money and without cost.2 "Why do you spend money for what is not bread, and your wages for what does not satisfy? Listen carefully to Me [LORD God], and eat what is good, and delight yourself in abundance. **3 "Incline your ear and come to Me. Listen, that you may live; and I will make an everlasting covenant with you, according to the faithful mercies shown to David...6 Seek the LORD**

while He may be found; call upon Him while He is near. [7] Let the wicked forsake his way and the unrighteous man his thoughts; and let him return to the LORD, and He will have compassion on him, and to our God, for He will abundantly pardon. [8] "For My thoughts are not your thoughts, nor are your ways My ways," declares the LORD. [9] "For as the heavens are higher than the earth, so are My ways higher than your ways and My thoughts than your thoughts. [10] "For as the rain and the snow come down from heaven, and do not return there without watering the earth and making it bear and sprout, and furnishing seed to the sower and bread to the eater; [11] So will My [LORD God's] word be which goes forth from My mouth; it will not return to Me empty, without accomplishing what I desire, and without succeeding in the matter for which I [LORD God] sent it…"

TEST, TEST, THIS IS A TEST!

When I was in medical school we met in a large lecture hall with about 200 students and typically one lecturer. As the lecturer would teach on the topic of the day they would often repeat the points that they would be tested us on; that is to say, the lecturer would emphasize the points that we would be questioned on. When there was a repeating point we would whisper and nudge our neighbor saying **"Psssst! test, test this will be on the test", and those who regarded the call would prepare so as to pass the test.** In the same way, as I was led by the LORD to Numbers 19 and 20 "the Ordinance of the Red Heifer" the LORD was instructing me regarding tests. Numbers 19 address the need for water for purification regarding dealing with the bodies of the dead. As I read "dead body, water, bathe, wash, water, bathe, wash, water, dead body, water, water, bathe, bathe, wash..." God was showing me that in the same way that our medical school instructors were preparing us for a test, He was preparing the children of Israel for a test regarding purification, water and a dead body. In essence, what I was hearing from the LORD was **"Psssst! test, test, this will be on the test, and those who regarded the call would prepare so as to pass the test."** Water was required by the LORD as well as the ashes of the burnt offering "Red Heifer". As is always the case there was a test, though the flesh of man would be concerned with water for the purpose of drinking and survival, the Spirit would be concerned with water for the purpose of being pure and obedient before the LORD. That is to say one need would override the other, either the concern for water for the purposes of drinking or for the purpose of being cleansed and obedient before the LORD. In the presence of much water the test would be limited as there was enough water for both drinking and spiritual purification, but in the absence of much water the human heart could be tested. If there were only enough water to either drink or to be spiritually pure, the question is begged, which would be regarded as the priority; the flesh or the Spirit? **Or perhaps greater still what if there were no water at all** and there were a dead body, what would cry of the people be? We need water to drink or we need water to be pure before the LORD; that question would expose their heart. In Numbers Chapter 19 the children of Israel were presented with the laws concerning the handling of the dead, and their need for water for the purpose of purification, they were prepared for the test as they were given the test question. In Numbers Chapter 20 they were tested, in verse 1 "Miriam died", there is your dead body, and verse 2, there was "no water". Here lies the test, here the heart of the people will be exposed, will they cry for water for the purpose of purification before the LORD, a cry from the Spirit, or will they be more concerned with the flesh, what will we drink? In Numbers Chapter 20:4 the assembly of people gathered and "assembled themselves against Moses and Aaron... [and they complained, that there is no food] nor is there water to drink". It is sad to see that their response was not "how will we do as You commanded regarding purification?"

"All the commandments that I am commanding you today you shall be careful to do, that you may live and multiply, and go in and possess the land which the Lord swore *to give* to your forefathers. You shall remember all the way which the Lord your God has led you in the wilderness these forty years, that He might humble you, testing you, to know what was in your heart, whether you would keep His commandments or not. He humbled you and let you be hungry, and fed you with manna which you did not know, nor did your fathers know, that He might make you understand that man does not live by bread alone, but man lives by everything that proceeds out of the mouth of the Lord. Your clothing did not wear out on you, nor did your foot swell these forty years. Thus you are to know in your heart that the Lord your God was disciplining you just as a man disciplines his son. Therefore, you shall keep the commandments of the Lord your God, to walk in His ways and to fear Him.

Deuteronomy 8:1-6

"THANK YOU!!" TWENTY YEARS LATER

       I was driving in the car early one morning in 2010. I sensed that the LORD reminded me of a good deed that I had done some twenty years earlier while in Papua New Guinea on a missionary trip in 1990. While traveling to the highlands of the Enga province we came upon a large group of people, it was very hot and a lady had passed out, she was laying on the ground and nobody was helping her. I checked to see if she was alive, I moved her into the shade and cooled her with some water. Over time her condition improved, she was conscious, she looked stable and in good hands so I left her my fresh water and we left. For the most part I had forgotten about the event for 20 years, until the LORD reminded me of it on this day. I remember smiling, nodding my head and saying "oh yah that's right! I remember that", and I wondered why I had remembered that now after all of these years. At that point I sensed that the LORD was saying that He reminded me of the event simply that He may say "THANK YOU!" Can you imagine that? You're welcome LORD!

Hebrews 6:9-12

But, beloved, we are convinced of better things concerning you, and things that accompany salvation, though we are speaking in this way. **For God is not unjust so as to forget your work and the love which you have shown toward His name, in having ministered and in still ministering to the saints.** And we desire that each one of you show the same diligence so as to realize the full assurance of hope until the end, so that you will not be sluggish, but imitators of those who through faith and patience inherit the promises.

THAT GREAT NIGHT WITH HANNAH, "FOR SIGNS AND FOR SEASONS"

One night in the "dead of winter" my favorite daughter Hannah and I decided that we would go and see AVITAR. It was very unusual for me to do that kind of thing on a whim at that point (not now), as it turned out the LORD made it a most interesting and entertaining evening. The LORD dazzled us with His signs as the LORD's entertainment far outdid anything that Hollywood could do-even AVITAR. After deciding to go to the movie we jumped into the car in the dead of a very cold Minnesota winter. I looked into the sky as we drove and I noted that the moon was brilliant and it appeared to be very large in the eastern sky. I pointed out the moon to Hannah and we both marveled at this awesome sight of the huge moon in the sky, it looked too large to be real. Hannah and I talk about the LORD and how He had created the stars and the planets "for signs and for seasons" (See Genesis 1:14) and we commented that this huge moon was one very cool sign to us to see.

"Then God said, 'Let there be lights in the expanse of the heavens to separate the day from the night, and let them be for signs and for seasons and for days and years; [15] and let them be for lights in the expanse of the heavens to give light on the earth'; and it was so. [16] God made the two great lights, the greater light [sun] to govern the day, and the lesser light [moon] to govern the night; *He made* the stars also. (Genesis 1:14-16)

God's signs and wonders was the topic of our discussion as Hannah and I traveled. After talking about the stars, the planets and God's great signs we drove to the theater with the moon now to our back. Then we looked at the moon again and it was much different from how it appeared a minutes earlier. The moon had appeared huge a few minutes earlier and now was reduced to a fraction of what it had been just a few moments before. **Amazing! Hannah and I looked at** each other and wondered how that was possible. **It was wonderful to share that experience together-thank you Lord.** The movie was good too!

Ecclesiastes 12

Remember God in Your Youth

¹ Remember also your Creator in the days of your youth, before the evil days come and the years draw near when you will say, "I have no delight in them"; ² before the sun and the light, the moon and the stars are darkened, and clouds return after the rain; ³ in the day that the watchmen of the house tremble, and mighty men stoop, the grinding ones stand idle because they are few, and those who look through windows grow dim; ⁴ and the doors on the street are shut as the sound of the grinding mill is low, and one will arise at the sound of the bird, and all the daughters of song will sing softly. ⁵ Furthermore, men are afraid of a high place and of terrors on the road; the almond tree blossoms, the grasshopper drags himself along, and the caperberry is ineffective. For man goes to his eternal home while mourners go about in the street. ⁶ *Remember Him [YHWH, LORD God]* before the silver cord is broken and the golden bowl is crushed, the pitcher by the well is shattered and the wheel at the cistern is crushed; **⁷ then the dust will return to the earth as it was, and the spirit will return to God who gave it. ⁸ "Vanity of vanities," says the Preacher, "all is vanity!"** ⁹ In addition to being a wise man, the Preacher also taught the people knowledge; and he pondered, searched out and arranged many proverbs. ¹⁰ The Preacher sought to find delightful words and to write words of truth correctly. ¹¹ The words of wise men are like goads, and masters of *these* collections are like well-driven nails; they are given by one Shepherd. ¹² But beyond this, my son, be warned: the writing of many books is endless, and excessive devotion *to books* is wearying to the body.

¹³ The conclusion, when all has been heard, *is*: fear God and keep His commandments, because this *applies to* every person. ¹⁴ For God will bring every act to judgment, everything which is hidden, whether it is good or evil.

THE AGE OF ACCOUNTABILITY

I believe that the LORD gave me insight regarding "the age of accountability". **The term "the age of accountability" referrers to the age at which people are accountable for their sin, this term is familiar within the "Christian community".** The common belief is that newborns, infants and young children are not accountable for their sin and at some point in their development they become "aware of the difference between right and wrong". Presumably at some moment in time the child or person is no longer exempt from the consequence of their sin, they become aware and accountable, hence **"the age of accountability"**. A common supportive passage with regard to newborns and infants being exempt from sin is 2nd Samuel 12:23. In this passage David had lost his newborn son as a result of David's sin, **David declares "why should I [David] fast? Can I bring him [the child] back [from death] again? I [David] shall go to him [the child], but he will not return to me."** Therefore David declared that he understood that this newborn baby would be with him at some point in the future. The question has often been raised as to when exactly is the "age of accountability". Think about this, as a newborn it is not unusual to be naked and unashamed, it is no big deal for the newborn or even the infant to go about naked and be unaware or unashamed-they just don't seem to care. However, at some moment in time a child becomes conscious of his or her nakedness and feels compelled to cover their "private parts". I believe that the LORD revealed to me that this "moment in time", the moment that we become aware of our nakedness is perhaps the moment of accountability. This notion is supported in Genesis 3:7, **"Then** [after the fall of mankind, after eating of the fruit that LORD God had said 'you shall not eat from'] **the eyes of both of them** [Adam and Eve] **were opened, and they knew that they were naked; and they sewed fig leaves together and made themselves loin coverings." (Genesis 3:7)... "And the LORD God made garments of skin for Adam and his wife, and clothed them** [representing the first shed blood covering for the first sin]**." (Genesis 3:21)**

³⁵ "[Jesus said] **Be dressed in readiness, and *keep* your lamps lit.** ³⁶ **Be like men who are waiting for their master when he returns from the wedding feast, so that they may immediately open *the door* to him when he comes and knocks.** ³⁷ **Blessed are those slaves whom the master will find on the alert when he comes; truly I say to you, that he will gird himself *to serve*, and have them recline *at the table*, and will come up and wait on them.** ³⁸ **Whether he comes in the second watch, or even in the third, and finds *them* so, blessed are those *slaves [that Jesus finds ready]*.** ³⁹ "But be sure of this, that if the head of the house had known at what hour the thief was coming, he would not have allowed his house to be broken into. ⁴⁰ You too, be ready; for the Son of Man is coming at an hour that you do not expect." ⁴¹ Peter said [to Jesus], "Lord, are You addressing this parable to us [the disciples], or to everyone *else* as well?" ⁴² **And the Lord said, "Who then is the faithful and sensible steward, whom his master will put in charge of his servants, to give them their rations at the proper time?** ⁴³ **Blessed is that slave whom his master finds so doing when he comes.** ⁴⁴ Truly I say to you that he will put him in charge of all his possessions. ⁴⁵ But if that slave says in his heart, 'My master will be a long time in coming,' and begins to beat the slaves, *both* men and women, and to eat and drink and get drunk; ⁴⁶ the master of that slave will come on a day when he does not expect *him* and at an hour he does not know, and will cut him in pieces, and assign him a place with the unbelievers. ⁴⁷ And that slave who knew his master's will and did not get ready or act in accord with his will, will receive many lashes, ⁴⁸ but the one who did not know *it*, and committed deeds worthy of a flogging, will receive but few. From everyone who has been given much, much will be required; and to whom they entrusted much, of him they will ask all the more.

THE ANGEL AT BURGER KING

　　We had decided to move our Friday night Bible study from Carlos and Lucy's apartment to a local Burger King to provide the kids with a play area to entertain them. Our first meeting at the new location, it was winter and snowing; those meeting that night included: Hannah and me, Carlos, Lucy, little Lucy and their youngest daughter Dianna, Sarah, Eddie and Josh. As we arrived in the parking lot I saw a large man who looked to be in his 60s, he was moving very slowly from near the bus stop toward us as though he were headed toward Burger King. This large man was carrying large bags, he was moving very slowly and he looked like he was limited in his ability to move due to hip or knee injury. Though this man looked to be in such dire straits, he was large and moved so slowly yet he had a joy about him that was extraordinary. **I recall quietly saying "LORD is that an angel?"-a strange question.** As we moved toward the Burger King entrance we somehow got to the door at the same time as this "man" and we opened the door for him and he passed by with a nice greeting and he sat down at a table. I walked over to him and talked to him as I wanted to see how it was that a man in his condition could have such joy. **I knew that this guy must know the LORD and in our conversation he shared that he indeed knew the LORD-he continued to glow.** I invited him to sit with us and he joined us and he smelled very bad. I was disgusted with myself for being bothered by his body odor; as he joined in the discussion he spoke in what felt like Holy blasts of profound truth and then he smiled or wink. It was clear to me that there was a lot more to this guy than meets-the-eye. After the Bible study had ended the group got up and mingled, at some point the man wondered back to where he had been sitting, again, it was evening and there were not many people in the restaurant. I walked over to talk to him at his table and he was not there, though his bags and things were there. I looked all around the Burger King and I could not find this man, I went to the bathroom expecting to find him there and he was not there, this slow moving man had literally vanished from our midst and had left his things behind. **We were all in wonder and we felt that it was very possible that we had entertained an angel.** As I got into the car I asked the LORD "LORD, if that was an angel please talk about an angel in the next song on the radio". The next song on the radio was indeed about angels.

Hebrews 13

¹Let love of the brethren continue. ²Do not neglect to show hospitality to strangers, for by this some have entertained angels without knowing it. ³Remember the prisoners, as though in prison with them, and those who are ill-treated, since you yourselves also are in the body. ⁴Marriage is to be held in honor among all, and the marriage bed is to be undefiled; for fornicators and adulterers God will judge. ⁵Make sure that your character is free from the love of money, being content with what you have; for He Himself has said, "I WILL NEVER DESERT YOU, NOR WILL I EVER FORSAKE YOU," ⁶so that we confidently say,
"THE LORD IS MY HELPER, I WILL NOT BE AFRAID.
WHAT WILL MAN DO TO ME?" ⁷Remember those who led you, who spoke the word of God to you; and considering the result of their conduct, imitate their faith. ⁸Jesus Christ is the same yesterday and today and forever.

THE ANGEL WITH THE GREAT BIG BOOK

     I have not written much about other people's experiences with the LORD to this point, however, this is a great dream, vision or insight. A friend of mine relayed his dream to me. In his dream he was standing and in front of him was an angel sitting at a desk with a giant book, the book was about the size of a garage, the angel's back was to my friend. The angel was writing in the book and my friend stood behind the angel and he said to the angel "what are you doing?" the angel stopped writing, turned to my friend and said "I [the angel] am writing down everything that you have ever thought".

Romans 2:16

"on that day when, according to my gospel, God, through Jesus Christ, will judge the secret thoughts of all."

THE ANT -THE LIGHTNING BOLT - AND THE BLACK LEATHER SHOES.

Lance is Eddie's dad and a friend to several of us in the ministry; Lance was not working due to an injury and he was staying with Sarah who was helping him through his recovery. Lance and I began to meet with the intention of studying through the Bible and we had decided to begin with the Book of Genesis. Lance and I took our Bibles and went out to the back yard of the apartment to study on the grass. As we were reading about the Creation of the world I noted an ant climbing from the top of the page and walking straight down to the place that I was reading. I can recall smiling and thinking **"what is up with this ant LORD, I am trying to study Scripture with Lance and You [God] are goofing around with me?" The ant seemed as though it were on a mission as it walked straight down the page and it turned at what seemed to be a perfect right angle.** The ant then walked a circle around the very place that I was reading the words **"...everything that creeps on the ground..." (See Genesis 1:25)** As I was reading the words the ant circled around the words "...that creeps..." I asked Lance if he saw what had happened and explained what I saw. As I explained what had happened the ant did it again. **The ant creped around the words "that creeps" as I read the words "that creeps" and then it departed.**

Lance and I had a great laugh and a moment to appreciate the detail of the LORD over nature. We continued to meet weekly in the late afternoon for Bible study at Sarah's apartment. Sarah would typically take her two boys out so that Lance and I could have a quiet environment for prayer and study. On one occasion we met inside and shared prayer needs and then we prayed together. As the prayer time seemed to be drawing to an end I sensed that the LORD was prompting me to ask Him for a sign of His presence. **I hesitated and then stepped out in faith and asked the LORD out loud to "please show us a sign of His presence" and the room was salient for a few seconds. After a**

193

pause of 2-3 seconds we heard a rumble at a distance and then an immediate explosion of a lightning-bolt outside the window shaking the apartment. I looked at Lance and Lance looked at me-we agreed and thanked God for this great sign

Job 28:26

"…He [LORD God, YHWH] set a limit for the rain, and a course for the thunderbolt [lightning]"

Lance and I continued to meet for Bible study and on one of the days I arrived wearing a pair of black leather slip-on loafers, they were wing-tip with two tassels and had an unusual design around the front of the shoe made up of bent over and carved or split leather-they were very unusual. As I was leaving Lance commented that he really liked my shoes. I could see the Holy Spirit in this and I said **"Lance let's pray that God will provide you with a pair of shoes like these"**. I did not give Lance my shoes as I wear a size 9 shoe and Lance wore a size 12-14. Lance agreed and we prayed right-there-and-then for a pair of shoes like mine for Lance. **When I got home that evening my Mom greeted me and said that my brother-in-law had gone through his things and he had a pair of shoes that he wanted to give away, they were size 12-14 black wingtips exactly like mine**. With excitement I looked at the shoes that were just like brand-new, the same exact style of the shoes that we had prayed for: tassels, loafers, winged tip and even had the bent over and carved or split leather. **They fit Lance perfectly.** Praise the LORD.

Matthew 7:7-12)

"[Jesus said] Ask [In the Greek present tense ,"keep asking"] and it will be given to you; seek ["keep seeking"] and you will find; knock ["keep knocking"] and the door will be opened to you. For everyone who asks receives; the one who seeks finds; and to the one who knocks, the door will be opened. Which of you, if your son asks for bread, will give him a stone? Or if he asks for a fish, will give him a snake? If you, then, though you are evil, know how to give good gifts to your children, how much more will your Father in heaven give good gifts to those who ask him!"

THE BEETLE-THE STRANGER-AND, THE BROTHERS IN THE PARK.

Doing ministry has so many tangible and practical benefits. God finds ways to put His people to work and He rewards and protects them along the way. One day while doing ministry in St. Paul I was in the middle of the day after a full morning and I had nothing to do for several hours. I had to pick up Hannah in the afternoon and I went to the park to study and nap-two things that I enjoy. I was near a park in St. Paul, MN that is located on a small island that is accessible by way of a bridge that crosses a shallow area on the west side of the lake. There is an eagle's nest on the northern border of the lake overlooking Highway 61, the park is on the east side of this lake. I keep a blanket in the trunk of the car for times like these so I grabbed the blanket and my Bible and off I went. After I crossed over the bridge I saw all kinds of barriers and cordoned off areas. They were doing work in the park and it looked like a modified maze. I found an open area though it felt more like a construction area than a park; nevertheless it worked for me. I laid down with my Bible, read and fell asleep praying. While I was sleeping I was awakened by a big flying beetle or Junebug. **This beetle was so persistent as it flew around my head and around my ear; I tried to wave it away with no success. Finally I got up and I said out loud "WHAT!! WHAT IS IT!!" as though this was someone getting me out of bed.** Once I was committed to getting up I saw the beetle fly away as if to say, "mission accomplished, you are awake". **When I woke I turned and looked across the park, walking toward me was a man with a stick or branch or club in his hand; he looked like he was up to no good. As soon as I made eye contact with the man he turned and walked away. I suspect that he intended to beat me with the stick; his mission was thwarted by the buzz of one very persistent beetle. Thank You LORD!**

Psalm 105:14-15

He [LORD God] permitted no man to oppress them [His people], and He reproved kings for their sakes: 'Do not touch My anointed ones, and do My prophets no harm.'

In the same park several of us got together, we laid out a blanket and opened our Bibles for a study of the Book of James. We worked our way through the first three chapters and began to debate some subject and it became more argumentative than any of us had hoped for. Finally we realized that we were being pulled out into the deep-water of the flesh; we stopped, apologized and prayed together. After our prayer we reopened our Bibles and picked up where we had left off with James chapter 4:1, and read the following words, "**What is the source of quarrels and conflicts among you?...**" To say that we were humbled would be a gross understatement. God declared His presence with us right there in the park. Thanks again LORD!

THE BENEVOLENT FUND

When I first became a follower of Jesus some 40 years ago I had a small catering truck that I would drive on a route in East St. Paul, MN near the Lafayette Bridge and Plato Blvd. When I became a follower of Jesus my value system changed, I seemed to have new burdens to give beyond my tithe (literally "a tenth") what seemed to be a lot of money-at least it was a lot for me. I asked for advice and It was suggested that I establish my weekly need and open a separate bank account, and anything over that needed amount could be filtered into a designated account to give to others, "the benevolence fund". This seemed like a good idea and I opened the "the benevolent fund" account and I prayed that the LORD would bless me according to His will and that any amount over and above a set amount that I needed would go into the benevolent fund. Again, this was over and above my tithe and other monthly expenses. I recall looking at what I needed for my monthly expenses and I perceived that my expenses were so high that it was doubtful that anything would get to the benevolent fund. As I recall almost immediately after opening the benevolent fund my business grew and the amount that I was putting into the benevolent fund was greater than that deposited into my personal needs account. In essence my income more than doubled in what seemed to be over night-God supplied abundantly.

2 Corinthians 9

6Now this I say, he who sows sparingly will also reap sparingly, and he who sows bountifully will also reap bountifully. 7Each one must do just as he has purposed in his heart, not grudgingly or under compulsion, for God loves a cheerful giver. 8**And God is able to make all grace abound to you, so that always having all sufficiency in everything,** you may have an abundance for every good deed;

197

⁹as it is written,
**"HE [LORD God] SCATTERED ABROAD, HE GAVE TO THE POOR,
HIS RIGHTEOUSNESS ENDURES FOREVER."**

¹⁰Now He who supplies seed to the sower and bread for food will supply and multiply your seed for sowing **and increase the harvest of your righteousness; ¹¹you will be enriched in everything for all liberality, which through us is producing thanksgiving to God.** ¹²For the ministry of this service is not only fully supplying the needs of the saints, but is also overflowing through many thanksgivings to God. ¹³Because of the proof given by this ministry, they will glorify God for your obedience to your confession of the gospel of Christ and for the liberality of your contribution to them and to all,

¹⁴**while they also, by prayer on your behalf, yearn for you because of the surpassing grace of God in you. ¹⁵Thanks be to God for His indescribable gift!**

THE BIBLES AND THE SIGNATURE

Shortly after surrendering "my life" to the LORD He gave me two miracles that standout amongst so many. I have referred to these two miracles on many occasions. This testimony addresses the Bibles sent overseas and the other addresses the signature of the government official that was sitting right next to me on my plan trip to Papua New Guinea. Both of these miraculous events are too great to be simply referred to and would seem like making reference to "the Crossing of the Red Sea", "the falling of the wall of Jericho" or "David's defeat of the giant Goliath" without its own written account. Therefore, at the risk of being redundant, here is my account of this wonderful event.

While married, my wife Linda and I seemed equally yoked and we both had a gift of giving. On one occasion my wife and I were at a church meeting, there was a speaker that was involved in smuggling Bibles into countries that were closed off to the gospel and the speaker shared several ways that we could be involved in that ministry. One opportunity for support was to cover the cost of Bibles to be brought in, the other was to smuggling in Bibles. When I heard this presentation there was an immediate tug at my heart to send 300 Bibles-I recognize now that this prompting was from the Holy Spirit. After the prompting I put off doing as I was being lead to do, the timing seemed bad, I did not have the funds...and the burden to send the Bibles seemed to increase with time-I was being tested. As time passed the burden to send the Bibles became so great that I was having difficulty sleeping; sending these Bibles seemed to always be on my mind. **I felt the Spirit move me to faith, and I needed to send these Bibles at all cost.** I resolved to get the order forms in place and I move forward, when I received the Bible order form I filled in the space ordering 300 Bibles and I then calculated the postage expense, I totaled the amount and resolved to send the check-come what may. I felt that I would make this my priority and would put all other commitments on the back burner. I tucked the completed order form into the envelope and wrote the check, as I recall it was **$657.27.** Immediately after I had signed the check my Grandma who had walked to the mail-box said out loud "Todd, you have something in the mail, and it looks like a check", I was not expecting money from anyone. My first thought was "this must be for the Bibles". My Grandma handed me the envelope that I was not expecting nor was it ever explained to me, it was a government refund check, (at the time I had a small business and I did not ever get a refund). None the less I was holding an envelope in my hand for a refund and I was thankful; and the timing was perfect as I had received it seconds after signing the check for the Bibles. **As I opened the check I looked at the amount of the refund check, $657. 27, it looked surprisingly familiar, I had just written that same amount. I held in one hand the refund check and I held in the other the check for the Bibles that I had just written a few seconds before, and they were for the same amount, to the penny. I recall showing my wife the two checks for the same amount and I said "look at this, remember this, there may be a day when we question whether this really happened", but it did.** My Grandma gave me a stamp, I stamped and sealed the envelope and off it went.

2 Kings 22

The Lost Book
[8]Then Hilkiah the high priest said to Shaphan the scribe, "I have found the book of the law in the house of the LORD." And Hilkiah gave the book to Shaphan who read it. [9]Shaphan the scribe came to the king and brought back word to the king and said, "Your servants have emptied out the money that was found in the house, and have delivered it into the hand of the workmen who have the oversight of the house of the LORD." [10]**Moreover, Shaphan the scribe told the king saying, "Hilkiah the priest has given me a book." And Shaphan read it in the presence of the king. [11]When the king heard the words of the book of the law, he tore his clothes. [12]Then the king commanded** Hilkiah the priest, Ahikam the son of Shaphan, Achbor the son of Micaiah, Shaphan the scribe, and Asaiah the king's servant saying,[13]**"Go, inquire of the LORD for me and the people and all Judah concerning the words of this book that has been found, for great is the wrath of the LORD that burns against us, because our fathers have not listened to the words of this book, to do according to all that is written concerning us."**

THE MAGIC TWIG, or, THE BRANCH
IN MY OWN EYE

Jesus said "Why do you look at the speck [twig] that is in your brother's eye, but do not notice the log [branch or plank] that is in your own eye? "Or how can you say to your brother, 'Let me take the speck out of your eye,' and behold, the log is in your own eye?" Matthew 7:3-4
Up until a few years ago I went for a long walk almost daily. I typically walked on the road then onto a paved path through a residential area and around a golf course. Around several portions of the path are trees that tower over the path. On one occasion as I was walking I was reviewing a conversation that I had had with my good brother in the LORD; I was frustrated by what seemed like a casual regard for the things of the LORD by my friend-at least that is how he sounded to me. I was upset and continued to mull over the conversation to the point that I was becoming very judgmental. I could feel and sense that the LORD was telling me that I was being judgmental though I justified my anger as being "righteous judgment" (See John 7:24). **As I was walking and judging my brother, I reviewed our conversation again and focused on the path in front of me; I was walking full stride when a small branch hit me in the eye from above.** The interesting thing is that I was wearing my glasses and the twig hit me from above my eye. Think about it, I was walking full stride wearing glasses, a twig broke off far above me, the twig dropped and fell precisely between my forehead and my glasses it then navigated around my eyelashes hung in midair and then was redirected backward into my eye. It seems quite impossible when I think through this. **As soon as I felt the twig drop into my eye I was reminded that before I attempt to remove the speck or twig from my brother's eye I need to remove the: log, twig, or plank from my own eye. I got the message loud-and-clear LORD-thank You.**

Matthew 7

[1]"[Jesus said]Do not judge so that you will not be judged. [2]"For in the way you judge, you will be judged; and by your standard of measure, it will be measured to you. [3]**"Why do you look at the speck [twig] that is in your brother's eye, but do not notice the log [branch] that is in your own eye?** [4]**"Or how can you say to your brother, 'Let me take the speck out of your eye,' and behold, the log is in your own eye?** [5]"You hypocrite, first take the log out of your own eye, and then you will see clearly to take the speck out of your brother's eye.

THE CHARGING DOG

I was on a long walk through the golf course in the late fall or early winter, there were no people on the course at all, the golf course is surrounded by large homes and I was facing the back of the homes. As I was walking I was asking the LORD to show me something and to please reveal Himself-I recall expecting to see some wild animals... As I was walking I heard a dog barking from a distance with the bark of anger and defense. As I looked I could see a large dog running off of the deck of a home near me and it was running full speed right toward me-it looked angry. I looked around hoping to see someone that would control the dog or call it away from charging me but that did not happen. **The dog continued to run at me full stride and it showed no sign of fear or hesitation and as it seemed to get closer to me it looked to be escalating into an attack mode-it looked fierce to me and I was scared. I looked around and it seemed senseless to run as there was nowhere to run to safety. I suddenly became very bold and felt the spirit of God move me to faith, I looked at the dog running at me, I pointed at the dog and I boldly yelled as loud as I could "En El Nombre De Jesus". The moment that I pointed at the dog and yelled the words "En El Nombre De Jesus" the dog stopped and looked at me with a confused expression on its face, as if it were asking "WHAT WERE WE DOING HERE AGAIN? The dog then looked away and voiced a confused yelp, and turned and trotted home. I laughed as the dog turned and went home and I went on my way without incidence.**

"En El Nombre De Jesus" is Spanish for "In the name of Jesus"

"...at the name of Jesus every knee should bow, of things in Heaven and things on earth and things under the earth."

THE CHOCOLATE COVERED TURD

This may sound vulgar, however, it's not meant to be crude. God showed me a graphic vision of a hand holding a thread, dangling from this thread was a clump of human waste-"a turd". The turd was in the shape a small round glob about the size of a piece of candy; the turd was then dunked into a vat of melted chocolate and lifted out, it was literally a chocolate covered turd that looked like a chocolate candy. The LORD showed me that this is analogous to the tactic of the enemy who will promise a treat as he draws us into his trap, however, what we receive is a toxic mess-just beyond the candy coated surface is a deadly poison. **To reiterate, the enemy of our soul will offer what looks like a pleasant and delicious reward and he entices us to bite deeply into the world system. The promise of the enemy is for something sweet and satisfying, however after biting into the world system we find that it is smoke-and-mirrors, distasteful and toxic. What the enemy of our soul offers to us is much like a "chocolate covered turd".**

Revelation 19

[20]And the beast was seized, and with him the false prophet who performed the signs in his presence, by which he deceived those who had received the mark of the beast and those who worshiped his image; these two were thrown alive into the lake of fire which burns with brimstone. [21]And the rest were killed with the sword which came from the mouth of Him who sat on the horse, and all the birds were filled with their flesh.

Revelation 20

[10]And the devil who deceived them was thrown into the lake of fire and brimstone, where the beast and the false prophet are also; and they will be tormented day and night forever and ever.

THE CROSS IN THE SKY

When my dad was eight years old he traveled into the "Bible belt"-Texas, as I recall. My dad reflects on this experience often and he describes it in detail recalling the names of the people he had known at that time. While in the South my dad was exposed to a "Southern Baptists" tent revival, and he recalls going night after night carrying his Bible and, according to my mother, he even endured some criticism by family and friends as a result of his zeal for God. While in Texas "unrelated" to these revival meetings my dad seriously injured and almost lost his leg during the time of the tent revival. After his injury my dad recalls a man "laying his hands" on him and praying that the LORD would heal his injured leg. My dad describes being in what sounds like a state of shock and infection while this man prayed over him-today dad's leg is fine, he was healed. My question to my dad was **"which of your great working legs was in need of prayer Dad?"** From my perspective my dad has a difficult time expressing his faith in the LORD, though he sees Scripture all over in the house, and he will even support our efforts in ministry-I see dad moving in the right direction, toward God. I continue to see people of the LORD brought into my dad's path, and I believe that I can see the LORD's hand continuing to reach out to my dad. At times my dad may seem oblivious to God's signs-but not always.

There have been times that I have been sharing the LORD with my dad and I watched as God was reaching out to him. As I recall I was driving him into work early one morning as we were talking of the LORD I commented that "if you [dad] received the LORD as a child and even though you [dad] may have walked away" when I said the words "you may have walked away" my dad turned his head to the left and he respectfully said very seriously "I never walked away". I acknowledged his statement, I thanked the LORD and I looked at the car directly in front of us, and I pointed out to my dad that the car in front of us had my dad's initials MDC on the license plate and an Icthus (a Christian symbol of a fish) on the bumper. Dad said that he noted

207

that as well as he seemed to smile, this is significant to me. On another occasion I walked downstairs and noted my dad outside on the patio seemingly staring into the sky, something that I have done on many occasions, as have the Old Testament prophets (See 2 Kings 1:9). I walked out to see my dad as he looked to be at great peace staring into the sky. **I walked out and looked up to where my dad was looking and there was a huge cross in the sky that had been formed by the crossing of two jets. My dad sat staring in to the sky at a large cross and he said "do you see that?" Thank You LORD!**

2 Chronicles 15

[1] Now the Spirit of God came on Azariah the son of Oded, [2] and he went out to meet Asa [the king of Judah] and said to him, **"…the LORD is with you when you are with Him. And if you seek Him, He will let you find Him; but if you forsake Him, He will forsake you.** [3] For many days Israel was without the true God and without a teaching priest and without law. [4] **But in their distress they turned to the LORD God of Israel, and they sought Him, and He let them find Him.** [5] In those times there was no peace to him who went out or to him who came in, for many disturbances afflicted all the inhabitants of the lands. [6] Nation was crushed by nation, and city by city, for God troubled them with every kind of distress. [7] **But you, be strong and do not lose courage, for there is reward for your work."**

2 Chronicles 16

[7] At that time Hanani the seer came to Asa king of Judah and said to him, **"Because you have relied on the king of Aram and have not relied on the LORD your God, therefore the army of the king of Aram has escaped out of your hand.** [8] Were not the Ethiopians and the Lubim an immense army with very many chariots and horsemen? **Yet because you relied on the LORD, He delivered them into your hand.** [9] **For the eyes of the LORD move to and fro throughout the earth that He may strongly support those whose heart is completely His.** You have acted foolishly in this. Indeed, from now on you will surely have wars."…[11] Now, the acts of Asa from first to last, behold, they are written in the Book of the Kings of Judah and Israel. [12] In the thirty-ninth year of his reign **Asa became diseased in his feet. His disease was severe, yet even in his disease he did not seek the LORD, but the physicians.**

THE DIRT-BIRD

I was driving on a highway during the winter and praying to the LORD, regarding life being tough. I recall saying things like, **"O LORD how long will we be here? When will we go and be with you, it seems like this life is taking so long. Why does it have to be this long? O LORD…"** While I was reflection on what seemed our long lives and quite frankly I was complaining to the LORD He drew my attention to a large black bird sitting on the shoulder of the road in front and to the right of me-I could see the bird very clearly. My attention was fixed on the bird **"do you see?"** asked the LORD, "yes LORD I see the bird" I replied. As I drove another few seconds my eyes fixed on the bird, I watched as the once very clear bird was not a bird at all but was a pile of black ice and snow and I heard **"do you see?"** I responded "yes LORD I see that it is not a bird but a chunk of ice and snow in the shape of a bird". I continued to drive a few more seconds and watched as the ice and snow shaped bird was looking more like a pile of dirt and I quickly drove past and heard again **"do you see"**. **I replied to the LORD "yes LORD I saw the bird turn into a pile of dirt within seconds and right before my eyes".** I do not recall hearing anything more from the LORD but the message to me was clear and comforting, **"This is how it is with you, you are here then turned again to dust in a blink of an eye".** Reflection back on this I have often asked myself which of the three was really at the side of the road for those few seconds; I believe that they were all there, first the bird, then the dirty snow and ice and then the dirt.

Genesis 2

[7] Then the LORD God formed a man from the dust of the ground and breathed into his nostrils the breath of life, and the man became a living being.

[19] *[The LORD said to Adam] by the sweat of your face you will eat*
bread, till you return to the ground,
because from it you were taken; for you are dust,
and to dust you shall return."

THE DOG AND THE FOOD NUGGET

With regard to our training, the LORD gave me an analogy of a trained dog. It is my observation that the most difficult command for our dog to obey is "STAY". After commanding our dog to "stay" it seems that she "stays" as long as she can see me watching her, however, as soon as I am out of her sight she takes off. My dog's obedience is short lived. We humans are similar to my dog. God will command us to "BE STILL", STAY" or "BE QUIET" and in no time we lose faith, jump ship, question the Master and we begin to: speak, act, and do stuff impulsively. Recall the, **if you will** then **I will** promises of the LORD **"The LORD will fight for you [His part] while you keep silent [our part]" (Exodus 14:14).** God has created us with strong desires, these "strong desires" (Greek, epithumia) is translated "lust". Lust goes far beyond sexual strong desire to include desire for: power, material goods, education, entertainment, security.... I believe that God uses our strong desires or "lusts" to test and train us, and the enemy does as well.

Consider a well trained dog sitting while its master places a food nugget on its nose. The nose is the sensory organ, resting food on the nose would cause an undisciplined animal to struggle and fail the "sit", "stay", and "wait" test, yet the master of the animal works to train the dog to override its desire to eat. The dog is tempted to eat the food nugget that is on its nose, but in obedience the dog waits for the command of the master. **The animal gives regard to the master rather than serving its fleshly "strong desires [lusts]"; it overrides its instincts and in obedience it trusts in its master.** The animal and the master wait with patience as the dog sits and stays with a food nugget resting on its nose, this is not to say that the animal does not "lust for" or have "strong desires" for the food; yet the animals overriding devotion is shown by its willingness to "SIT STILL" and "STAY". At the moment determined by the master the command is given to eat, the dog eats and the dog and master erupt in joy. **So it is to be between**

211

us and our Master. We are to be so trained as to disregard our lust (strong desires), and to obey our Master's command.

1 Samuel 15

²²Samuel said,
"Has the LORD as much delight in burnt offerings and sacrifices
as in obeying the voice of the LORD?
Behold, to obey is better than sacrifice,
and to heed than the fat of rams.
²³"For rebellion is as the sin of divination,
and insubordination is as iniquity and idolatry
because you have rejected the word of the LORD,
He has also rejected you from being king." ²⁴Then Saul said to
Samuel, "I have sinned; I have indeed transgressed the command of
the LORD and your words, because I feared the people and listened to
their voice.

Psalm 32:9

Do not be as the horse [impulsive] or as the mule [stubborn,
resistant] which have no understanding,
Whose trappings include bit and bridle to hold them in check,
Otherwise they will not come near to you.

THE BEAR AND THE "JESUS NOISE"

I had a dream that I was out in a large open country setting-it looked like a State Park. I was able to see cleared area all around for quite a distance, there were people sparsely scattered throughout the park picnic area. It looked as though we were out West near some mountains and I seemed to be a long distance from any shelter. From far out in the distance I could see a bear emerge from the woods slowly making its way toward me and I began to feel vulnerable. I began to take a step backward while keeping my eyes on the bear. As the bear moved in my direction I saw several more bear emerge from the woods both to the right and to the left of me, and like the others they seemed to be making their way in my direction. I became concerned, fearful and I began to take another step backward while I was watching all of the bear moving toward me. As I took steps backward I felt something right behind me and I could see peripherally that there were bear immediately to my rear and on both sides, in fact I felt that I was literally stepping back pressing into one of them. I stopped in my tracks and I was unable to speak due to fear; at this point there were bear all around to the front, sides and immediately behind me-and they were on their haunches. **As I opened my mouth and I tried to scream for help or to rebuke the bear, I forced out a barking screech of a noise that almost sounded mechanical in nature-it was loud and strange. At the moment that I made the sound the bears retreated and scattered from me running back into the woods. I felt empowered in the process. Some people came over to me and enquired about "the noise" and the power of the noise; my response to them was "OH, THAT WAS THE JESUS NOISE"**

Luke 10

[17]The seventy returned with joy, saying, "Lord, even the demons are subject to us in Your name." [18]And He said to them, "I was watching Satan fall from heaven like lightning. [19]"Behold, I have

213

given you authority to tread on serpents and scorpions, and over all the power of the enemy, and nothing will injure you. [20]**"Nevertheless do not rejoice in this, that the spirits are subject to you, but rejoice that your names are recorded in heaven."** [21]At that very time He rejoiced greatly in the Holy Spirit, and said, "I praise You, O Father, Lord of heaven and earth, that You have hidden these things from the wise and intelligent and have revealed them to infants. Yes, Father, for this way was well-pleasing in Your sight. [22]"All things have been handed over to Me by My Father, and no one knows who the Son is except the Father, and who the Father is except the Son, and anyone to whom the Son wills to reveal Him." [23]Turning to the disciples, He said privately, **"Blessed are the eyes which see the things you see,** [24]for I say to you, that many prophets and kings wished to see the things which you see, and did not see them, and to hear the things which you hear, and did not hear them."

THE DREAM OF THE CRUMBLING TOWER

I had an interesting dream that is going to be tough to describe, but here goes. I was in a framed tower, the floor was plywood, and the walls were simply framed as there were wood beams but no walls and open air all around. There were two stair cases on each floor, one on one wall and the other across from it on the opposite wall. The floors were about 15' x 15' square and we were 5-10 stories high with quite a few floors above us. I was not feeling comfortable with the height on the open platform-I was scared. I recall that there were one or two other people with me and I do not know who they were. We were standing firmly on the floor and for no reason known to me the floor that I was standing on began to break away much like thin ice on a lake. As the floor below was breaking I stepped forward trying to find solid footing and then I was falling forward and grabbing the floor in front of me in a bit of a panic as it all crumbled as soon as put any pressure on it.

I believe that this physical floor that I am describing represents the world system that we see with our physical eyes, it is: fake, phony and it cannot be trusted.

As the floor and the surrounding walls of this tower were crumbling around me, it was defying my understanding of what I saw, felt and trusted in to support me. It made no sense to me that I could not stand upon that which looked to be solid and stable. As I leaned forward in the midst of a panic with the floor crumbling around me I fell outside of the confines of the walls into the open air away from the building and far above ground, and instead of falling to the ground I floated. While in the open air I was able to move, navigate and maneuver with relative ease floating, soaring and moving about through the air-it defied my senses.

I believe that the open air outside of the floors represents the kingdom of God, available to us now, for those who believe and

215

care to accept it. This represents that which is believed in with our spiritual eyes, and our spiritual senses.

Though I recognized the contrast between these two worlds, the floor of the tower being that which I/we have grown accustom to trust. I/we have been programmed from birth to trust in that which we can see with our eyes and feel with our hands, this we have been persuaded to put our faith in. That very foundation was failing to support me at a critical moment and was nothing more than an illusion. On the other hand, once I found myself outside of the confines of the earthly structure I was free to maneuver with relative ease and precision, floating, soaring and flying-it was wonderful. The thing that was so surprising to me was that although I recognized the contrasts of the two systems, I continued to return to the crumbling tower in spite of its relative instability. I would continually fight for stable footing until I was thrust back out into the open air where I began to: soar, maneuver and fly in comfort. And then I would look and see myself flying far above the ground and I then became intimidated by what I saw with my physical eyes. I was fearful and I returned to that which made physical sense to me, even though it was continually breaking into pieces under my feet - it could not be trusted.

Matthew 14:26-31

When the disciples saw Him [Jesus of Nazareth] walking on the sea, they were terrified, and said, "It is a ghost!" And they cried out in fear. But immediately Jesus spoke to them, saying, "Take courage, it is I; do not be afraid." Peter said to Him, "Lord, if it is You [Jesus], command me to come to You on the water." And He said, "Come!" And Peter got out of the boat, and walked on the water and came toward Jesus. But seeing the wind, he became frightened, and beginning to sink, he cried out, "Lord, save me!" Immediately Jesus stretched out His hand and took hold of him, and said to him, "You of little faith, why did you doubt?"

THE DREAM OF HANNAH LITERALLY "STEPPING OUT IN FAITH"

I had completely forgotten about this dream when my daughter Hannah said to me today "hay Dad [this is], just like that dream that you had about me stepping out of the car by faith". Hannah reminded me of this great dream and I knew that I needed to write this one down- amazing.

The dream that I had was as follows; Hannah and I were being driven in a car, there was a driver and a passenger in the front seats. Hannah and I were in the back seat, I was behind the driver's seat and Hannah was behind the passenger seat. We were traveling westbound on 694 as we approached Silver Lake Road at a rate of about 65 miles per hour. As we were driving someone commented that they needed something that was in the trunk of the car. We were talking of pulling over to get into the trunk when Hannah said that she would go to the trunk while we were driving and that "there was no need to pull over". I questioned Hannah and I was very reluctant to see her step out of the car as our car was moving about 65 mph down the freeway. Hannah opened the door of the car and stepped out of the car making her way to the trunk, slowly moving toward the trunk of the car while we were traveling at freeway speed. We all watched in amazement and I was freaking out. Again, Hannah stepped out of a car moving 65 MPH and she walked to the trunk on a pillow of air. When Hannah had safely reached the back of the car and began to open the trunk I became very fearful, I panicked at that point and I demanded that the driver pull the car over that we could help Hannah though she was doing just fine. Hannah had great faith while I was fearful.

The Triumphs of Faith

¹Now faith is the assurance of things hoped for, the conviction of things not seen. ²For by it the men of old gained approval. ³By faith we understand that the worlds were prepared by the word of God, so that what is seen was not made out of things which are visible.

⁴By faith Abel offered to God a better sacrifice than Cain, through which he obtained the testimony that he was righteous, God testifying about his gifts, and through faith, though he is dead, he still speaks. ⁵By faith Enoch was taken up so that he would not see death; AND HE WAS NOT FOUND BECAUSE GOD TOOK HIM UP; for he obtained the witness that before his being taken up he was pleasing to God.

⁶And without faith it is impossible to please Him, for he who comes to God must believe that He is and that He is a rewarder of those who seek Him. ⁷By faith Noah, being warned by God about things not yet seen, in reverence prepared an ark for the salvation of his household, by which he condemned the world, and became an heir of the righteousness which is according to faith.

THE DREAM OF OUR GLORIFIED BODIES

The LORD gave to me a great dream. I was standing in a heavenly garden in front of my wife Linda, **we were facing each other in our new and heavenly bodies.** The new bodies were: youthful, joyful, perfect…and they looked similar to our earthly bodies though they were young, and we were naked. Though we were not clothed there was no sense of sexual arousal or embarrassment, and I do not recall seeing any sexual markers like nipples or pubic hair. We were: young and at peace, without body defects. Our bodies were not excessively muscular and there was no overt vanity of hair style or makeup, we were simple, natural, plain, youthful and perfectly innocent looking. I looked at my wife and I kissed her with a kiss of affection apart from any sexual connection or agenda, I then stepped back and I said to Linda "I am not ashamed". **My statement "I'm not ashamed" seemed to be inclusive of both the fact that I had kissed my wife, and that we were not clothed as if to say that we may have been without clothing and yet we were not naked, exposed and or embarrassed or ashamed in any way-I really don't know why I said "I'm not ashamed". I woke feeling that I had had a glimpse of our heavenly bodies, and then I opened my Bible and I read this passage.**

"Then the Lord God took the man and put him into the Garden of Eden to cultivate it and keep it... And the man and his wife were both naked and were not ashamed." (Genesis 2:15, 25)

2 Corinthians 5

The Temporal and Eternal
[1] For we know that if the earthly tent which is our house is torn down, we have a building from God, a house not made with hands, eternal

219

in the heavens. ² **For indeed in this *house* we groan, longing to be clothed with our dwelling from heaven, ³ inasmuch as we, having put it on, will not be found naked.** ⁴ For indeed while we are in this tent, we groan, being burdened, because we do not want to be unclothed but to be clothed, so that what is mortal will be swallowed up by life. ⁵ Now He who prepared us for this very purpose is God, who gave to us the Spirit as a pledge. ¹⁷ **Therefore if anyone is in Christ, *he is* a new creature; the old things passed away; behold, new things have come. ¹⁸ Now all *these* things are from God, who reconciled us to Himself through Christ and gave us the ministry of reconciliation, ¹⁹ namely, that God was in Christ reconciling the world to Himself, not counting their trespasses against them, and He has committed to us the word of reconciliation.** ²⁰ Therefore, we are ambassadors for Christ, as though God were making an appeal through us; we beg you on behalf of Christ, be reconciled to God. ²¹ He made Him who knew no sin *to be* sin on our behalf, so that we might become the righteousness of God in Him.

THE DREAM OF THE GREAT HARVEST

When I began in the ministry I had a dream of grain-trucks lined up to my right, my left in front and behind me. In the dream I was a spectator and I was standing in the middle of long lines of gigantic grain trucks. The full-to-overflowing grain trucks were sitting still in the beginning of my dream and I stood in a safe place and looked in amazement as the trucks began to move in an orderly fashion like solders moving out in rank. The grain trucks were so full that they were overflowing with grain as though they had been completely buried or immersed in grain; as the trucks drove away the grain was literally falling to the ground with every move that the trucks made.

Matthew 9

[36] Seeing the people, He [Jesus] felt compassion for them, because they were distressed and dispirited like sheep without a shepherd. [37] Then He said to His disciples, "The harvest is plentiful, but the workers are few. [38] Therefore beseech the Lord of the harvest to send out workers into His harvest."

Revelation 14

The Reapers
[14]Then I looked, and behold, a white cloud, and sitting on the cloud was one like a son of man, having a golden crown on His head and a sharp sickle in His hand. [15]And another angel came out of the temple, crying out with a loud voice to Him who sat on the cloud, "Put in your sickle and reap, for the hour to reap has come, because the harvest of the earth is ripe." [16]Then He who sat on the cloud swung His sickle over the earth, and the earth was reaped. [17]And another angel came out of the temple which is in heaven, and he also had a sharp sickle. [18]Then another angel, the one who

has power over fire, came out from the altar; and he called with a loud voice to him who had the sharp sickle, saying, "Put in your sharp sickle and gather the clusters from the vine of the earth, because her grapes are ripe." [19]So the angel swung his sickle to the earth and gathered the clusters from the vine of the earth, and threw them into the great wine press of the wrath of God. [20]And the wine press was trodden outside the city, and blood came out from the wine press, up to the horses' bridles, for a distance of two hundred miles.

THE DREAM OF THE LESS TRAVELED ROAD

"The road" and "the path" are a common theme of my dreams lately. I had a dream that I was walking on a matted down path wide enough for a small car to drive on. There were lush fields on either side of the path with tall grass, walking the path, there were two other people out in front of me, one person in front about twenty feet and another person was ahead and off to the right of me. While walking the path we were: observant, silent and at peace.

My stand-out impression of this dream was that this was an infrequently traveled path as only few were walking on it, and the path was not well worn. While walking the path there was a sense of great peace and discovery amongst us as we traveled. And, we were not walking together, we walked alone as we silently reflected.

Matthew 7

The Narrow and Wide Gates
[13]"Enter through the narrow gate; for the gate is wide and the way is broad that leads to destruction, and there are many who enter through it. [14]"For the gate is small and the way is narrow that leads to life, and there are few who find it. [15]"Beware of the false prophets, who come to you in sheep's clothing, but inwardly are ravenous wolves. [16]"You will know them by their fruits. Grapes are not gathered from thorn bushes nor figs from thistles, are they? [17]"So every good tree bears good fruit, but the bad tree bears bad fruit. [18]"A good tree cannot produce bad fruit, nor can a bad tree produce good fruit. [19]"Every tree that does not bear good fruit is cut down and thrown into the fire.

THE DREAM OF THE MARTYRED SAINT

This dream was in the setting of a large secluded wooded area, there was a cleared area in the woods, and it looked to be used for some type of ceremonial purposes-perhaps sacrifices. There was a man dressed in a religious outfit and he looked like a Pope or a Cardinal, he was holding what looked like a shepherd's staff and he was wearing a decorated robe and the tall headpiece, there were two men assisting the man dressed like a Pope. Between the man dressed as the Pope and the two men assisting him was a humble looking man kneeling in prayer near a prepared fire pit, it was clear that this was a man of God. The man dressed as the Pope was raising his free hand as though he were praying and giving a command to the two that were assisting him, as the command was given they approached the man kneeling in prayer. The order that was given to the two men by the man dressed as the Pope was that the man of God was to be burned-at-the-stake for his testimony regarding the LORD Jesus Christ. As the man dressed as the Pope gave the order and the two men approached the man of God, I screamed "NO!!" and then I prayed "LORD may the men involved be saved as a result of the testimony of this martyred saint". And I woke up crying and screaming.

(A disclaimer. I am not attacking the Catholic Church or any other group, I am just sharing my dream as accurately as possible. Note that the man dressed as the Pope may or may not have been the Pope.)

Revelation 6

The Fifth Seal--Martyrs

⁹When the Lamb broke the fifth seal, I [John] saw underneath the altar the souls of those who had been slain because of the word of God, and because of the testimony which they had maintained;
¹⁰and they cried out with a loud voice, saying, "How long, O Lord,

holy and true, will You refrain from judging and avenging our blood on those who dwell on the earth?" **¹¹And there was given to each of them a white robe; and they were told that they should rest for a little while longer, until the number of their fellow servants and their brethren who were to be killed even as they had been, would be completed also.**

Revelation 20

¹Then I saw an angel coming down from heaven, holding the key of the abyss and a great chain in his hand. ²And he laid hold of the dragon, the serpent of old, who is the devil and Satan, and bound him for a thousand years; ³and he threw him into the abyss, and shut it and sealed it over him, so that he would not deceive the nations any longer, until the thousand years were completed; after these things he must be released for a short time. **⁴Then I saw thrones, and they sat on them, and judgment was given to them And I saw the souls of those who had been beheaded because of their testimony of Jesus and because of the word of God, and those who had not worshiped the beast or his image, and had not received the mark on their forehead and on their hand; and they came to life and reigned with Christ for a thousand years.**

THE DREAM OF THE ROMAN PARTY

Our church group meets in homes, parks…for our Sunday services. When our groups multiply (as they should do) we generally divide into two smaller groups. Several years ago we as a group were faced with this good dilemma and at the time of our church split I had a repeating dream, and I was reminded of Joseph's statement to Pharaoh regarding "repeating" dreams in Genesis chapter 41 "[Joseph said] Now as for the repeating of the dream to Pharaoh twice, it means that the matter is determined by God, and God will quickly bring it about. Now let Pharaoh look for a man discerning and wise, and set him over the land of Egypt" (Genesis 41:32-33) The point made by Joseph I believe applies **"[Joseph said] Now as for the repeating of the dream…twice, it means that the matter is determined by God".** My dream repeated and was back-to-back with little change in the details.

This dream looked to be a combination of modern time's décor and Roman times dress. There was a large palace that was very beautiful with large white granite pillars and a huge staircase. There was a costume party or gathering of people, it was very colorful, very controlled, the people were well behaved. There was a mix of people that were very elegantly dressed, and there was a large contingent of solders mingling with the crowd. The soldiers were dressed in armor and they had their helmets removed, they had swords but they were not drawn-the soldiers were relaxed. In other words these soldiers were at ease, eating, drinking and, distracted, they were far from being "on guard" or "alert". It was my impression that these soldiers represented the present day saints of the LORD. While the soldiers were at rest and at ease the enemy who looked dirty and evil broke through the doors and began firing on the party members and on the soldiers, they were gunning down the saints of the LORD with what looked like an antiquated machine gun that shot bolts. I recall that in the assault we lost two key soldiers in one dream and three key soldiers in the second dream. It is interesting that during our planned church split there were two or three church leaders that were hurt and offended by our talk of splitting the group for the purpose of growth and outreach.

Luke 21

The Return of Christ

[25]"There will be signs in sun and moon and stars, and on the earth dismay among nations, in perplexity at the roaring of the sea and the waves, [26]men fainting from fear and the expectation of the things which are coming upon the world; for the powers of the heavens will be shaken. [27]"**Then they will see THE SON OF MAN [JESUS THE ANOINTED KING] COMING IN A CLOUD with power and great glory. [28]"But when these things begin to take place, straighten up and lift up your heads, because your redemption is drawing near."** [29]Then He told them a parable: "Behold the fig tree and all the trees; [30]as soon as they put forth leaves, you see it and know for yourselves that summer is now near. [31]"So you also, when you see these things happening, recognize that the kingdom of God is near. [32]"**Truly I say to you, this generation will not pass away until all things take place.** [33]"Heaven and earth will pass away, but My words will not pass away. [34]"**Be on guard, so that your hearts will not be weighted down with dissipation and drunkenness and the worries of life, and that day will not come on you suddenly like a trap; [35]for it will come upon all those who dwell on the face of all the earth.** [36]"**But keep on the alert at all times, praying that you may have strength to escape all these things that are about to take place, and to stand before the Son of Man."** [37]Now during the day He was teaching in the temple, but at evening He would go out and spend the night on the mount that is called Olivet. [38]And all the people would get up early in the morning to come to Him in the temple to listen to Him.

THE DREAM-THE SCHOOL FOR YOUNG PROPHETS

I had a dream that I was alone and quiet on a school campus, the school was a one level brick building on a large grassy lot on a hill that was separated from anything else. I was on the school campus, alone, quiet, listening and observing. While I was alone and quietly observing and in prayer, several bus loads of young people drove onto the campus. The bus loads of young people were screaming and talking loud, they were excited and screwing around as they were driven onto the campus. The young people on the bus were let off and they were loaded onto a smaller vehicle pulling cars to sit on, it looked like a little train, they were then driven around as though they were given a tour of the campus. I stood alone while I quietly observed the young people who looked to be a generation or two below me, as I recall some were my son Philip's close friends. While I observed these young people I noted that some were writing: verses, prophetic words and messages on the sidewalks while others were speaking prophesy. **It was clear to me that this was a school for young prophets, and that this young entering class of prophets was talking much and listening little and I was the guy that was there to quietly train them.**

1 Samuel 10

Saul among Prophets
[1] Then Samuel [a prophet of the LORD God] took the flask of oil, poured it on his [Saul's] head, kissed him and said, "Has not the LORD anointed you a ruler over His inheritance [Israel]?...[5] **Afterward you will come to the hill of God where the Philistine garrison is; and it shall be as soon as you have come there to the city, that you will meet a group of prophets coming down from the high place with harp, tambourine, flute, and a lyre before them,**

and they will be prophesying. ⁶ Then the Spirit of the LORD will come upon you mightily, and you shall prophesy with them and be changed into another man. ⁷ **It shall be when these signs come to you, do for yourself what the occasion requires, for God is with you...**

⁹ Then it happened when he turned his back to leave Samuel, God changed his heart; and all those signs came about on that day. ¹⁰ When they came to the hill there, behold, a group of prophets met him; and the Spirit of God came upon him mightily, so that he prophesied among them. ¹¹ It came about, when all who knew him previously saw that he prophesied now with the prophets, that the people said to one another, "What has happened to the son of Kish? Is Saul also among the prophets?" ¹² A man there said, "Now, who is their father?" Therefore it became a proverb: "Is Saul also among the prophets?" ¹³ When he had finished prophesying, he came to the high place.

THE DREAM OF THE SLOW
BOAT- HEADED TO HELL

I had a dream; in the dream I was quietly observing on what seemed to be a very nice and very large cruise ship. This cruise ship was far more comfortable than any that I have ever seen. The passengers on the ship seemed to be relatively moral people; I did not see any drunkenness, pornography, gambling... The passengers were all very busy and they seemed consumed with activities like: painting, arts and crafts, music...and all at their own private activity stations. These activity stations were in the open but it seemed clear that they were meant to be kept relatively private and undisturbed by others. From the world's perspective these stations were private for the purpose of private quiet time, from my perspective they were meant to keep people isolated from others and absorbed in their activity. Again, the passengers seemed to be moral people busy in activities such as: music, art and crafts... they seemed very well cared for by the ships staff. The ships staff was very accommodating and they seemed content to serve the guests as long as the guests remained busy in their activity and remained relatively isolated from others. As an aside, I recall hearing someone talk of gambling and someone say that they should not gamble; my question to them was "why should you not gamble?" I feel that my response to the gambling question was as if to question their hypocrisy regarding **their comfort with their comfort and entertainment** as well as their apparent desire to sound and appear "moral". This very easily may have been a "Christian cruise". Recall that Jesus said, **"Enter through the narrow gate; for the gate is wide and the road is easy [comfortable] that leads to destruction, and there are many who take it. For the gate is small and the way is narrow [difficult] that leads to life, and there are few who find it"** (Matthew 7:13-14)

As I observed we were slowly traveling, the crew was tending to the needs of the passengers and the passengers were content in their: art, music and seemingly "moral" entertainment, and as I

231

recall there seemed to be talk of sports... At the end of the dream it was revealed to me that this cruise ship was headed to hell and that the attendants were demons in disguise. This cruise ship was on a slow and comfortable course to hell as the enemy was entertaining people to death one second at a time.

Matthew 24

[32] "[Jesus said] Now learn the parable from the fig tree: when its branch has already become tender and puts forth its leaves, you know that summer is near; [33] so, you too, when you see all these things, recognize that He is near, *right* at the door. [34] Truly I say to you, this generation will not pass away until all these things take place. [35] Heaven and earth will pass away, but My words will not pass away. [36] "But of that day and hour no one knows, not even the angels of heaven, nor the Son, but the Father alone. [37] For the coming of the Son of Man will be **just like the days of Noah. [38] For as in those days before the flood they were eating and drinking, marrying and giving in marriage, until the day that Noah entered the ark, [39] and they did not understand until the flood came and took them all away; so will the coming of the Son of Man be. [40] Then there will be two men in the field; one will be taken and one will be left. [41] Two women *will be* grinding at the mill; one will be taken and one will be left.**

[42] "Therefore be on the alert, for you do not know which day your Lord is coming. [43] But be sure of this, that if the head of the house had known at what time of the night the thief was coming, he would have been on the alert and would not have allowed his house to be broken into. [44] For this reason you also must be ready; for the Son of Man is coming at an hour when you do not think *He will.* [45] "Who then is the faithful and sensible slave whom his master put in charge of his household to give them their food at the proper time? [46] Blessed is that slave whom his master finds so doing when he comes. [47] Truly I say to you that he will put him in charge of all his possessions. [48] But if that evil slave says in his heart, 'My master is not coming for a long time,' [49] and begins to beat his fellow slaves and eat and drink with drunkards; [50] the master of that slave will come on a day when he does not expect *him* and at an hour which he does not know, [51] and will cut him in pieces and assign him a place with the hypocrites; in that place there will be weeping and gnashing of teeth.

THE DREAM OF THE TRAIN

I had a dream of a large army being transported in a train, the uniforms of the soldiers and the train itself was consistent with that of the Civil War era. I was a bystander and I was moving about in the train observing the army, the train was moving very fast and it seemed to be traveling quickly between battles; the soldier's in the train were at rest. I observed that the soldiers were resting, their weapons were disassembled and being cleaned; I can distinctly recall seeing soldiers lying around campfires in the train cars, they were at ease and completely unprepared for attack as they were steaming down the tracks. **It was clear that these soldiers were in wartime, they seemed safe from attack they were unprepared and resting.** As the train was speeding down the track I looked to my left and the train car door slid open, I stepped out of the way as many enemy soldiers darted onto the train car hunched over and moving quickly carrying their rifles with fixed bayonets. It was interesting that the enemy was dressed in the same uniforms of the army riding on the train though they were imposters; they were armed and rushing in to take possession of the train and of the army that travelled in it. **The message to me seemed clear. The enemy is waiting to infiltrate the army of the LORD; the enemy of the LORD will attack in a time that God's people will least expect it, and while God's people are at rest, and, the enemy will be disguised as the children of light.** As I type this I realize the LORD may be communicating information regarding His return as well, "like a thief in the night". **See Matt 24:43**

[14]No wonder, for even Satan disguises himself as an angel of light. [15]Therefore it is not surprising if his servants also disguise themselves as servants of righteousness, whose end will be according to their deeds.

Luke 21

The Return of Christ

[25]"There will be signs in sun and moon and stars, and on the earth dismay among nations, in perplexity at the roaring of the sea and the waves, [26]men fainting from fear and the expectation of the things which are coming upon the world; for the powers of the heavens will be shaken. [27]"Then they will see THE SON OF MAN COMING IN A CLOUD with power and great glory. [28]"But when these things begin to take place, straighten up and lift up your heads, because your redemption is drawing near." [29]Then He told them a parable: "Behold the fig tree and all the trees; [30]as soon as they put forth leaves, you see it and know for yourselves that summer is now near. [31]"So you also, when you see these things happening, recognize that the kingdom of God is near. [32]"Truly I say to you, this generation will not pass away until all things take place.

[33]"Heaven and earth will pass away, but My words will not pass away. [34]"[Jesus said] Be on guard, so that your hearts will not be weighted down with dissipation and drunkenness and the worries of life, and that day will not come on you suddenly like a trap;

[35]for it will come upon all those who dwell on the face of all the earth.[36]"But keep on the alert at all times, praying that you may have strength to escape all these things that are about to take place, and to stand before the Son of Man."

THE DREAM OF THE UNWANTED RESCUE

I had a dream last night; in the dream I was overlooking a large outdoor mall, there were three or more large outdoor fountains on the mall, people were collected together near the fountains. There was a large group of people gathered in the center of the mall area and they had assembled around one particular fountain area, they seemed content in their mingling and talking together. I was standing some distance from them and I was with a group of plain clothed "special forces" type of people. From where we were watching the group we could see that they were in grave danger from outside forces. As we moved in toward them and finally reached them, I addressed the crowd with an absolute sense of urgency. I was pleading with them and I explained that we were there to help them and that I had been shot. My being wounded intensified my sense of urgency in the matter. I asked for their cooperation to expedite their rescue. They seemed to listen carefully, and after explaining the plan for their rescue I was shocked by the fact this large group of people lingered casually and even wandered over to a nearby booth that a "famous author" had set up for a book signing event. I was pleading for the people to hurry as they were in danger and many lingered on by the booth and asked if they "could just stay long enough to get the autograph of this popular author". **The people were more concerned about the things of this world (getting an autograph) than for their rescue and salvation, it amazed me at how easily they were drawn away from their rescue and quietly lulled into danger simply by wasting their time in folly and entertainment. And so it is today it seems.**

Genesis 19

The Doom of Sodom
[1] Now the two angels came to Sodom in the evening as Lot was sitting in the gate of Sodom. When Lot saw *them*, he rose to meet them

and bowed down *with his* face to the ground. ..[12] Then the *two* men said to Lot...we are about to destroy this place, because their outcry has become so great before the LORD that the LORD has sent us to destroy it." **[14] Lot went out and spoke to his sons-in-law, who were to marry his daughters, and said, "Up, get out of this place, for the LORD will destroy the city." But he appeared to his sons-in-law to be jesting. [15] When morning dawned, the angels urged Lot, saying, "Up, take your wife and your two daughters who are here, or you will be swept away in the punishment of the city." [16] But he hesitated.** So the men seized his hand and the hand of his wife and the hands of his two daughters, for the compassion of the LORD *was* upon him; and they brought him out, and put him outside the city. [17] When they had brought them outside, one said, "Escape for your life! Do not look behind you, and do not stay anywhere in the valley; escape to the mountains, or you will be swept away." **[18] But Lot said to them, "Oh no, my lords!** [19] Now behold, your servant has found favor in your sight, and you have magnified your lovingkindness, which you have shown me by saving my life; but I cannot escape to the mountains, for the disaster will overtake me and I will die; [20] now behold, this town is near *enough* to flee to, and it is small. Please, let me escape there (is it not small?) that my life may be saved." [21] He said to him, "Behold, I grant you this request also, not to overthrow the town of which you have spoken. [22] Hurry, escape there, for I cannot do anything until you arrive there." Therefore the name of the town was called Zoar.

[23] The sun had risen over the earth when Lot came to Zoar. [24] Then the LORD rained on Sodom and Gomorrah brimstone and fire from the LORD out of heaven, [25] and He overthrew those cities, and all the valley, and all the inhabitants of the cities, and what grew on the ground. [26] But his wife, from behind him, looked *back*, and she became a pillar of salt. [27] Now Abraham arose early in the morning *and went* to the place where he had stood before the LORD; [28] and he looked down toward Sodom and Gomorrah, and toward all the land of the valley, and he saw, and behold, the smoke of the land ascended like the smoke of a furnace. **[29] Thus it came about, when God destroyed the cities of the valley, that God remembered Abraham, and sent Lot out of the midst of the overthrow, when He overthrew the cities in which Lot lived.**

236

THE DREAMS OF THE BAPTISMAL WATERS

I was in prayer regarding baptisms and waters used for baptisms; my particular point of concern was that there didn't seem to be many open places for baptisms. During that time I had three very colorful and interesting back-to-back dreams regarding potential baptism waters.

Dream 1

There were three large and expensive homes built on a prized and coveted circles elevated and overlooking the ocean. The ocean waves were crashing onto the shore below on what looked to be the Pacific Northwest Highway on the California coast. Though the three homes looked like prized and perfect properties from a distance the lives of those living in the homes were in utter chaos. **I felt that the LORD was pointing out that although this picture looked great from the outside it was in complete chaos on the inside-things are certainly not all that they seem. Again, the best that the world can offer is chaotic, dark and disturbing.**

Dream 2

I was on a docked pirate ship in a port of call and I was observing the lives of the pirates-it was very colorful. The pirates seemed to be docked in a busy port of call and it looked like they were stirring up trouble in this otherwise relaxed fishing port. I seem to remember being with a guide or a helper who was explaining things to me about the pirates. **It seemed clear that the pirates represented demons.**

Dream 3

I was on a long thin piece of land that was developed with houses on three sides of a strip of land surrounded by water. There were pirates wandering and scattered around on the land and again I was with a guide that was answering my questions regarding the things that

I was observing. As we were talking something that looked like a man walked out of the water on one side of the strip of land, it was hunched over with seaweed draped over it. This creature walked directly to the other side of the strip of land, it avoided the other pirates or creatures; this hunched over creature was grumpy and the other pirates avoided him. My guide was referring to the creature and said "O don't worry about that guy". **The message seemed clear (at the time) that the sites of water were highly coveted by the enemy as he wants to seize our baptismal options. It also seemed quite possible that there are "marine spirits" or demons that live in water, or at least that there are different types and ranks of spirits.**

Acts 8:29-39

Then the Spirit said to Philip, "Go up and join this chariot." Philip ran up and heard him reading Isaiah the prophet, and said, "Do you understand what you are reading?" And he [the Ethiopian eunuch] said, "Well, how could I, unless someone guides me?" And he invited Philip to come up and sit with him.

Now the passage of Scripture which he was reading was this: "HE [Jesus of Nazareth, the Sacrificial Lamb] WAS LED AS A SHEEP TO SLAUGHTER; AND AS A LAMB BEFORE ITS SHEARER IS SILENT, SO HE DOES NOT OPEN HIS MOUTH. [33]"IN HUMILIATION HIS JUDGMENT WAS TAKEN AWAY; WHO WILL RELATE HIS GENERATION? FOR HIS LIFE IS REMOVED FROM THE EARTH."

The eunuch answered Philip and said, "Please tell me, of whom does the prophet say this? Of himself or of someone else?" Then Philip opened his mouth, and beginning from this Scripture he preached Jesus to him. **As they went along the road they came to some water; and the eunuch said, "Look! Water! What prevents me from being baptized?" [And Philip said, "If you believe with all your heart, you may [be baptized]." And he answered and said, "I believe that Jesus Christ is the Son of God."] And he ordered the chariot to stop; and they both went down into the water, Philip as well as the eunuch, and he baptized him.** When they came up out of the water, the Spirit of the Lord snatched Philip away; and the eunuch no longer saw him, but went on his way rejoicing.

THE ENEMY AT THE DOOR

Scene One

I had a dream that was in three parts or scenes, all three scenes addressed the enemy. In the first scene I was walking down the middle of the road, there was no traffic, it was dark and the streetlights were on I was walking with a large group of men, almost like you would picture a gang walking together in the streets. I was out in the front of the rest of the group, there were people to both sides and behind me and they were walking a half step behind me. I felt that my group represented the saints of the LORD. At a distance in front of us was another gang, Satan was leading a similar group and they were walking towards us as you would imagine gangs of two opposing groups approaching one another for a confrontation. **As our group walked towards the opposing group we were all silent and bold yet we silently agreed to allow each other to pass by without engaging in battle.** As we passed by we walked within inches of one another, we walked face to face with our enemy cautious as we passed. As soon as our enemy passed beyond our peripheral vision the enemy reneged on our agreement and engaged us in battle with the Saints.

Scene Two

I was walking in a lower middle class urban community of small but nicely kept older homes on very small lots. I was examining the area as the enemy had recently passed through. **I was struck by the cruel nature of the enemy of God as he and his army had killed children in the front yards of their mother's homes.** This scene was very disturbing and gave me an appreciation of how diabolic, ruthless and hatful our enemy is, however, this is what we are dealing with.

Scene Three

I continued to move about in the neighborhood of the battle zone and I came to a house and Satan himself was standing at the front door steps of one of the saints. **The enemy was standing poised as though he were waiting for people to walk out of the door. As he stood at the front door he was standing still and silent, he was dressed like a joker in a white jumpsuit, the white jumpsuit had very thin random splashes of bright red blood stains that looked like red pinstripes all over his jumpsuit.** As the enemy stood poised at the front door he was standing on one leg with one leg bent and his arms were held up above his head; he looked poised, self-assured and defiant. When the enemy was exposed he left very quickly dashing through the back yards-for some reason there was a pool in the back yard of this home (potential baptismal waters perhaps).

Psalm 17

[6]I have called upon You, for You will answer me, O God; incline Your ear to me, hear my speech. [7]Wondrously show Your lovingkindness, O Savior of those who take refuge at Your right hand from those who rise up against them. [8]Keep me as the apple of the eye; hide me in the shadow of Your wings, [9]from the wicked who despoil me, my deadly enemies who surround me. [10]They have closed their unfeeling heart, with their mouth they speak proudly. [11]They have now surrounded us in our steps; they set their eyes to cast us down to the ground. [12]He is like a lion that is eager to tear, and as a young lion lurking in hiding places. [13]Arise, O LORD, confront him, bring him low; deliver my soul from the wicked with Your sword, [14]from men with Your hand, O LORD, from men of the world, whose portion is in this life, and whose belly You fill with Your treasure;

they are satisfied with children, and leave their abundance to their babes. [15]As for me, I shall behold Your face in righteousness; I will be satisfied with Your likeness when I awake.

THE SMILING-FACE IN THE SPILLED POP

God plays with us like we are His kids-because, we are His kids.

One of the many times that the LORD manifested Himself to us as a family was while we were in the kitchen and I was with my kids Hannah and Philip. The three of us were goofing around with each other, one of the kids was drinking a can of grape pop. While we were goofing around the pop was spilled onto the white counter. We all stopped and looked at the large puddle of pop that had settled on the counter-and then we looked at each other. The pop had spilled in a round head-shaped pool with three open spots toward the middle to form a face, two eyes and a mouth. The mouth was shaped to form an "O" with a smile as if it were commenting on the spill or just engaging in our playtime. It was truly hilarious. Recall that I had earlier said "The three of us were goofing around with each other", well that statement was way off as **the four of us were goofing around together** and the LORD would not be outdone. God has a great sense of humor.

Job chapter 29

¹And Job again took up his discourse and said,
²"Oh that I were as in months gone by,
As in the days when God watched over me;
³When His lamp shone over my head,
And by His light I walked through darkness;
⁴As I was in the prime of my days,
When the friendship of God was over my tent;
⁵When the Almighty was yet with me,
And my children were around me;
⁶When my steps were bathed in butter,
And the rock poured out for me streams of oil!

THE PROMPTING TO PRAY FOR A CRUMBLING ECONOMY

It was late 2007 and I was prompted to pray for the American economy to crumble. It was a detailed message; I was to pray that God would remove the thing that had become the focus of our nation's attention-our prosperity, the economic idol of America. **I was being called to pray that there would be an economic crisis in our nation to such an extent that many families would occupy one household, and that there would be a shift of recourses from the hands of the ungodly to the hands of those that know the Lord. That the ungodly would be moved to seek recourses, food and shelter... from the Godly, and that the ungodly would be pulled toward the Godly in mass numbers much like iron toward a magnet for the purpose of mass evangelism and salvation. In essence, I was called to pray that God would make the spiritual battlefield smaller and more confined in order to save souls.** I recall specifically asking the LORD that many would live in one household for the purpose of this mass evangelism. I had a vision of formerly "well-to-do" people being humbled and forced into food lines or food shelves...that the people of God would show agape' love and mercy to them. This vision was very profound and included people stepping over people in homes, people scattered across floors crouched against walls, people sneaking outside like rats through broken places in broken buildings, going out onto cold and quiet streets looking much like ghost towns.

At the time of this of this vision I was so moved that I was compelled to stop what I was doing and call my Pastor/mentor to share this vision with him and a few others. The bright spot of this vision was that the children of the LORD were giving to the needy and boldly preaching the Gospel with their words and their deeds. I began to pray and the "Great Recession" ensued.

"The Great Recession-which officially lasted from December 2007 to June 2009-began with the bursting of an 8 trillion dollar housing bubble. The resulting loss of wealth lead to sharp cutbacks in consumer spending."

The state of Working America, The Great Recession, Wikipedia

"Surely the Lord God does nothing Unless He reveals His secret counsel To His servants the prophets. A lion has roared! Who will not fear? The Lord God has spoken! Who can but prophesy?"
Amos 3:7-8

THE FACE OF MY MOM AS A CHILD

My mom and my daughter Hannah were talking in the kitchen, as the conversation took a slightly negative turn it became respectfully argumentative, and then heated. As I listened to their debate I observed Hannah backing off opting for peace rather than "winning" this argument. Plain and simple, Hannah the younger of the two at age 14 chose the "high ground" in this case. My first impulse was to be disappointed in Mom, and unlike other times I choose to take the high ground as well, I was quiet and still before the LORD, and I said nothing. I finished what I was doing and slipped down stairs and prayed asking the LORD "what was happening here? What was going on LORD, why is it that my mom at 76 years old was acting like a child?" I decided to take a shower and get ready for whatever it was that I was going to do. As I was scrubbing my face with my eyes closed a clear black and white image of what looked to be a face appeared and then the clear image of a little girl's face came into clear view. **While my eyes were closed I focused in on the features of the little girls face and I asked "what is this LORD?" and then I recognized that the little girl was my mom when she was 3-5 years old.** The message and interpretation was clear that there is a difference between chronological and spiritual age. Though my daughter Hannah was 13 years old she was the spiritual elder and the more mature of the two at that moment, while my mom though older chronologically was the younger spiritually at that moment-Mom was in her spiritual infancy at that time.

It is interesting to me that over the past few years my mom has grown in the LORD, she shows signs of internal and external fruit and she was recently baptized. Thank you LORD!

[17]The seventy returned with joy, saying, "Lord, even the demons are subject to us in your name." [18]And He said to them, "I was watching Satan fall from heaven like lightning. [19]"Behold, I have given you authority to tread on serpents and scorpions, and over all the power of the enemy, and nothing will injure you. [20]"Nevertheless do not rejoice in this, that the spirits are subject to you, but rejoice that your names are recorded in heaven."

[21]At that very time **He [Jesus of Nazareth] rejoiced greatly in the Holy Spirit, and said, "I praise You, O Father, Lord of heaven and earth, that You [YHWH, LORD God] have hidden these things from the wise and intelligent and have revealed them to infants. Yes, Father, for this way was well-pleasing in Your sight.** [22]"All things have been handed over to Me by My Father, and no one knows who the Son is except the Father, and who the Father is except the Son, and anyone to whom the Son wills to reveal Him."

[23]Turning to the disciples, He said privately, **"Blessed are the eyes which see the things you see, [24]for I say to you, that many prophets and kings wished to see the things which you see, and did not see them, and to hear the things which you hear, and did not hear them."**

THE FLASH

In 2003 I had been a believer in the LORD for about 20 years. If asked I would have told you that "oh yes I was a strong believer". I had had a radical conversion, I was quite different from my former state, I had done some missionary work, and I had even lost some friends over my faith in Jesus-some didn't want to talk to me anymore. In my opinion I was a serious disciple of Jesus. From the outside looking in my life looked good; I was a Dr. and I had plenty of money, homes and all the things of the world. However, on the inside my life was a mess as my wife had left me, I had drifted from the LORD. I was abusing prescription pain medications and I was involved in several sexual relationships. I had set up "a practice" I had an office and I saw patients around the clock but didn't keep good records, pay bills, or sleep. I had made my choice, I chased after the things of the world, and it was a slippery slope that led to darkness. I had been deceived into thinking that if I was a Medical Doctor and did all the things that went with worldly success that I would be happy-I was wrong. I was circling-the-drain and out of control. I didn't know what to do or how to keep everything from falling. My foresight was correct and over the next few years I would lose my: ability to think clearly, my medical license, and my freedom… **I knew that I needed God, I knew that I wanted His help, and I needed more than just religious people saying religious things. At that moment I needed something big from the LORD to sustain me through that time, and for me to reflect on later-I needed a miracle.**

It was sometime in the early afternoon and I was driving north near my home in Saint Paul, MN. I was passing a small lake on the left and to the right was a suburban neighborhood. There was nothing unusual about what I am describing, I had driven that road many times before and many times after this event. But as I was driving this day I saw a flash, and though it was visual I also saw it in my mind. **The flash lasted about a second, it was gold in color and bright; during the** flash I could see the area around me though through a gold colored lens. Though the landscape, the wooded area…was essentially the same, there was no street, no lake and it was very beautiful, clean and bright. It looked uniform with regard to its light. I do not recall seeing shadows and there was no sun, only a uniform radiance. That flash that I saw was from the LORD, He gave me that gift, He got my attention, and that one second flash has helped me to see God's personal hand in my life-thank You!

Revelation chapter 21

[1]Then I [John] saw a new heaven and a new earth; for the first heaven and the first earth passed away, and **there is no longer any sea…**[3]And I heard a loud voice from the throne, saying, **'Behold, the tabernacle of God is among men, and He will dwell among them, and they shall be His people, and God Himself will be among them…'** [18]The material of the wall was jasper; and **the city was pure gold, like clear glass…**[21] And the twelve gates were twelve pearls; each one of the gates was a single pearl. And the street of **the city was pure gold, like transparent glass.** [22]I saw no temple in it, **for the Lord God the Almighty and the Lamb are its temple.** [23]**And the city has no need of the sun or of the moon to shine on it, for the glory of God has illumined it, and its lamp is the Lamb…** [25]In the daytime (for there will be no night there) its gates will never be closed; [27]**and nothing unclean**, and no one who practices abomination and lying, shall ever come into it, but only those whose names are written in the Lamb's book of life.

God communicated volumes in that silent moment, it was powerful and timely. It gave me hope as the bottom was falling out of my life-a heavenly distraction. That flash that lasted no more than a second helped me to see with my eyes what my heart was hopping for-God was present at my time of need. It was wonderful. I have asked the LORD why He would give me such a great gift at such a disobedient time in my life. It seems rhetorical; because He is good! **"…while we were yet sinners Christ died for us." See Romans 5:8**

THE FLIP OF A COIN, AND
THE SOVRENTY OF GOD

The Biblical term "casting lots" is used to describe a practice similar to "drawing straws". Casting lots, drawing straws or even flipping-a-coin are all ways of determining Gods will if accompanied by faith. In these situations we are resting in Him to lead and determine the outcome. This is quite different from: arm-wrestling, thumb wrestling, racing or any competition to determine "the best" or "the winner". This was the case with the sailors on the ship with Jonah, the disobedient prophet of the LORD; recall the sailors sought a word from the LORD, they were asking direction from Him and they "cast lots" or drew straws too discern the will of God. There have been times that my kids and I have prayed and flipped a coin in order to determine God's will in a matter. I believe that this is honoring to the LORD if faith is applied and the outcome is honored.

Proverbs 18

[18]To cast lots puts an end to disputes and decides between powerful contenders.

On every occasion that my daughter and I have used this method to determine the LORD's will, the LORD has confirmed the matter through His great signs and wonders. On one occasion I had just picked up Hannah from Stillwater/Hugo for the weekend and she had no sooner settled into our house in Brooklyn Park, MN and she asked me if she could spend the night with a friend in Oakdale near Stillwater. Hannah clearly made the point that she really wanted to go, and she felt that it was God's will for her. My initial reaction was "we just got home from a long drive from there" and I wanted to spend time with her; we were on opposite ends of the decision spectrum and we agreed to ask of the LORD that His will be made known by means of the flip of a coin. I was thinking that I my choice of not to go had the upper-hand as it made no sense to me to travel back to the very place that we had just returned from. With a prayer and the flip of a coin it was determined that God indeed willed us to pack up and head back out to the area from whence we came. While making the long drive Hannah and I had a nice talk and we prayed that the time would be fruitful. After about 35-40 min we had arrived at the entrance of the apartment building of Hannah's friend, as I was pulling into the parking lot my son Philip called and asked if I could meet him and a friend as his friend was feeling broken, and open and wanted to talk about the things of the LORD. I asked where he was and he happened to be about one mile west of us at a Caribou coffee, we were able to be there in a matter of minutes-Hannah and her friend joined us. While we were meeting with Philip and his friend Tamara we found this young lady wearing a wig as she had lost her hair due to a drug overdose in an attempt to take her own life. Tamara was terminally ill, estranged from her family and eager to talk of the things of the LORD. As our fruitful time came to an end Hannah gave Tamara her Bible and laid her hand on Tamara as we ended our time in prayer. It was clear to see in all of this that the sovereignty God was demonstrated and greatly appreciated-and preceded by the flip of a coin.

Jonah 1

[7]Each man said to his mate, **"Come, let us cast lots so we may learn on whose account this calamity has struck us " So they cast lots and the lot fell on Jonah.** [8]Then they said to him [Jonah], "Tell us, now! On whose account has this calamity struck us? What is your occupation? And where do you come from? What is your country? From what people are you?" [9]**He [Jonah] said to them, "I am a Hebrew, and I fear the LORD God of heaven who made the sea and the dry land."** [10]Then the men became extremely frightened and they said to him, "How could you do this?" For the men knew that he was fleeing from the presence of the LORD, because he had told them. [11]**So they said to him, "What should we do to you that the sea may become calm for us?"--for the sea was becoming increasingly stormy.** [12]**He said to them, "Pick me up and throw me into the sea. Then the sea will become calm for you, for I know that on account of me this great storm has come upon you."**

THE FOOD SHELF AND
THE SHOPPING CARTS

The food shelf began in about 2010. We essentially put up a few tables in the hall of a strip mall turned church, we set out: bread, can-goods and a few other things. The people came by word-of-mouth, and they would fill a bag or a box as they walked along the table pushing the box and picking goods from the table. The process of filling boxes while pushing, carrying or dragging them was cumbersome and dangerous as people were tripping over the boxes as they moved. As the food shelf grew, we began to pray for shopping carts, though at the time it seemed a long-shot as we had no funds to work with. At some point one of the workers at the food shelf contacted a local Target store manager and shared information about the food shelf ministry, in the process we gained the favor of the LORD through Target stores. Target offered to lend 12-15 shopping carts to the food shelf for a "short time" with the agreement that we would return them by a date determined by the store manager. We were thrilled to have the shopping carts as they worked out great, though we knew that this arrangement was only for the short term. The time to return the carts approached and even passed by a few days, the LORD prompted me to get involved and I followed up with the store manager regarding the carts. I called and left a massage with the manager and I apologized that we had neglected to return the carts on time and I made arrangements to return the carts. We were in prayer for favor. When I received a return call from the Target manager I was busy and I missed the call; I was prompted to faith and to prayer before returning the managers call. Again I asked the LORD for favor, and I reminded the LORD of His promise in **Proverbs 21:1 "a king's heart is like channels of water in the hand of the LORD and He [LORD God] directs it [the heart] whichever way he chooses"**, I asked the LORD for shopping carts and that God's will to be done in this matter, **"let Your will be done LORD". I called the manager and apologized again for our late return of the carts; as the store manager and I**

251

talked we talked about his good Biblical name, John (Greek, "God has been gracious to me"). John did not seem to be familiar with the things of the Scripture though he seemed polite and willing to listen; at some point in the conversation he asked if the carts had been helpful to the ministry, and I explained that the carts had been a blessing and at that point the store manager said that we could "use the carts indefinably", and we had since been given more carts. Wahoo!

Deuteronomy 8

[1] "All the commandments that I [LORD God] am commanding you today you shall be careful to do, that you may live and multiply, and go in and possess the land which the LORD swore *to give* to your forefathers. [2] *You shall remember all the way which the LORD your God has led you in the wilderness these forty years, that He might humble you, testing you, to know what was in your heart, whether you would keep His commandments or not.* [3] He humbled you and let you be hungry, and fed you with manna which you did not know, nor did your fathers know, *that He might make you understand that man does not live by bread alone, but man lives by everything that proceeds out of the mouth of the LORD.* [4] Your clothing did not wear out on you, nor did your foot swell these forty years. [5] Thus you are to know in your heart that the LORD your God was disciplining you just as a man disciplines his son. [6] *Therefore, you shall keep the commandments of the LORD your God, to walk in His ways and to fear Him.* [7] *For the LORD your God is bringing you into a good land, a land of brooks of water, of fountains and springs, flowing forth in valleys and hills;* [8] *a land of wheat and barley, of vines and fig trees and pomegranates, a land of olive oil and honey;* [9] *a land where you will eat food without scarcity, in which you will not lack anything;* a land whose stones are iron, and out of whose hills you can dig copper. [10] When you have eaten and are satisfied, you shall bless the LORD your God for the good land which He has given you.

THE FOOL HAS SAID IN HIS HEART THAT THERE IS NO GOD

I believe that most people will not allow the LORD to test them on a deeper level, that is to say, most of us will become faint of heart at the slightest of tests and most of us will retreat when we are really tested by the LORD. When our following of the LORD begins to include a cost to us though the question may well be, did you labor for the wealth of the world, that is silver, gold, recognition of men, comfort, entertainment, and vanity? Or did you pick up your cross "death stake" and follow Me [Jesus] **(Matthew 10:38)**? In other words the question is not who did you say that you follow, but, who did you really follow?

We may say with the words of our mouth "MASTER" but the works of our hands may be given to another "master". Realize that what we say with our lips, as important as that is, ought to be substantiated by the work of our hands, our giving, our expressions of love, time, and our willingness to be doers of the word and not simply hearers of the word. **"But prove yourselves doers of the word, and not merely hearers who delude [deceive or miscalculate] themselves" (James 1:22).** We ought not misrepresent the LORD by inviting people to come and see of the goodness of the LORD and then to beat, attack, and mistreat them along the way. This may be counterproductive to the Kingdom, and is nothing less than disregard of the truth, that is, blatant misrepresentation of the LORD to others. That is to say, we may be well intended in our giving food to the poor, but if we disregard them with hurtful words and looks while in line for their food we have missed the point, we have fallen into sin, we have effectively made them slaves to a hurtful task-master, a false-master, a pseudo-Christ, or anti-Christ. Though we may have cast a line for the LORD, and perhaps with good intention, yet along the way we may have fallen into the flesh, succumbed to: pride, pressure, distraction or even busyness; and effectively, what was a line cast for the LORD wound up a catch for the enemy. Ministries may have originated in the Spirit and ended in the flesh. Recall that "The fool" referred to by the Psalmist was not saying with his mouth that there is no God, in fact he may have regarded the LORD with his words, but in his heart, that is in the deepest places of his or her life, in his or her behavior, in the real places where the truth would be known; the very place that the LORD searches, knows and tests us (1st Chronicles 28:9, Psalm 139:23, Jeremiah 17:10), "The fool has said in his heart, 'There is no God." (Psalm 14:1). Let us not invite people to come "IN THE NAME OF THE LORD" and then serve the meal in the name of the liar that is the false Christ. Let us not do dead works but repent, or turn away from these dead works and become mature in our actions, let us press on to maturity as a result of practice (Hebrews 5:11-6:12). Let us speak truth in love and follow through with life giving works, "recall, "a live dog is better than a dead lion" (Ecclesiastes 9:4). And recall the teaching of the Lord Jesus regarding the hypocritical religious leaders 'THIS PEOPLE HONORS ME WITH THEIR LIPS, BUT THEIR HEART IS FAR AWAY FROM ME. 'BUT IN VAIN DO THEY WORSHIP ME, TEACHING AS DOCTRINES THE PRECEPTS OF MEN.'" (Matthew 15:8-9) Perhaps we ought to be reminded of the need to start well, and end well; "how blessed [happy] are those who keep justice, who practice righteousness at all times" (Psalm 106:3). It's time to grow up.

Hebrews 5

8 Although He [the LORD Jesus] was a Son, He learned obedience from the things which He suffered. 9 And having been made perfect, He became to all those who obey Him the source of eternal salvation, 10 being designated by God as a high priest according to the order of Melchizedek. *11 Concerning him we have much to say, and it is hard to explain, since you have become dull of hearing. 12 For though by this time you ought to be teachers, you have need again for someone to teach you the elementary principles of the oracles of God, and you have come to need milk and not solid food. 13 For everyone who partakes only of milk is not accustomed to the word of righteousness, for he is an infant. 14 But solid food is for the mature, who because of practice have their senses trained to discern good and evil.*

254

"Therefore leaving the elementary teaching about the Christ, let us press on to maturity, not laying again a foundation of repentance from dead works and of faith toward God"

THE CERAMIC FROG

The Spirit of God is not limited and seems to move in the most unusual ways at times; when we begin to "tune in" to the Spirit it can seem confusing, illogical at times and can be confused with "our own thoughts"... It takes practice and a certain amount of willingness to step out in faith and test-to-see if we are indeed hearing from the LORD or are we "imagining thing in our head". If we choose to take a step of faith we will often find that we have indeed been hearing from the LORD-at least that has been my experience. On one of many occasions we were in prayer in a meeting, we were asking the LORD to reveal Himself to us through the Spirit by a word, visions, prophecy, images... As we were praying I saw "in my mind's eye" a clear picture of a green ceramic frog with big eyes and a big exaggerated smile. I was uncomfortable with the idea of telling the group that I saw a frog as it sounded silly to me, though I felt convicted for being silent. After our prayer time I continued to feel convicted for not sharing my vision, I pulled two people aside and explained that I had seen a green ceramic frog and though it made no sense to me I felt that I needed to share it with them. One of the people immediately said **"oh that's [about] Grandma Foggy"** my response was "who is grandma Froggy?" and she explained that Grandma Froggy was Shannon's Grandma. It was clear that the LORD had a plan in mind for us to meet with Grandma Froggy. As it turned out we began to meet on a weekly basis with Grandma Froggy and we continued to meet with her for almost two years. During that time Grandma Froggy grew in her relationship with the LORD, she testified of the LORD and she studied through her Bible-and then she died. This seemed to be fruitful time in the LORD, and the LORD was seen in it by His leading.

1 Corinthians 12

¹Now concerning spiritual gifts, brethren, I do not want you to be unaware. ²You know that when you were pagans, you were led

257

astray to the mute idols, however you were led. ³Therefore I make known to you that no one speaking by the Spirit of God says, "Jesus is accursed"; and no one can say, "Jesus is Lord," except by the Holy Spirit. **⁴Now there are varieties of gifts, but the same Spirit. ⁵And there are varieties of ministries, and the same Lord.** ⁶There are varieties of effects, but the same God who works all things in all persons. **⁷But to each one is given the manifestation of the Spirit for the common good.** ⁸For to one is given the word of wisdom through the Spirit, and to another the word of knowledge according to the same Spirit; ⁹to another faith by the same Spirit, and to another gifts of healing by the one Spirit, ¹⁰and to another the effecting of miracles, and to another prophecy, and to another the distinguishing of spirits, to another various kinds of tongues, and to another the interpretation of tongues.¹¹But one and the same Spirit works all these things, distributing to each one individually just as He wills. ¹²For even as the body is one and yet has many members, and all the members of the body, though they are many, are one body, so also is Christ. ¹³For by one Spirit we were all baptized into one body, whether Jews or Greeks, whether slaves or free, and we were all made to drink of one Spirit.

THE FRUITFUL CROP

Recall that Joseph was the son of the Patriarch Jacob, Jacob was later renamed Israel. Joseph found himself in a pit at the hands of his jealous and deceptive brothers. While Joseph's brothers were eating a meal near the pit containing their brother Joseph, they made further plans for their brothers future. Joseph was then sold to slave traders and was brought into Egypt. Joseph was sold to a band of slave traders for sharing a dream similar to the one that I now share. I had a dream that I was alone in a huge rolling field with beautiful and colorful vegetables as far as I could see; it was a very lush and colorful scene. The vegetables were clean, shiny, ripe and very large-and the weather was perfect. For some reason I felt that the fields were mine and somehow indoors though it looked like we were outdoors and again these fields were expanded as far as I could see. From a distance I could see my: Mom, my sister Sue and brother-in-law, and others, and though they were quite a distance from me they were moving in my direction through the field and I was moving in their direction to meet them. **I was watching my family as they walked through the fields toward me, I was thrilled as they were looking at and marveling at the various vegetables before them, they were literally in the process of examining the fruit of my life in Christ as they were moving in my direction-it was wonderful. It felt like heaven to me.**

Psalm 1

[1]**How blessed [happy] is the man [person]** who does not walk in the counsel of the wicked,
Nor stand in the path of sinners,
Nor sit in the seat of scoffers!
[2]**But his delight is in the law of the LORD,
And in His law he meditates day and night.**

³He will be like a tree firmly planted by streams of water,
Which yields its fruit in its season
And its leaf does not wither;
And in whatever he does, he prospers.
⁴The wicked are not so,
But they are like chaff [the worthless portion thrown to the wind or
thrown into the furnace] which the wind drives away.
⁵Therefore the wicked will not stand in the judgment,
Nor sinners in the assembly of the righteous.
⁶For the LORD knows the way of the righteous,
But the way of the wicked will perish.

THE FLOATING FUZZ IN THE RAINSTORM

I live with my parents in their home and I have a room on the lower-level facing west where my view includes: a wide grassy area, some large trees and a few homes in the background. I spend a lot of time praying while looking out the window. Prior to knowing the Lord I would do very much the same thing though instead of prayer-time I called it "my thinking time". While laying quietly I would think through complicated questions, like, how is it that trees are balanced with weight equally distributed and the answers seemed to "just come to me". I remember laying for hours thinking of things, reasoning through things as I attributed insight and revelation to my own ability. I have since come to appreciate that the Lord was communicating with me and teaching me as a good father teaches his children. On one occasion I was praying and watching a rainstorm, it was raining very hard and the rain drops were very large. It was unusual to see so much water fall and bombard the grass with such force-it was impressive. As I watched the rain I noted a large glob of fuzz rise in the middle of the rain out in front of me; this fuzz looked like it was from a plant of some kind, almost like the small top from a dandy-lion or a Cottonwood plant or tree. The fuzz rose in front of me in the rain and I wondered how this was possible, knowing that if one of those large raindrops hit the fuzz it would drop to the ground, so, I watched and waited. **I then sensed that the Lord was at work and that He was showing me His great hand at work almost as though He were just showing off His ability (I mean that with the greatest respect for the Lord).** I watched in absolute amazement as this fuzz rose and moved in and out of the raindrops with relative ease without being touched; it then continued to hover out a ways in plain sight and weaving in and out between the raindrops, I could almost see the Lord smiling. The fuzz then floated away as if in total defiance of the rain drops-no problem for the Lord. All things are possible with God.

261

Psalm 91

[1]He who dwells in the shelter of the Most High will abide in the shadow of the Almighty. [2]I will say to the LORD, "My refuge and my fortress, my God, in whom I trust!" [3]For it is He who delivers you from the snare of the trapper and from the deadly pestilence. [4]He will cover you with His pinions, and under His wings you may see refuge; His faithfulness is a shield and bulwark. [5]You will not be afraid of the terror by night, or of the arrow that flies by day; [6]of the pestilence that stalks in darkness, or of the destruction that lays waste at noon. [7]A thousand may fall at your side and ten thousand at your right hand, but it shall not approach you. [8]You will only look on with your eyes and see the recompense of the wicked. [9]For you have made the LORD, my refuge, even the Most High, your dwelling place. [10]No evil will befall you, nor will any plague come near your tent. [11]For He will give His angel charge concerning you, to guard you in all your ways. [12]They will bear you up in their hands, that you do not strike your foot against a stone. [13]You will tread upon the lion and cobra, the young lion and the serpent you will trample down. [14]"Because he has loved Me, therefore I will deliver him; I will set him securely on high, because he has known My name. [15]"He will call upon Me, and I will answer him; I will be with him in trouble; I will rescue him and honor him. [16]"With a long life I will satisfy him and let him see My salvation."

THE GAP BETWEEN MIRACLES

I asked the LORD into my life when I was about 22 years old and prior to that I had been involved in: organized gambling, drug dealing, fornication…you name it and I was likely in it. I had a dramatic conversion, I was radically changed and I assumed that I had experienced all of the LORD that was possible this side of heaven. After about ten years of what I thought was walking with the LORD I began to follow my strong desire to go to Medical School and become a Dr. I made a choice to pursue a medical career and though I did not consciously determine to forsake the LORD I know now that I placed my agenda above His. For the next seven years of my life I felt dead in my spirit, my life literally unwound and spun completely out of control, **I had cut loose my Anchor.**

While I was literally on the brink of losing my: family, my homes, my freedom, my career and my reputation, I would soon be reporting to jail for a sentence of 1 year or 8 months if for "good behavior". I was lying on the deck of my soon to be foreclosed on home and I was thinking on the things of the LORD. I recall that at that moment the LORD was more real to me then I had experienced in a long time. God was in my thoughts at that time. I was reflecting on all that seemed to be accessible to me through Him and all that He was so willing to share. I then thought of how little I seemed to really pursue the things of God; my life felt fruitless, useless and empty to that point in time

My comment to the LORD "LORD you have so much to offer and we seem so little in our asking, in our pursuit of You, we are so small in our faith, I have so little to offer You at this point in my life, but if You can use me in this state please feel free, please use me. And things began to change, and have not been the same since then..

Thank you LORD.

Job 19:23-26

23"[Job says]Oh that my words were written!
Oh that they were inscribed in a book!
24"That with an iron stylus and lead
They were engraved in the rock forever!
25"As for me, I know that my Redeemer lives,
And at the last He will take His stand on the earth.
26"Even after my skin is destroyed,
Yet from my flesh I shall see God;

Job 42:5

"I [Job] have heard of You [LORD God] by the hearing of the ear.
But now my eye sees You [LORD]."

THE LAUGHING SKIPPING
AND LEAPING ZEBRA

One Saturday afternoon we drove a car load of Hannah's friends out to the Como Park Zoo. As we wandered around the zoo we came into one popular building that housed giraffes and zebras; the building was essentially divided down the middle separating the giraffes on one side and the zebra on the other. As you walk into the building you first visit the giraffes and then move toward the zebras. As the girls and I were looking at the amazing giraffes and then the zebra's fine and detailed stripes we began to talk about the greatness of God in His creation. We then talked about how ridicules it was to think that anyone but the Devine Creator Himself could be credited for such great things as this. **We began to laugh at the silliness of people to discredit the LORD by giving glory to "chance events"-and we laughed hard. At that very moments that we began to laugh out loud the zebra began bucking, leaping and bounding from front to back opening its mouth, laughing along with us and we all stood laughing together. This was one of the funniest things that I have ever seen-a zebra laughing.**

Job 12

⁶"The tents of the destroyers prosper,
and those who provoke God are secure,
whom God brings into their power.
**⁷"But now ask the beasts, and let them teach you;
and the birds of the heavens, and let them tell you.
⁸"Or speak to the earth, and let it teach you;
and let the fish of the sea declare to you.**

**⁹"Who among all these does not know
that the hand of the LORD [YHWH, God] has done this,
¹⁰In whose hand is the life of every living thing,
and the breath of all mankind?**

¹¹"Does not the ear test words,
as the palate tastes its food?
¹²"Wisdom is with aged men,
with long life is understanding.

THE LICENSE PLATE

I have been divorced for twenty years and yet I feel no less bound to my wife now than the day that we were married. This has nothing to do with me or my impressive devotion to my wife, but it does have everything to do with the LORD. Let me clarify; there are entirely different rules that govern the world system and the High Courts of the LORD. I believe that in the High Court of the LORD we remain married regardless of what any human courts may say or do. I believe that God continues to confirm this to me even after being apart from my wife for these twenty plus years.

On one occasion while I was driving with my daughter in the Shoreview area I noticed the car directly in front of us as we were driving westbound on Highway 96 (a two lane Highway). The car directly in front of us had a license plate with the letters TCR- followed by three numbers that I do not recall. The "TCR" reminded me of my name, **T**odd **C**rawford, hence "TCR" and I said to my daughter Hannah, "hay who does that [license plate] remind you of?" and she said "TCR oh that's you dad". I then began to think of my wife and talk to the LORD quietly in my mind. I was saying to the LORD "LORD it doesn't seem fair to me that I should have to think of my wife day-in and day-out while she probably doesn't think of me at all." And then I said to the LORD **"LORD, it's not fair, I wish that you would give her a license plate like the one in front of me [TCR-...] so that she would have to be reminded of me every time that she gets into her car"**. I know that this may seem like an outrageous way to be talking to the LORD but the LORD knows my heart, He knows that I have been hurt by the divorce and thankfully He has great patience. While I was stating my case before the LORD the car in front of me with the license plate TCR-..., signaled left and then moved into the left hand lane slowed down and moved about 5 feet to my left. I looked at the driver and to my amazement it was my wife Linda, I nudged my daughter to my right and I said

267

"Hay Hannah look, it's your Mom" **my wife was driving that very car, as it was her car. The very car that had the plate TCR-... was the very person that I was praying would have those plates.** Thank you LORD for your strong support, indeed what God has joined together, let no man [no man can] separate. :)

"Come now, and **let us reason together**, says the Lord, though your sins are as scarlet, they will be as white as snow; though they are red like crimson, they will be like wool." **Isaiah 1:18**

"[God says] Put Me in remembrance, let us argue our case together; state your cause, that you may be proved right." Isaiah 43:26

¹When Jesus had finished these words, He departed from Galilee and came into the region of Judea beyond the Jordan; ²and large crowds followed Him, and He healed them there. ³Some Pharisees came to Jesus, testing Him and asking, "Is it lawful for a man to divorce his wife for any reason at all?" ⁴And He [Jesus of Nazareth] answered and said, "Have you not read that He who created them from the beginning MADE THEM MALE AND FEMALE, ⁵and said, 'FOR THIS REASON A MAN SHALL LEAVE HIS FATHER AND MOTHER AND BE JOINED TO HIS WIFE, AND THE TWO SHALL BECOME ONE FLESH'? ⁶**"So they are no longer two, but one flesh.** What therefore God has joined together, let no man separate." **Matthew 19**

THE LITTLE-BOY AND HIS WAGON

During a pivotal point in my life, when I was being stripped of: the things of this world, my career, my houses, my pride, and my freedom, I was receiving new-to-me revelation from the LORD.

At that time I received a very clear picture in my "mind's eye" of little boy walking on a sidewalk, to the little boy's left was his father and to the left of them was a large wooded area and a pond. The boy and his dad were quietly walking and making their way down the sidewalk, the little boy was pulling a red wagon filled with his most valued worldly possessions: toys, books, string…the stuff that a 5 year old boy would value and collect. As the two were walking along the concrete path a storm began to blow in from the west and they continued their walk. As the two were walking it became clear that the storm was building. The wind was picking up, leaves and twigs were blowing and the little boy reached out to his dad with one hand, both were still quiet; dad was walking holding the hand of his son while his son pulled his wagon with his other hand. As the storm was building the little boy looked to his father who was holding the boys hand, and dad was holding out his free hand for the child to accept or to deny in favor of his worldly possessions contained in the wagon. It was hard for the little boy to let go of the handle of the wagon so he choose to hold his father's hand with one hand as he continued to pull the wagon with the other hand. The storm became more violent, rain began to fall, the wind was gusting blowing leaves and twigs and the sky looked increasingly threatening. Again the little boy's father held out his free hand to the little boy as the little boy continued to pull the wagon, now focusing less of his attention on the wagon and more onto his father. The little boy wrestled with the decision at hand, to let go of his things and fully embrace his father or to continue to pull his wagon with one hand and hold his father's hand with the other. Reaching out to his father with both hands would mean letting go of all of his things. While holding onto his things meant that

269

he could hold onto his father but only to a lesser degree, the embrace of one would mean to compromise the other. Again, the little boy was at a point in his journey that he needed to decide and act; the full embrace of one would mean the denial or letting go of the other, he could not have the full benefit of both, the little boy needed to choose then act accordingly.

In my vision, the father stood still holding the little boys hand with one hand while extending his free hand to the little boy. The winds blew harder and harder until the little boy let go of the handle of the wagon, he extended his now free hand toward his father who grabbed his hand and lifted him to safety as the little boy was now able to experience the full embrace of the father-both were unhindered by the things of the world.

Matthew 6

[19"] [Jesus said] Do not store up for yourselves treasures on earth, where moth and rust destroy, and where thieves break in and steal. [20"]But store up for yourselves treasures in heaven, where neither moth nor rust destroys, and where thieves do not break in or steal... [24"]No one can serve two masters; for either he will hate [disregard] the one and love the other, or he will be devoted to one and despise the other You cannot serve God and wealth.

THE MAN, THE SHIRT, AND THE SHELTER

My good friend and ministry brother Jeremiah was in town and we had plans to go into a Saint Paul homeless shelter in order to pray, minister and see what the LORD had in mind for us for the day. Jeremiah is a bold witness in the LORD, he has infiltrated homeless shelters around the Midwest for the purpose of reaching the lost. Jeremiah has done street ministry, preached on street corners with a "mega phone" and preached until he was forced to leave by the police. He has passed out Scripture to thousands and he seems to be living up to his good name, Jeremiah means "to exalt the LORD". Jeremiah spent the night on our hide-a-bed in the family room of our home and we woke up early to head for the shelter. **As I was getting ready I put my favorite T-shirt on and I sensed that the LORD was telling me to put another T-shirt on under the one that I was wearing. I shared the thought or word that I had regarding the T-shirt with Jeremiah and before heading out to the homeless shelter I went back to the closet and did as I was told-I put a T-shirt on under my favorite T-shirt (note that there was nothing special about my favorite T-shirt). I then told Jeremiah that the LORD would likely be requiring my favorite T-shirt today at the homeless shelter,** though I did not know the details-we laughed and headed out. We arrived at the shelter in the morning and there was a crowd of people in the courtyard. Jeremiah and I were not sure what we were to do so we walked and we prayed and look for opportunities. We continued to walk and pray and we eventually felt that it was time for us to leave and we began to walk past the courtyard with the intention of going to the car and leaving. At that point I was wondering if I would be called on to give up my shirt as I had thought. I was feeling relieved as this was my favorite T-shirt and one of my few shirts. As we took one last look through the courtyard fence and we made our way to the car I noted a man with his leg bandaged and he was reading a Bible. I asked him about his injury and about what he was reading and we ended our conversation with prayer for his injured leg and for help from the

LORD with regard to this man's homeless condition. As we ended our prayer we said "goodbye" and we began to walk away. **After about 10 steps, as we walked toward the street in route to the parking lot I heard the man call to me from through the fence "HAY, [I turned around and I looked at him] I LIKE YOUR SHIRT!"** As he said "I like your shirt" Jeremiah and I looked at each other and laughed and we walked back to the man. We told him the story of the word regarding the shirt and I took the shirt off and gave it to him. Though the shirt has been long since gone, the memory is not, the test was great, as was the witness that we all shared regarding God Who speaks to us. It seems that "the man at the shelter" was "in the shelter of the Most High" (See Psalm 91). Thank you LORD.

Psalm 91:1

"He [or she] who dwells in the shelter of the Most High will abide in the shadow of the Almighty"

Matthew 5

[3] "[Jesus said] Blessed are the poor in spirit, for theirs is the kingdom of heaven. [4] "Blessed are those who mourn, for they shall be comforted. [5] "Blessed are the gentle, for they shall inherit the earth. [6] "Blessed are those who hunger and thirst for righteousness, for they shall be satisfied. [7] "Blessed are the merciful, for they shall receive mercy. [8] "Blessed are the pure in heart, for they shall see God. [9] "Blessed are the peacemakers, for they shall be called sons of God.

272

THE MAN HEADED FOR THE CROSS

I had a dream that I was on the outskirts of what looked like a large festival. I was sitting on a hill and I was looking west over a valley into an old city, the people's clothing, the building, means of transportation and the streets all looked to be consistent with the time of Christ. In the center of a huge group of people were several men that were being led to a place of crucifixion, this looked like a type of festival, some type of religious ceremony commemorating the Crucifixion of the LORD. My focus was fixed upon one man, he was: slim, dark, young, early to mid-thirties, hurting and very focused; he was surrounded by people that looked to be moving him and maybe even assisting in getting him to the place that his crucifixion was to take place. My heart went out to this man; I walked through the crowd and stood right in front of him asking by gesture if there was anything that I could do to help him. **The man in my dream was headed for the cross and for his own crucifixion, he looked past me almost as though he didn't see me. To say that he looked focused is a huge understatement. When I reflect on the details of this dream I wonder, I seriously wonder if I wasn't actually sitting on the Mount of Olives looking across the Kidron Valley right into Jerusalem at the time of Jesus' crucifixion. This dream was so real.**

Matthew 20:17-19
[17]As Jesus was about to go up to Jerusalem, He took the twelve disciples aside by themselves, and on the way He said to them, [18]"Behold, we are going up to Jerusalem; and the Son of Man will be delivered to the chief priests and scribes, and they will condemn Him to death, [19]and will hand Him over to the Gentiles to mock and scourge and crucify Him, and on the third day He will be raised up."

273

Luke 9:51

"When the days were approaching for His [Jesus'] ascension, He was determined to go to Jerusalem"

GOD'S MESSENGER THE BIRD-AND MY DISOBEDIENT NATURE

While I was working in the plastics factory it was not uncommon for the LORD to meet me in very personal and creative ways-ways that boggled my mind and even made me question my sanity at times. I have since become dependent upon the presence of the LORD and His signs and wonders. I now wonder what I did for enjoyment prior to experientially knowing the LORD. On one occasion I was standing at my work station near the northern most wall of the factory. The north wall of the plastics factory had a few large windows that could be opened to the outside. It was not uncommon for birds to fly into the factory through the shipping and receiving doors on the other end and become trapped in the factory. These birds would fly around the inside of the building and they distracted us from the loud and monotonous factory work. On one occasion I was standing at my post praying, and I was lamenting over the relative disregard of people for the LORD, especially those who claim to follow Jesus. In the midst of my sadness I recall hearing the loud chirps of a bird as though it was calling out to me. I can recall saying out loud "oh that [bird chirping a message] is for me". Responding to the chirp I looked over to the bird that was perched on the window looking at me and chirping. I felt that this bird chirped to get my attention and I recognized that the LORD was up to something interesting. As I looked I felt compassion for the bird and I wanted to set it free, so I prayed and walked toward the bird with the intention of opening the window that stood in the way of its freedom. Initially the bird seemed comfortable with my walking toward it. As I walked closer to the window the bird became nervous and eventually flew away in an impulse before I could get to the window. I recall stepping back and feeling frustrated that I was unable to help the bird; it felt ironic to me that the very hand that intended to help the bird was the hand that the bird was fearful of. **I stated my case to the LORD "LORD, I have compassion for the bird, the bird is trapped and I** want to help, I want to set it free; but every time I get close it flies away in fear". The LORD's response to me was "that is how it is with you [humans] toward Me [YHWH, God]." He gets close, and we get uncomfortable and run.

Psalm 124:7-8

Our soul has escaped as a bird out of the snare of the trapper;
the snare is broken and we have escaped.
Our help is in the name of the LORD [YHWH],
who made heaven and earth.

Luke 5:8

But when Simon Peter saw that [Jesus' miracle], he fell down at Jesus' feet, saying, 'Go away from me Lord, for I am a sinful man!'

THE MOVIE AND THE SAFETY-PIN

After the LORD met with me in a personal way I felt compelled to erect as a memorial-I set up an altar. I have a bookshelf with a board over it and draped over the board is a red plaid blanket with hundreds of safety pins pinned into it. The pins represent miracles that the LORD has shown to me or done through me. Safety pins are very personal to me in the LORD.

In the evenings I typically sit with my parents from about 6:30-8:00 P.M. as it seems to be a time that we can spend together; my folks usually like to watch old movies.

We were watching an old movie and I was in prayer and quite board watching this particular "corny" old movie, the "stars" were Bing Crosby and Rhonda Fleming, the movie, A Connecticut Yankee in King Arthur's court. I began to ask the LORD to please reveal Himself to me. At that moment in the movie two people were sitting in an uncovered horse drawn carriage and the carriage was pulled over to the side of the road. The man in the carriage, it may have been Bing Crosby, was romancing a the lady sitting next to him, he was talking to her as though he was ready to propose marriage to her, and in the midst of the drama he reached into his pocket opened his hand and presented to her a gift from the heart-**a SAFETY PIN. :)**

Psalm 4

A Psalm of David.

[1]I waited patiently for the LORD;
And He inclined to me and heard my cry.
[2]He brought me up out of the pit of destruction, out of the miry clay,
And He set my feet upon a rock making my footsteps firm.
[3]He put a new song in my mouth, a song of praise to our God;

Many will see and fear
And will trust in the LORD.
**⁴How blessed [happy] is the man [person] who has made the
LORD his trust,**
And has not turned to the proud, nor to those who lapse into falsehood.
**⁵Many, O LORD my God, are the wonders which You have done,
And Your thoughts toward us;
There is none to compare with You
If I would declare and speak of them,
They would be too numerous to count.**
⁶Sacrifice and meal offering You have not desired;
My ears You have opened;
Burnt offering and sin offering You have not required.
⁷Then I said, "Behold, I come;
In the scroll of the book it is written of me.
⁸I delight to do Your will, O my God;
Your Law is within my heart."

THE NOW-VACANT-DESK

There have been times that the LORD has prompted me to say and do things that seemed odd and may have even tested social boundaries at times. I understand that "here lies the test". That is, God calls us out of our comfort zone at times perhaps to test our commitment to Him. In these situations the LORD confronted me with the question **"do you love Me more than these?" (See John 21:15),** with "these" being: relationships, reputation, comforts, securities... The question asked of the LORD in these cases, "are you willing to risk: relationships, reputation, comforts, securities...for your obedience to Me?" This question was fitting as the Old Testament prophets seemed to be people who were misfits in this world as are modern day prophets. These prophets were and are called to a higher calling, they were and are called to speak and act in ways that may seem odd to the world system. On one occasion while I was working at the plastics factory I began to meet with Eric who was a temporary employee and he had great zeal for the LORD. I watched as Eric become energized when he would talk to people about the LORD. Eric seemed to be an evangelist and watching him work with such boldness and enthusiasm encouraged me. Eric and I began to meet at lunchtime outside for Bible study and prayer with hopes of reaching others for the LORD (See Matthew 4:19, Mark 1:17). There was a lady by the name of Sheryl who worked near Eric's station, she seemed to be in the position of authority over Eric, a type of supervisor in Eric's department. Eric had early conflicts with Sheryl and he could see that the enemy was trying to divide them-we began to pray for Sheryl. Soon Sheryl began to sit near us while we had our noontime Bible study, and then she became a regular in our small group lunch meeting. Sheryl seemed to be moving in the right direction though it was tough to read Sheryl's regard for the LORD. In that context the LORD in His "still small voice" (see 1st Kings 19:12) told me that the enemy was poised to attack Sheryl, that she needed to be warned of the pending attack, and called to a more serious place. I took a deep breath and brought the message to Sheryl. I boldly presented the Gospel of Christ, and I warned Cheryl of her need for a quick response; Sheryl finished her cigarette then looked at me and walked away. Sheryl died shortly after our discussion. God knows the outcome.

2 Samuel 1:14

"…Yet God does not take away life, but plans ways so that the banished one will not be cast out from him."

THE PALM-READER

We were at our Monday morning men's-group and one of the men brought up the subject of a palm reader on Lexington Ave. in Saint Paul, MN. I felt a burden at that point to pray for the palm reader and to lovingly confront her, and present the Gospel of Jesus to her. I told the other men at the meeting about my burden, we prayed and I asked the LORD for a specific sign to confirm His will. I asked to see a "VKP" on a license plate on my way home indicating that the LORD wanted me go to the palm reader's house. I saw the "VKP [P for palm reader]" on my way home and I received that as a sign of the LORD's will. The next day I headed over with my Bible, I let my mentor Dan know the details and he said that he felt that I should not park in front of the house but "around the back" as he was concerned about possible witchcraft directed at my car. I arrived at the palm readers house, all of the parking spots in the rear were occupied by cars except for one spot, I pulled into the only open spot and noted the license plate in front of me, "VKD [D for Dan]" I laughed and took a picture and sent it to Dan, it was good confirmation for me and for Dan. I walked to the house with my Bible and I knocked on the door. A young lady opened the door, the environment in the house looked dark and there was a toddler walking around at the feet of the young lady. The toddler made eye contact with me as if to be asking for my help, the young lady politely said that she was not the palm reader and she closed the door. I prayed for the house and for the child, and then I headed home. I felt compelled to return to the house as I did a few days later, as I walked to the house this second time I was met by a patron of the palm reader, he was standing at the door as I walked up. The patron said that he was there for "insight" and we began to talk about the LORD. This man was familiar with the things of the LORD, he looked as though he felt convicted for his being there, he was willing to pray to the LORD as we did on the front steps of the palm reader's home. It was Interesting timing meeting the Christian guy there. We then said goodbye and I left as my mission seemed to have been completed.

281

¹⁶ Then the king gave orders, and Daniel was brought in and cast into the lions' den. The king spoke and said to Daniel, "Your God whom you constantly serve will Himself deliver you." ¹⁷ A stone was brought and laid over the mouth of the den; and the king sealed it with his own signet ring and with the signet rings of his nobles, so that nothing would be changed in regard to Daniel. ¹⁸ Then the king went off to his palace and spent the night fasting, and no entertainment was brought before him; and his sleep fled from him.

¹⁹ Then the king arose at dawn, at the break of day, and went in haste to the lions' den. ²⁰ When he had come near the den to Daniel, he cried out with a troubled voice. The king spoke and said to Daniel, "Daniel, servant of the living God, has your God, whom you constantly serve, been able to deliver you from the lions?" ²¹ Then Daniel spoke to the king, "O king, live forever! ²² My God sent His angel and shut the lions' mouths and they have not harmed me, inasmuch as I was found innocent before Him; and also toward you, O king, I have committed no crime." ²³ Then the king was very pleased and gave orders for Daniel to be taken up out of the den. So Daniel was taken up out of the den and no injury whatever was found on him, because he had trusted in his God. ²⁴ The king then gave orders, and they brought those men who had maliciously accused Daniel, and they cast them, their children and their wives into the lions' den; and they had not reached the bottom of the den before the lions overpowered them and crushed all their bones. ²⁵ Then Darius the king wrote to all the peoples, nations and *men of every* language who were living in all the land: "May your peace abound! ²⁶ I make a decree that in all the dominion of my kingdom men are to fear and tremble before the God of Daniel; **for He is the living God and enduring forever, and His kingdom is one which will not be destroyed, and His dominion *will be* forever. ²⁷ "He delivers and rescues and performs signs and wonders in heaven and on earth, who has *also* delivered Daniel from the power of the lions."** ²⁸ So this Daniel enjoyed success in the reign of Darius and in the reign of Cyrus the Persian.

THE PANTS, "YOU BOUGHT THEM!!

After years of thinking that I was my provider the LORD persuaded me differently. God was training me to recognize His voice and He was providing for my needs just as He said that He would-and I was beginning to see things more clearly. At about that time, my mother was in what seemed to be the early stages of her faith, she commented that "I needed new pants" and "why don't we get some from a second-hand store as that would be cheaper". I challenged her thinking and said that God could provide pants if we asked Him to do that. She said to me "what is He going to do bring them in from nowhere?" my response was, "sure, if He wants to". We stood in the entry way of their home and prayed asking God to provide "two pairs of jeans for work and the ones with the little pocket on the side would be nice". It wasn't long before someone unrelated to us who had not been told about our request gave me two pair of pants. They asked me if I thought that they would fit and my response was "oh I'm sure that they will fit". The pants fit great and one pair had that little pocket on the side that I had asked the Lord for.

Psalm 37:4
"Delight yourself in the LORD; and He [YHWH, LORD God]
will give you the desires of your heart."

God provided all of my clothing needs for quite some time-it was our little thing. One day my mom and I passed by a church "garage-sale" and I allowed myself to be pulled in to buying some jeans for a few bucks a pair. The whole time that I was going through this stack of jeans I was hearing the LORD remind me that He is my provider. I tried the jeans on and they fit well, **I caved into temptation and bought the jeans with His money and without His approval.** After I got the jeans home I tried them on again and this time they did not seem to fit very well-they were too tight. I went for a walk with the jeans on and I was complaining to the LORD for a good half-an-hour. As I continued to walk I complained that these size 34 jeans were

283

"too tight", I was doing all the talking until I heard the LORD say in a voice that sounded like my own, **"you bought them"**. I laughed when I heard the LORD's response but at the same time I realized that the money was not mine to spend and it could have gone to feed the poor... I regretted buying the pants. I continued walking parallel to 85th Ave. a busy boulevard and I saw out in the middle of the road something mashed down wet and run over; it looked flat like a shingle in the street. I had no reason to think that it was anything special. I continued walking and then turned around sensing that the LORD had something for me if I were willing to go get the thing in the road. I went back, waited for traffic to clear and picked up the thing in the road and I realized that the thing in the road was a pair of men's jeans. These jeans were very nice and stylish, size 36 (go figure), I delighted and thanked the LORD and returned home with His gift. I walked in the door and shared how God had provided in such a great and funny way. I washed the jeans and it came to no surprise at all that they fit perfectly. It's funny that the brand of the Jeans was Retro Fox as Todd means "foxy" or "crafty"; recall the name of the fox in Disney's The Fox and the Hound? It was Todd.

Matthew 6:25-28

"For this reason I [Jesus] say to you, do not be worried about your life, as to what you will eat or what you will drink; nor for your body, as to what you will put on. Is not life more than food, and the body more than clothing?

284

ELLEN, THE PAPER LADY

As I have alluded to in the past I am part of a home church group that meets in a tailor in the Hilltop community near Columbia Heights MN. Though our congregation may be few in number we have a great group and a wide range of people at many places on the spectrum of maturity. I love these folks and these folks love the LORD and they love each other. In our home church we aspire to be lead by the Holy Spirit; we typically share, pray, sing, eat and study through the Scriptures together. I seemed to have assumed the role of the Pastor of this wonderful little gathering though I feel that I am more of a facilitator. Recently I have questioned the LORD's purpose for me and I have questioned whether I am "the right person for the job of Pastor". About a week and a half ago I was engaged in a conversation with a local Pastor of a traditional church and we discussed our home church gathering, at one point in the conversation I told him that I frequently felt ill-equipped for the job but due to the lack of support from those more suited I was meeting the call. I then repeated three times that the laborers were "few, few, few" that are working the fields for the LORD. **I left the conversation feeling a bit discouraged and I questioned the LORD as to whether I was "in the right place'".** While at church Sunday a heated discussion began during our study of Acts chapter 5:1-11 discussion of the deaths of both Ananias and Sapphira, a objection was raised by one of the congregation that had interpreted this as harsh treatment by the LORD. It seemed to be a reasonable and healthy discussion that quickly escalated into a loud argument between two of those in leadership. **I left the gathering that day feeling a bit discouraged and I questioned the LORD again as to whether I was "in the right place and the right person for this job?", My specific question to LORD had been "who am I LORD, what is my job here LORD"?**

Early this morning I prepared the Bible study lessons and scriptures to bring to my son Philip for his distribution at work. After an initial problem with the computer it seemed that the LORD was telling me to "leave now with what I had" so I did just that. I stepped into the garage, opened the door and as the garage door opened I saw a van parked near the base of the driveway. I recognized the van as the newspaper delivery lady's van. I had said hello to her on several occasions and had acknowledged that she was listening to Christian radio and I may have said "LORD bless you" on one occasion, beyond this I do not recall saying much in our few encounters. When I first saw her van I had no reason to believe that she wanted to talk to me, as I pulled up near her I planned to get the papers for those in the cul-de-sac and I said "are you ok? Need any help?" As I stepped up to the van she said that the LORD had directed her to "talk to me" as she "had a word from God" for me and she politely said in the form of a question "You're a Pastor". I then explained that I was a leader of a small home church group in a tailor park and she nodded with a sense of confirmation and smiled. The paper lady politely stopped me and said **"No, I'm not asking if you are a Pastor, I'm telling you. You are a Pastor!"** She then explained that the LORD was moving in great ways in her life, I acknowledged the same in mine. Earlier that morning Ellen had gotten all the way home and felt compelled to drive back and share the word with me. **I then was reminded of my questioning the LORD regarding His will for me and the paper lady said to me again "the LORD told me that you are a Pastor" as she spoke she was making a statement as to my place rather than asking me a question. This message communicated volumes to me, God made His point well known to me at that moment in the statement "YOU ARE A PASTOR", I am a pastor, and I receive that loud and clear.**

Jeremiah 1

Jeremiah's Call and Commission

[1]The words of Jeremiah the son of Hilkiah, of the priests who were in Anathoth in the land of Benjamin, [2]**to whom the word of the LORD came** in the days of Josiah the son of Amon, king of Judah, in the thirteenth year of his reign...[4]**Now the word of the LORD came to me saying,** [5]**"Before I formed you in the womb I knew you, and before you were born I consecrated you; I have appointed you a prophet to the nations."** [6]Then I said, "Alas, Lord GOD! behold, I do not know how to speak, because I am a youth." [7]But the LORD said to me, "Do not say, 'I am a youth,' **because everywhere I send you, you shall go, and all that I command you, you shall speak.** [8]**"Do not be afraid of them, for I am with you to deliver you," declares the**

LORD. ⁹Then the LORD stretched out His hand and touched my mouth, and the LORD said to me,
"Behold, I have put My words in your mouth. ¹⁰"See, I have appointed you this day over the nations and over the kingdoms, to pluck up and to break down, to destroy and to overthrow, to build and to plant.

THE PATH AND THE SERPENT

I had a dream that I was walking along a path with two other people walking in front and to the right of me. On both sides of the path were fields, grass and trees for as far as I could see. As we were casually walking along the path, we seemed to be in no real hurry to get anywhere and the path seemed wide enough for a car to drive, the path was not paved and our staying on the path seemed to be the order of the day. As we were walking I looked off to the left of the path and I saw a reflection. I walked over to the far left side of the path and without stepping off of the path I looked down and saw the flickering of light as though it were reflecting off of snake skin. The snake skin was only exposed in a very small place under a leaf and some twigs; I suspected that there was a very small snake under a small pile of leaves and grass in front of me. **I commented out loud to myself and to others "oh a serpent!" and expecting it to be a small snake I bent over to touch it. As I leaned over still standing on the path I touched the small piece of the exposed snakeskin expecting a small snake to slither away. What happened next was surprising, as I touched the snake the entire landscape to the left of the path moved away from me as if the snake were fearful of me and it was now exposed. I thought that it was interesting that the serpent was fearful of me while I was on the path and I was not threatened by it. The entire landscape to the left was a serpent camouflaged and poised waiting for me or one of the others to step off of the path.**

Revelation 12

[7]And there was war in heaven, Michael and his angels waging war with the dragon. The dragon and his angels waged war, [8]and they were not strong enough, and there was no longer a place found for them in heaven. [9]**And the great dragon was thrown down, the serpent**

of old who is called the devil and Satan, who deceives the whole world; he was thrown down to the earth, and his angels were thrown down with him. [10]Then I heard a loud voice in heaven, saying, "Now the salvation, and the power, and the kingdom of our God and the authority of His Christ [Jesus the anointed King] have come, for the accuser of our brethren has been thrown down, he who accuses them before our God day and night. [11]"And they overcame him because of the blood of the Lamb and because of the word of their testimony, and they did not love their life even when faced with death.

[12]"For this reason, rejoice, O heavens and you who dwell in them Woe to the earth and the sea, because the devil has come down to you, having great wrath, knowing that he has only a short time."

THE PERFECT STORM

Hannah and her friends and a few others from church were going to a Christian music festival on Herriot Island in Saint Paul. The event, "ROCK THE RIVER" was promoted by the Franklin Graham Ministry and was "a very big deal". The morning of the event was very cloudy with a thick cloud cover and as I recall heavy rain was in the forecast. We were driving south with a carload of young people and I remember calling for the groups attention and praying that the LORD would clear the sky and provide good weather for the event. I reached my hands in the air and I called the others to do the same saying "come on!", I grabbed at the air from right to left or west to east-I motioned pulling at the air as though to push the clouds away from west to the east. At that time all that I could see was a sky filled with dark thick clouds. I seemed to have a mustard seed of faith at that moment-not much more. We almost immediately turned left, headed east and drove for about 1/4 of a mile, for about 2 minutes; we then turned right heading south once again. As we turned right I looked at the sky that we had prayed over a few minutes before, then dark and densely clouded. **As I looked again toward the west, a front, running like a straight line as far as I could see was pushing the clouds from west to east just as we had asked the LORD a few minutes before, it cleared the sky for the most part and provided clear weather for the great concert. Thank You LORD!**

Matthew 17

[20]*And He [Jesus the Christ the anointed King said]...for truly I say to you, if you have faith the size of a mustard seed, you will say to this mountain, 'Move from here to there,' and it will move; and nothing will be impossible to you.*

AND THE LIGHT-SHOW

On another occasion, in the summer of 2010, as though it were God's great encore; I was headed to Willmar, MN to the Sonshine Music Festival for the day, the night, and to help take camp down the next day. I had dropped off Hannah and a few friends along with the rest of the church group a day or two before. About midway through the two hour trek to Willmar I received a text from my good brother Erik at about 3 P.M. asking me to pray to the LORD that He might send a storm onto Willmar and that it would end by 8:00 P.M. **I have learned to trust Erik and I prayed as he had asked that God would please send a storm and that it would end by 8:00 P.M.** I arrived in Willmar at the campsite and all was well. Sarah and her two boys, Eddie and Joshua had decided to stay in a hotel for the weekend and had invited people to come to the room, it was a nice break from the heat of the day, showers etc. We were at Sarah's hotel room by about 5:00 or so when a storm rolled-in. The storm that hit Willmar that evening was the greatest storm that I had seen in my life and is one that people from Willmar are still talking about, I know this to be true as I had recently talked to some people from Willmar who remembered the storm. It is hard to describe this storm without feeling that I am understating it. Lightning was fleshing and exploding all around, wind was blowing, hail and rain were falling... The hotel called a mandatory evacuation of everybody and we were all instructed to gather in the lower level. The evacuation seemed to last about a half an hour to 45 minutes, the winds the rain and the lightning passed toward the campsite. We gathered together at the room when the evacuation ended, and then went out to see what the storm had left behind. There were branches, leaves and twigs thrown around, the sky looked like it had just been badly beaten and bruised and was flashing with lightning bolts every few seconds. At least a few "thunderbolts" came in real close, right across and into the adjacent field as we watched through the main level door and window. By about 7:00 we made our way back to the campsite where we saw people coming out of the shelter of the nearby school. Things and tents were toppled bent and rolled all around. We met with our group who reported that as the storm had rolled in and people were evacuated into the nearby school. The storm was still rumbling and throwing lightning bolts and seemed to be moving away from the stage and the campground and hovered just adjacent to the stage far enough to miss any rain and close enough to appreciate the lightning show throwing bolts to and fro. It was going on 8:00 if not 8:00 P.M. exactly when we approached the stage, people stopping and staring into the sky in marvel, the music was blaring giving praises to God. The lightning was flashing with the music and I don't recall hearing any thunder, the sky was a blaze-red; people were stopped all over gazing at the sky almost in disbelief and in reverence of this great sight. The praise music went on for hours; the lightning show went on far longer into the night. God would not and could not be outdone by any performance of man-before our eyes the lightning flashed and pulsated with the music.

Job 28

[20]"Where then does wisdom come from?
And where is the place of understanding?
[21]"Thus it is hidden from the eyes of all living and concealed from the birds of the sky.
[22]"Abaddon and Death say, 'With our ears we have heard a report of it.'
[23]"God understands its way, and He knows its place.
[24]"For He [YHWH, LORD God] looks to the ends of the earth and sees everything under the heavens.
[25]"When He imparted weight to the wind and meted out the waters by measure,
[26]When He set a limit for the rain and a course for the thunderbolt,
[27]Then He saw it and declared it;
He established it and also searched it out.
[28]"And to man He said, 'Behold, the fear of the Lord, that is wisdom;
And to depart from evil is understanding.'"

THE PICTURE OF THE LITTLE
ANGEL BEHIND ME

In 1989 I had the pleasure of going to Papua New Guinea on a missionary trip. While in route to New Guinea my travel partner and I spent a few days in Guam visiting with a young missionary couple. As we explored Guam we were taken though a local church and though there were no people in the congregation I stepped up to the pulpit holding a Bible in one hand and pointing in dramatic fashion with the other hand. I was pretending that I was preaching and my travel partner took a picture of me pretending to preach at the pulpit, the picture has been in a photo album for thirty plus years and I have looked at it many, many times. Let me say that again, I have looked at that picture many, many times. During a time of recent revelation by the LORD He directed me to the photo album of the Guam and Papua New Guinea trip. **While I was looking at the picture album and this particular picture I saw something that I had never seen before, standing behind me and to the left of me in the photo is a little girl that looks to be about three to five years old, she is wearing a dress and the photo is of her literally hanging in mid-air with her arms stretched to the heavens and her feet above the ground, she is literally flying and she looks like a little angel.**

Romans 16

[24][The grace of our Lord Jesus Christ be with you all. Amen.] **[25]Now to Him who is able to establish you according to my gospel and the preaching of Jesus Christ, according to the revelation of the mystery which has been kept secret for long ages past,** [26]but now is manifested, and by the Scriptures of the prophets, according to the commandment of the eternal God, has been made known to all the nations, leading to obedience of faith; [27]to the only wise God, through Jesus Christ, be the glory forever. Amen.

Note the little girl in the back

THE PINS AND THE ORDER FORM

I carry in my pocket a handful of safety pins. As you may know I have a blanket draped over an alter in my room; on the blanket are hundreds if not thousands of pins that each represent miracles, that is, every time that the LORD gives me a miracle, He then gives the word that it is "pin worthy". When I receive the word that a miracle is "pin worthy" I attach a pin to my shirt and I later pin it to the blanket. This is a tangible way for me to mark the wonders of the LORD. My first purchase of pins was a lot of "ten gross" 1440 pins, as I recall. As these pins were used up and are now on the blanket I was asking the LORD how to proceed as I was out of pins, my question to the LORD, "LORD is it your will that I continue?". As I recall that very day an order form for safety pins came in the mail addressed to me, and my Dad offered to buy another "lot [1440]" of pins.

2 Chronicles 16

⁷At that time Hanani the seer came to Asa king of Judah and said to him, "Because you have relied on the king of Aram and have not relied on the LORD your God, therefore the army of the king of Aram has escaped out of your hand. ⁸"Were not the Ethiopians and the Lubim an immense army with very many chariots and horsemen? Yet because you relied on the LORD, He delivered them into your hand.

⁹"**For the eyes of the LORD move to and fro throughout the earth that He may strongly support those whose heart is completely His.** You have acted foolishly in this. Indeed, from now on you will surely have wars."

THE PROMPTING "TO THE PARK"

As I was driving and doing ministry with my brother in the LORD, Jeremiah, we were prompted to "go to the park". I knew that "the park" referred to a local Saint Paul park that our church group had assembled at in the past. I told Jeremiah that we were to go to the park though I had no understanding of why we were being called there as it was early on a weekday. Yet the prompting was clear, "go to the park", so we went to the park. As Jeremiah and I pulled up we could see that the park was covered with hundreds of kids that seemed to be engaged in play and organized activity, there were also scattered men and women supervising and observing and they looked like they were secret service officers as they were serious and on-guard. As I recall we prayed for God's leading and with our Bibles in hand we set out into the park. As we walked toward the center of the park we began to hear the beating of an evil sounding drum, it was interesting as we had earlier identified a similar sound of a drum that was related to some very dark demonic behavior. Jeremiah and I walked in the middle of these hundreds of kids and we began to ask questions regarding who they were and why they were there. The kids communicated to us that they were from a local Muslim school and they had gathered for a day of recreation. Jeremiah and I understood that we were to pray and witness for the LORD Jesus in that place. As we observed we prayed, we anointed the ground with oil and found ourselves in the presence of a man in the center of the park. While we were there we talked in detail with this man about his beliefs and ours, we were all respectful and kind, and we then discussed his position with the school that was represented in the park that day. **As it turned out this man was the founder of the local school and seemed to hold a high position with the local Muslim community. I do not recall exactly what was said however I do recall affirming with Jeremiah that our appointment from the LORD felt fruitful, our witness for Jesus was conducted in love and respect and most importantly we were obedient to the prompting to "go to the park". We both left the park saying in tandem "WOW"!**

¹Now the Spirit of God came on Azariah the son of Oded, **²and he went out to meet Asa and said to him, "Listen to me, Asa, and all Judah and Benjamin: the LORD is with you when you are with Him and if you seek Him, He will let you find Him; but if you forsake Him, He will forsake you.** ³"For many days Israel was without the true God and without a teaching priest and without law. **⁴"But in their distress they turned to the LORD God of Israel, and they sought Him, and He let them find Him.** ⁵"In those times there was no peace to him who went out or to him who came in, for many disturbances afflicted all the inhabitants of the lands. ⁶"Nation was crushed by nation, and city by city, for God troubled them with every kind of distress." **⁷"But you, be strong and do not lose courage, for there is reward for your work."**

THE APOSTLE AND THE ROOF

I am blessed to know Dennis, a man who claims to be an Apostle. God has confirmed Dennis' claim of Apostleship to me through a number of signs and wonders as well as through Dennis' understanding that his appointment is not about him but about God. Not long after meeting Dennis I was led to take him to breakfast to get to know him, we agreed on a time and I picked him up at the place that he was staying. As we left his home Dennis asked me if we could stop at a friend's house, for prayer. Dennis explained that his friend and his wife have a ministry to young people, though it may seem like a "daycare" it is Christ-centered, kids are taught about the LORD in this place, kids grow up in the LORD and return to this place to lead others to the LORD. Dennis and others have shared that kids will come into this place as small children and they are taught about the LORD, they are raised in the LORD here, and many leave as young adults and return as volunteers. I have spent time watching as large numbers of kids flow through this place, teachers of the LORD come and teach and outreach is happening; there is sense of peace in this place; the presence of the LORD is there. Dennis and I drove to the house, and we sat outside on the street, while we sat in the car Dennis explained that he had a great burden for the ministry here. Dennis explained that they needed a new roof and that someone had agreed to do the roof, they had removed the existing roof and then left the roof unprotected and with no plan to complete it. Dennis wanted to go and pray that the LORD would finish this roof soon somehow as rain was in the forecast. Dennis and I spent time reminding the LORD of the way this home is being used to advance His kingdom **"Present your case, the LORD says, bring forward your strong arguments..." Isaiah 41:21,** *"you who remind the LORD, take no rest for yourselves; and give Him no rest..." Isaiah 62:6-7*, we then left for breakfast. While at breakfast we continued to pray and talk about the roof and we prayed that the LORD would "hold back the rains" as the skies looked dark and threatening and heavy rain was in the forecast.

At this point there was no plan, no crew, no protection on the roof and we had absolutely no idea of where but to God to turn to for help-this was perfect for a miracle. As we talked and prayed for the roof to be replaced I felt the Spirit prompt me to boldness and I prayed out loud with Dennis that the roof would be completed "today" and I saw out the window of the restaurant a car driving by with a confirmatory "VKR-[R for roof]" on the license plate. Dennis was not familiar with the way the LORD speaks to me by way of "VKs" so I appreciated the conformation privately, I sensed that all would be fine. After our time together, we drove by the house once again, we stopped and we prayed, and again, there was no crew present and no plan for a crew to arrive that we knew of. I dropped off Dennis at his home and I went home and laid on my bed looking out at the dark skies, and I spent the day in prayer and I fell asleep. Later that afternoon I awoke from a nap, I was reminded of the roof, I looked at the dark skies and at some point I noted a few raindrops had fallen on the window, again I prayed and I felt otherwise helpless. A short time later I received a message from Dennis that it was beginning to rain out by him, that the roof was completed and done in time to beat the rain; I never did hear the details of how the LORD worked this out, but I know that He did.

Psalm 46

*[1]God is our refuge and strength, a very present help in trouble.
[2]Therefore we will not fear, though the earth should change, and
though the mountains slip into the heart of the sea; [3]Though its
waters roar and foam, though the mountains quake at its swelling
pride. Selah. [4]There is a river whose streams make glad the city of
God, the holy dwelling places of the Most High. [5]God is in the midst
of her, she will not be moved; God will help her when morning
dawns. [6]The nations made an uproar, the kingdoms tottered; He raised
His voice, the earth melted. [7]The LORD of hosts is with us; the God of
Jacob is our stronghold. Selah.
[8]Come, behold the works of the LORD, who has wrought desolations
in the earth. [9]He makes wars to cease to the end of the earth; He
breaks the bow and cuts the spear in two; He burns the chariots with
fire. [10]"Cease striving and know that I am God; I will be exalted
among the nations, I will be exalted in the earth."
[11]The LORD of hosts is with us; the God of Jacob is our stronghold.
Selah.*

THE PROPHET CAME TO ME

In the summer of 1995 I packed our belongings into a tailor and along with my wife Linda and son Philip we moved to Des Moines Iowa where I went to medical school. Linda and I had been living with my Grandparents at the time. The evening before we were to leave, a car pulled up in front of the house and Carl, a person that I had been an acquaintance of since junior high walked up and asked "could we talk for a minute?". Carl and I had grew up in the same area, I had been a friend and housemate of his brother Cliff who has since died. Carl had become a believer in the LORD about the time of Cliff's death and though we crossed paths and were friends we rarely spent time together, though I enjoyed his company when we did. I had not talked to Carl and had no idea how he knew where to find me, or how he may have known that I was leaving-this all seemed "very unusual". Nonetheless here was a brother who seemingly stopped over at the very time that I was moving, it seemed "quite random" yet perfect-the trailer was packed and we planned to leave in the morning. **We walked to Carl's car and sat in the front seat, Carl was very serious and he began to warn me of the things that would be happening to me if I let my guard down and took my focus off of the LORD in this next phase of my life. As I recall, he said that I "would be losing my wife and my family and that I would go through such pain as I had never experienced in my life", he was detailed in his description of what would soon be happening if I drifted from the Lord.** Carl's message was a warning, he did not make light of it and he did not apologies for it, he simply delivered it to me and then he said goodbye. After settling in Des Moines, IA I became busy in med school, we did not seek out fellowship and my disciplines of daily Bible reading/study and prayer and giving were replaced by an over whelming school load. As time passed Carl's massage stayed with me, I reviewed his message over and over and I seemed to almost consciously push it to the side. I resisted the warning, I did not realize that it was a prophetic warning-and I drifted

303

away from the LORD. What happened as time passed was exactly as it was delivered to the smallest detail, as I remember, I had been reminded by God of His kind warning to me but I was too much the fool to listen and like the Prodigal son I lost my focus, I spent my inheritance and I lost everything, and yes I experienced such pain as I have not before or since experienced. After about ten years and many reminders of Carl's prophetic word to me I called Carl and his wife to encourage them in the LORD. Carl had little to no recollection of the word, and it sounded to me like Carl too was drifting from the Lord as he too was entrenched in his career... How sad!

Amos 3:1-8

All the Tribes Are Guilty
Hear this word which the LORD has spoken against you, sons of Israel, against the entire family which He brought up from the land of Egypt: "You only have I chosen among all the families of the earth; therefore I will punish you for all your iniquities." Do two men walk together unless they have made an appointment? Does a lion roar in the forest when he has no prey?
Does a young lion growl from his den unless he has captured something? Does a bird fall into a trap on the ground when there is no bait in it? Does a trap spring up from the earth when it captures nothing at all?
If a trumpet is blown in a city will not the people tremble? If a calamity occurs in a city has not the LORD done it?
Surely the Lord GOD does nothing unless He reveals His secret counsel to His servants the prophets.
A lion has roared! Who will not fear [have great regard]?
The Lord GOD has spoken! Who can but prophesy?

THE PUPPIES ON THE CARD

In the past I have carried generic greeting and thank-you cards with me. I found that the LORD would open doors of opportunity and use these cards from time to time. I recall that they were most often used for sympathy type messages in response to loss of life situations. As I recall, at this particular time of my life I was feeling discouraged with regards to the relative lack of regard for the things of the LORD that I was seeing in the people that I was working with. I was having a hard time understanding why people simply didn't seem to see and appreciate the things of the LORD that I was so clearly seeing. On one occasion the LORD had me focus my attention on the front of one of these cards, the picture on the front of the card was of a basket of puppies, there were about 5-7 puppies and they were very cute. As the LORD had me focus on the puppies He said **"do you see the puppies?"** and I responded "yes LORD I see the puppies" and I noted that the eyes of the puppies were all closed, **I thought that it was odd that the eyes of the puppies were all closed, I noted it and said "LORD the eyes of these puppies are closed" and then I put the card down**. As a little time passed the card remained where I had left it on a workbench, a few minutes to an hour later I returned to the workbench where the same card was laying. Walking past the workbench I felt compelled to look at the same card again, the LORD said **"do you see the puppies?"**; as I looked at the same card I noted that all of the puppies eyes were now open and my response to the LORD was **"hay, the eyes of the puppies were closed and now they are open"**. **The LORD responded in a still small voice "in the same way, your eyes were once closed and now they have been opened [as well]"**

²⁴So a second time they called the man who had been blind, and said to him, "Give glory to God; we know that this man is a sinner." **²⁵He then answered, "Whether He is a sinner, I do not know; one thing I do know, that though I was blind, now I see." ²⁶So they said to him, "What did He [Jesus of Nazareth] do to you? How did He open your eyes?"** ²⁷He answered them, "I told you already and you did not listen; why do you want to hear it again? You do not want to become His disciples too, do you?" ²⁸They reviled him and said, "You are His disciple, but we are disciples of Moses. ²⁹"We know that God has spoken to Moses, but as for this man, we do not know where He is from." **³⁰The man answered and said to them, "Well, here is an amazing thing that you do not know where He is from, and yet He opened my eyes.**

THE SHADOW AND MY MOTHER

It is not uncommon for: me, my daughter Hannah, my mom and my dad to go to a local Vietnamese restaurant for dinner on Friday or Saturday nights. Most recently, as we were driving to the restaurant, Dad was driving and Mom was riding in the passenger seat, I was behind Mom and Hannah was behind my dad in the back seats. It was late afternoon to early evening as Dad likes to eat around 5:00 P.M. The sun was to the west and we were traveling south, the sun was to Mom's right casting a perfect shadow of the profile of her face to the finest detail onto the center armrest. I was unable to see Mom's real face but I could see her shadow off to my left on the armrest and it was as if the shadow was speaking to us as Mom spoke. As I could not see Mom but I could see her shadow face, I was directing my conversation to the center-armrest. As we talked I was watching the shadow of her face moving and showing all of the details of her face and mouth as she talked-it was cool. As Mom was talking I was watching her shadow and I could see her mouth and face moving to every word that she was speaking; it quite literally looked and sounded as though the shadow itself was speaking. Again, Mom's real face was not visible to me from my perspective as she was sitting directly in front of me facing forward. **I looked at the shadow and I began to think of how insignificant this shadow was, how temporary it was in spite of it seemingly speaking fluently. I also had thoughts of this shadow being somehow prideful though it was nothing more than a shadow.** At that moment, as I looked in amazement, God began to speak to me in what the Bible describes as "His still and small [quiet] voice [Hebrew, 'a gentle blowing']" See 1st Kings 19:12. He conveyed to me that **"we in this flesh are little more than this shadow"**. Though we have some substance to these bodies, we are little more than the dust that we are made from. I marveled as I was thinking of how we people make such a big-deal of ourselves and our "significant" lives while we are little more than a mere mist, a vapor, a shadow.

1 Chronicles 29:15

"For we [creatures] are sojourners before You [LORD, God], and tenants, as all our fathers were; our days on the earth are like a shadow, and there is no hope [apart from You Lord]."

James 4:14

"Yet you do not know what your life will be like tomorrow. You are just a vapor that appears for a little while and then vanishes away."

THE TAPE

God has a great sense-of-humor. As I recall, we were driving the girls to church when Megan asked in a very random moment "do you have any tape?" For some reason, and perhaps because of her questions randomness we laughed and I said "why would I have any tape" as it seemed at least at the moment one of the least likely things that I would have with me. Well what happened over the next few days was a series of similar questions regarding "do you [Todd] have any tape" from many unexpected people in many unexpected places until I eventually carried in the car, you guessed it, tape. Soon after the initial question of Megan "do you have any tape?" One of my kids walked into my room while the other was standing there as well and asked "DAD, DO YOU HAVE ANY TAPE?" and we all laughed at the randomness of the question and we recounted the events of Megan's initial question. Soon after, my friend Larry was having car problems, as I recall and in a manner that it seems that only Larry could do he asked "Hey Todd, do you have any tape?" my thought was why would I have tape. Shortly thereafter I was driving to a prayer meeting and it was in the dead of winter on a very cold day, I saw a man pulled over to the side of the road on an on-ramp headed east bound on I-94 off of White Bear Ave. in St. Paul. At first I drove past him as I was running close to the scheduled time for prayer, I then checked in with the group and shared that I felt compelled to return to the man stuck on the ramp. I drove back and found him under the hood working on the engine and I asked if there was anything that I could do to help him, he was holding battery cables as I recall. After asking him how I could help him I was thinking that he would ask for tools of some kind, he turned and looked me in the eye and said "DO YOU HAVE ANY TAPE?" I laughed to myself and shook my head and thought, why would I have any tape? Later I was sitting in a gas station parking lot as I was putting air into a slowly leaking tire, as I filled the tire with air a little boy came walking over to me and he said "HEY MISTER, DO YOU HAVE ANY TAPE?" God's humor-second to none.

⁵Just as you do not know the path of the wind and how bones are formed in the womb of the pregnant woman, so you do not know the activity of God who makes all things.

⁶Sow your seed in the morning and do not be idle in the evening, for you do not know whether morning or evening sowing will succeed, or whether both of them alike will be good.

⁷The light is pleasant, and it is good for the eyes to see the sun.

THE SIGNATURE AND THE BIBLES

Shortly after surrendering "my life" to the LORD He gave me two miracles that have been standout miracles amongst so many. I have referred to these two miracles on many occasions. This testimony addresses the signature of the government official, the other addresses the Bibles. On another occasion I made reference to both of these wonderful miracles that have been imprinted on my mind. Both of these are too great to be simply referred to and would seem like making reference to "the Crossing of the Red Sea", "the falling of the wall of Jericho" or "David's defeat of the giant Goliath" without its own written account. Therefore, at the risk of being redundant, here is my account of this wonderful event.

My wife and I were seeking the LORD regarding His will for us and we seemed to be surrounded by people bent toward foreign missions. Our best friends, and several very good friends, and many acquaintances were either on furlough from the mission field, in the field or preparing to leave for the mission field. We considered translating the Bible to an unreached people group, we recognized the immeasurable value in foreign missions, and quite frankly there was even a component of glamour and heroics that may have been driving our aspirations. At any rate we were seeking the LORD and we were giving careful consideration to foreign missionary work. We decided that I ought to go on a short-term mission's trip to check it out and an opportunity presented itself so we took the next step. A young man from the west coast was preparing to go to Papua New Guinea (PNG) to survey the interior of the Inga Province in the highlands of PNG, and he was willing to take me as his travel companion. As we moved forward in our plans everything seemed to fall into place, the money came in, I had my passport, I had the time freed up and the plans were all made. Everything was in place with the exception of the signature of a government official from a certain office in PNG, the signature

311

marked the official permission of the PNG government for me to be wandering about in their jungles. As I recall there were no fax machines available and it was getting close to the departure date and no written response had arrived, as the departure date approached and still I had no permission to be in PNG. The day to leave came and I decided to move forward though they could have sent me back home as soon as I stepped off of the plane. I boarded the plane in MN and I flew to California, then onto to Hawaii then to Guam for a layover and then onto Port Moresby, PNG. On the long flight from Hawaii to Guam I had plenty of time to talk with the man sitting next to me, he had a long flight to observe my travel companion and me as we related to others and to each other, and he made note of my Bible... Sometime in the course of our conversation we talked on a deeper level about our mission's plans and our destination. I recall inquiring of the man his destination as he said that he was from PNG and I asked if he could help me by directing me to the city that I would need to travel to in order to find the man that needed to sign my document. He asked me where I needed to go, I told him and he replied that he knew the area well as he worked there and lived nearby. **I gave him the specific office name and the name of their official and he told me that there was no need for me to travel to this office as he was indeed that very man that I was looking for. The one man in the world that I needed to sign my document before landing was the very man that the LORD had sitting in the seat next to me. That man gladly signed the document and then we landed. Praise the LORD!**

Joshua 3:5-17

Then Joshua said to the people, "Consecrate yourselves, for tomorrow the LORD will do wonders among you. **"And Joshua spoke to the priests, saying, "Take up the ark of the covenant and cross over ahead of the people." So they took up the ark of the covenant and went ahead of the people. Now the LORD said to Joshua, "This day I will begin to exalt you in the sight of all Israel, that they may know that just as I have been with Moses, I will be with you. "You shall, moreover, command the priests who are carrying the ark of the covenant, saying, 'When you come to the edge of the waters of the Jordan, you shall stand still in the Jordan.'" Then Joshua said to the sons of Israel, "Come here, and hear the words of the LORD your God."... "Behold, the ark of the covenant of the Lord of all the earth is crossing over**

312

ahead of you into the Jordan. "Now then, take for yourselves twelve men from the tribes of Israel, one man for each tribe. "It shall come about when the soles of the feet of the priests who carry the ark of the LORD, the Lord of all the earth, rest in the waters of the Jordan, the waters of the Jordan will be cut off, and the waters which are flowing down from above will stand in one heap."…

So when the people set out from their tents to cross the Jordan with the priests carrying the ark of the covenant before the people, and when those who carried the ark came into the Jordan, and the feet of the priests carrying the ark were dipped in the edge of the water (for the Jordan overflows all its banks all the days of harvest), **the waters which were flowing down from above stood and rose up in one heap, a great distance away at Adam, the city that is beside Zarethan; and those which were flowing down toward the sea of the Arabah, the Salt Sea, were completely cut off. So the people crossed opposite Jericho. And the priests who carried the ark of the covenant of the LORD stood firm on dry ground in the middle of the Jordan while all Israel crossed on dry ground, until all the nation had finished crossing the Jordan.**

THE SIN OF SODOM AND GOMORAH

As is too often the case we tend to read the Scriptures through the lens of our: self-righteousness, hypocrisy and rationalizations. We tend to read Jesus' rebuke of the Pharisees and think to ourselves "oh those rotten Pharisees" as we direct our thoughts onto others. Perhaps we ought to consider that we may be the ones in desperate need of change. A good question to ask is, are we the Pharisees?

As is most often the case when we refer to "the sin of Sodom and Gomorrah" we seem to refer to sexual sin and homosexuality. The men of Sodom were indeed engaged in such behavior as it is stated in the Book of Genesis: "Now the men of Sodom were wicked exceedingly and sinners against the LORD". **(Genesis 13:13).** "And the LORD [YHWH] said, 'The outcry of Sodom and Gomorrah is indeed great, and their sin is exceedingly grave.'" **(Genesis 18:20)** "…the men of the city, the men of Sodom, surrounded the house, both young and old, all the people from every quarter; [5] and they called to Lot and said to him, "Where are the men who came to you tonight? Bring them out to us that we may have [sexual] relations with them." [6] But Lot went out to them at the doorway, and shut the door behind him, [7] and said, "Please, my brothers, do not act wickedly." **(Genesis 19:4-7).** However as dark as those sexual sins may have been these are not the original sins of Sodom and Gomorrah as they are cited in Ezekiel 16. The original sin of Sodom and Gomorrah is referred to as "abominations" and it is inferred that this dark sin referred to is the beginning of a "slippery slope" that led to the sexual depravity. Note that "… **[Sodom] had arrogance, abundant food and careless ease, but she [Sodom] did not help the poor and needy. [50] Thus they were haughty [proud, self-absorbed] and committed abominations before Me [the LORD God].** The original sin of Sodom was that Sodom had "abundant [extra, more than what was needed] food, and careless ease, but she [Sodom] did not help the poor and needy". Consider that "abundance" is more than what is needed, abundance is "excess" or "extra" and in this passage refers to food. Now consider that essentially every home in America is equipped with both cupboards a refrigerator and freezer for storage of our "excess" food. That is, even our "poor" have excess, and "abundance" of food to the point that it is commonplace to store and waste our food. The implication of these passages is that when people are hard-hearted enough that they can have extra, and abundance while the poor are starving then other immoralities such as sexual sin…will follow leading to destruction. Are we like Sodom?

Ezekiel 16

48 As I [LORD God] live," declares the Lord GOD, "Sodom, your sister and her daughters have not done as you and your daughters have done. **49 Behold, this was the guilt of your sister Sodom: she and her daughters had arrogance, abundant food and careless ease, but she did not help the poor and needy. 50 Thus they were haughty and committed abominations before Me [LORD God].** Therefore I removed them when I saw *it*. **51** Furthermore, Samaria did not commit half of your sins, for you have multiplied your abominations more than they. Thus you have made your sisters appear righteous by all your abominations which you have committed. **52** Also bear your disgrace in that you have made judgment favorable for your sisters. Because of your sins in which you acted more abominably than they, they are more in the right than you. Yes, be also ashamed and bear your disgrace, in that you made your sisters appear righteous.

THE SOUND OF THE CRUMBLING BUILDING

The LORD had me fix my gaze onto a tall building in downtown Minneapolis, MN. As I was looking at this building I began to hear what sounded like grains of sand hitting paper. The only way that I can explain this would be to have you hold a piece of paper to your ear horizontally and drizzle a few grains of sand onto it from a few feet above the paper, it was like the soft tapping on a drum. As I was looking at the building and hearing the distant sound of sand dropping I asked the LORD what it was that I was hearing? **The LORD in His goodness simply stated "the buildings are slowly crumbling".** These buildings are crumbling, (it's just happening too slowly for us to easily appreciate), these bodies too are failing and fading, yet we seem to ignore it.

2 Corinthians 5

[1]For we know that if the earthly tent which is our house is torn down, we have a building from God, a house not made with hands, eternal in the heavens. [2]For indeed in this house we groan, longing to be clothed with our dwelling from heaven, [3]inasmuch as we, having put it on, will not be found naked.

THE SPIRIT OF GOD FALLING ON ME

The promise of the LORD is that He will give the Spirit to those who ask of Him (See Luke 11:13). I know by experience that this is true. Though I had asked the LORD to save me some twenty five years earlier, I had most recently become less distracted by the world; this did not come as a result of any noble act or choices on my part as it was the LORD Himself that removed the obstacles that were keeping me from Him. The things that were receiving my attention and my praise became idols that I had set up in my heart. The very things that I set my heart to possess were possessing me. I am not proud to say that I was giving myself over to the world system-I took the bait and I was being deceived. Though from the outside looking in it may have looked like "I had it all", a career, a title, homes and girlfriends...the reality is that I was intensely miserable and lost. I felt like I was treading water and going down for the proverbial "third time". And then the LORD God shook me free of all that possessed me and though it was very uncomfortable at the time it was analogist to the chastisement of a loving father. I lost my medical license, and I went to jail, but the difficult years past and then years of fruitful ministry and insight ensued. The year was around 2007, I was studying hard the word of God, God was showing me things in the Scriptures that I had never appreciated, I had become very serious with regard to my walk with the LORD. One night, as I recall, I had fallen asleep after reading from the Scriptures and a time in prayer. As I was sleeping it was as though I were "downloading information" from the LORD; I received a word from the LORD regarding my position and He referred me to a passage in Deuteronomy, as I transitioned from sleep to awake and alert the conversation with the LORD continued as though without missing a step. The LORD was asking me "do you understand" and even though I do not recall any specific instruction I was seemingly given my appointment. It was in the middle of the night and I was alone down stairs and I was crying and rocking and I kept repeating "yes LORD, I understand". Thank you Lord, I understand.

Job's Confession
¹*Then Job answered the LORD and said,*
²*"I know that You can do all things,*
and that no purpose of Yours [God] can be thwarted.
³*'Who is this that hides counsel without knowledge?'*
"Therefore I have declared that which I did not understand,
Things too wonderful for me, which I did not know."
⁴*'Hear, now, and I will speak;*
I will ask You, and You instruct me.'
⁵**"[Job declared] I have heard of You by the hearing of the ear;**
but now my eye sees You;
⁶*Therefore I retract,*
and I repent in dust and ashes."

THE TOWLS

Angie is a dear sister from our church and she seems gifted in the area of hospitality… In spite of their struggles Angie and her daughters have opened their home on a regular basis to people in need. I admire Angie as she places a higher value on people than she does on appearance or a clean house. Angie has shared in the past that she is in need of bath towels on an ongoing basis as a result of the many people that she has in her home. My parents and I live in a cul-de-sac and our neighbors host an annual garage sale, more than a few of the neighbors get involved in this effort. Today was the final day of the sale and my mom picked up a few bath towels for Angie from one of the neighbors and that prompted me to stop by and look for towels at the other garage sales. As I walked into a garage I was greeted by the daughter of the home owner, this lady looked to be in her forties, I did not know her. I looked over the thin selection of garage sale stuff and I explained that I was looking for towels for a struggling lady and her family from our church. The lady said that they didn't seem to have towels but she said that she would ask her mother as she was still bringing things out. She opened up the door from the garage into the main level and she yelled "Mom, there is a guy here looking for towels" and there was no reply so she said a little louder "MOM, THERE IS A GUY HERE LOOKING FOR TOWLS". As she was yelling her mother walked up a set of stairs from the lower level into the garage and her Mom was saying "what did you say?" as her Mom truly did not hear her request for towels, and as her Mom came into view much to our surprise her mother was carrying a nice set of bath towels priced and ready for sale. **The daughter looked puzzled and said "that's weird that as I yelled for towels Mom was carrying towels up the stairs" and I explained that it was the LORD and that He indeed had a great sense of humor and timing. She seemed to patronize me and said "yeah, ok" and then she repeated "yeah, but that was really weird [as her mom did** not know that I needed towels]" and again I explained that I was not kidding and that this was indeed the LORD and that He had a great sense of humor and timing. I bought the towels; I thanked them and I left praising the LORD for His great signs and wonders-and for the towels. As I got into the car I was still thanking the LORD for His great signs and I tuned into the song playing on the radio and I heard the singer singing about the great signs of the LORD adding to my joy. As I drove down the road I received a conformational "VKT [T for towels]..." and then I stopped at another sale, picked up another stack of towels, as I walked to the car, and I could see the mail truck pulling up to our mailbox, I noted the timing, it was perfect and wondered if the LORD had a gift for me in the mail. When I opened the mail I had indeed received a support check to cover the towels and then some by about 20 times; it is true that we cannot out give God. Praise the LORD for His great works.

2 Corinthians 9

⁶Now this I say, he [or she] who sows sparingly will also reap sparingly, and he who sows bountifully will also reap bountifully. ⁷**Each one must do just as he has purposed in his heart, not grudgingly or under compulsion, for God loves a cheerful giver.** ⁸And God is able to make all grace abound to you, so that always having all sufficiency in everything, you may have an abundance for every good deed; ⁹**as it is written,**
"HE SCATTERED ABROAD, HE GAVE TO THE POOR, HIS RIGHTEOUSNESS ENDURES FOREVER."
¹⁰Now He who supplies seed to the sower and bread for food will supply and multiply your seed for sowing and increase the harvest of your righteousness; ¹¹**you will be enriched in everything for all liberality, which through us is producing thanksgiving to God.**
¹²For the ministry of this service is not only fully supplying the needs of the saints, but is also overflowing through many thanksgivings to God. ¹³**Because of the proof given by this ministry, they will glorify God for your obedience to your confession of the gospel of Christ and for the liberality of your contribution to them and to all,**
¹⁴**while they also, by prayer on your behalf, yearn for you because of the surpassing grace of God in you. ¹⁵Thanks be to God for His indescribable gift!**

THE PICTURE PERFECT FACE OF THE DOG

From my bedroom I face a large wide open space, roughly 200 yards of cleared area, beyond that is a thin wooded strip then a residential area. In the thin wooded strip is a group of evergreens and in the center of the evergreens is a large tree that has grown to tower over the pines. This large tree looks very symmetrical with a huge sprawling top that looked perfect from my point of view, this must be the movie star of all trees, or at least it should be. In the fall this tree has a great and colorful appearance and it even seems to look good in the winter. I spend a lot of time lying on my bed on my left side looking out of the window praying to God as I face this great tree.

During the fall this tree explodes with color and on some occasions will look more like a painted picture than a real tree. On one of those occasions that I was praying and facing out toward the tree my dog jumped onto the bed as she often does. As she jumped up and laid down I began to thank the LORD for this dog that had become a little friend to me. I was thanking the LORD for this little friend and staring into the tree. As I was looking at the tree an image came into focus and was much like one of the hidden pictures that were so popular in the 1980s, the pictures that you would need to stare into until the hidden picture was revealed. The interesting thing about those pictures to me was that one minute I would be unable to see and appreciate the hidden picture and the next minute the "hidden picture" was all that I was able to see. **As I was staring into the tree and thanking the LORD for my little dog friend the colorful full tree began to reveal a hidden picture of its own. As the tree was yielding a hidden picture I mentally stood back and observed and with no imagination required, the detailed image of my dogs face appeared in the tree.** This image was not fleeting as it remained, there was no rush in my thoughts and I recall just lying there looking at the face of my dog in this tree and appreciating all of the fine details. I even recall saying or thinking "I am just going to lay here and look at this for a while". When I was done the image was gone.

Luke 1

Jesus' Birth Foretold

²⁶Now in the sixth month the angel Gabriel was sent from God to a city in Galilee called Nazareth, ²⁷to a virgin engaged to a man whose name was Joseph, of the descendants of David; and the virgin's name was Mary. ²⁸And coming in, he said to her, "Greetings, favored one! The Lord is with you." ²⁹But she was very perplexed at this statement, and kept pondering what kind of salutation this was. ³⁰The angel said to her, "Do not be afraid, Mary; for you have found favor with God. ³¹"And behold, you will conceive in your womb and bear a son, and you shall name Him Jesus. *³²"He will be great and will be called the Son of the Most High; and the Lord God will give Him the throne of His father David; ³³and He will reign over the house of Jacob forever, and His kingdom will have no end."* ³⁴Mary said to the angel, "How can this be, since I am a virgin?" ³⁵The angel answered and said to her, "The Holy Spirit will come upon you, and the power of the Most High will overshadow you; and for that reason the holy Child shall be called the Son of God. ³⁶"And behold, even your relative Elizabeth has also conceived a son in her old age; and she who was called barren is now in her sixth month. *³⁷"For nothing will be impossible with God."* ³⁸And Mary said, "Behold, the bondslave of the Lord; may it be done to me according to your word." And the angel departed from her.

THE TREE-FACE WITH THE WINKING-EYE

I was lying on my bed in prayer and looking out my bedroom window toward the impressive tree, a different occasion, a different miracle, but the same tree.

In the spring and summer when this tree is dressed out with leaves it looks thick and fluffy, in the late fall the tree loses it leaves. When all the leaves have fallen the tree resembles a huge face with a large bushy looking hairdo-this tree has a huge sprawling canapé much like a great Banyan tree. I do not recall when in the year it was that I was staring into this tree and praying though I do recall that there were leaves on the tree. The tree was full and the interesting thing was that there were two eye-shaped patches in the tree that were free of leaves; it looked very much like a face with a wild and symmetric hairdo. There were not small leafless patches in the tree they were large, perhaps 3 feet by 4 feet and looked like prefect elliptic leaf-free patches that looked like eyes. As I looked at the face in this tree I can recall praying to the LORD and thanking Him for all the great ways that He had shown Himself to me. I reminded Him of His great displays of His wonderful sense of humor and then I asked what I thought would be impossible or at least unlikely. I asked the LORD if He would please cause the face in the tree with its two large and wide open eye shaped patches to wink at me somehow and in some way. This request was for no other reason than to see the LORD do something amazing-just like asking my giant invisible friend to show me something cool. As I prayed, I hoped, I knew the LORD could and the question was, would He do such a thing as this-I did have doubt and then I fell asleep.

When I woke I thought of the request immediately and was hesitant to look as I had though and I wanted to languish in hope, when I did look at the tree I was happy to see the tree and the face in the tree looking at me had the left eye completely shut. I stared into the face trying to figure out how this had happened, how and what was

325

covering the once wide open spot in the tree that looked like an open eye. I finally stopped trying to figure out this great thing and simply received it as the great gift that it was. This tree that had had two eye-shaped open areas now had only one, and it remained that way for the duration of the season. Thank you again LORD, my Lord.

Ephesians 3

[20]Now to Him who is able to do far more abundantly beyond all that we ask or think, according to the power that works within us,

[21]to Him be the glory in the church and in Christ [the anointed King] Jesus to all generations forever and ever. Amen

THE TRUCK IN FULL AGREEMENT

It seems that only the human heart can rebel against the LORD. Not even trucks, gadgets, the weather nor trees and plants are exempt from the LORD'S control. This has been shown to me on many occasions and at times it is downright funny as the LORD revels Himself in whatever manner He chooses. On one occasion I was talking with someone about the LORD and I was shocked by their lack of regard for the LORD. As I recall this person claimed to be a believer in the LORD, which in and of itself means nothing as Satan himself believes in the existence of God (See James 2:19). I remained calm on the outside, as we were talking though in my Spirit I was: angry, sad and frustrated. When we were done with our conversation I left from the far western end of the building where there is a parking lot and a loading dock. Once outside of the building I shook my head in disbelief and blew a blast of air out of my mouth making a "Paaaa" kind of a sound. The "Paaaa" sound was my response to the conversation that I had just had-I was disappointed. At that moment from a truck some distance away the same noise occurred and it caught my attention, "Paaaaa" and I smiled. At that point I knew that the LORD was up to something and I thought I would try to have the last word and I again made the "Paaaa" noise, this time the sound was not out of disgust but in a playful and relaxed way as with the LORD. Again as soon as the stream of air shot from my mouth making the "Paaaa" sound the truck returned the sound from a distance as though it were in playful conversation with me. As I may have said before, the LORD plays with us like we are His children, because we are His children, and He had the last word.

2 Samuel 18

⁶Then the people went out into the field against Israel, and the battle took place in the forest of Ephraim. ⁷The people of Israel were defeated there before the servants of David, and the slaughter there

that day was great, 20,000 men. **⁸For the battle there was spread over the whole countryside, and the forest devoured more people that day than the sword devoured.**

THE VAN AND THE PAINT JOB

The Greek word "Ekklesia" is often translated "church", "gathering" or "assembly" and it is far too often interpreted to mean a building. The more accurate translation of "Ekklesia" is the "called out ones" or "the ones called out [for a purpose by God]". The word "koinonia" is often translated "fellowship" and is too often interpreted to mean getting together with other believers and: eating, drinking and talking about current events or things of the LORD. The Greek word literally means "a common sharing" or "all things commonly shared" to include: gifts, abilities and resources... This is a great example of "Koinonia [fellowship, a sharing of all things in common]" in the "Ekklesia [Church]".

I was standing outside of Perkin's restaurant where we meet throughout the week to have: Bible studies, Greek classes... God has used Perkin's and their staff in a great way. Angie is a waitress at Perkins and we were outside talking about her need for a van as her current van was "falling apart". Angie and I prayed that the LORD would provide a van for her "in a great way" and we believed that He would. We then entered the restaurant and I sat down, as I recall I prayed with a group of men at the table for a van for Angie, and, as we ended our prayer Eric from another table said "I just read that a family was willing to trade a paint job on their house for a nice van". Eric explained that he was thinking about doing the job for himself but saw it as the LORD's will that we do it for Angie. We called and made the necessary arrangements, we painted the house the next week and we received the very nice van for the work, and we gave the van to Angie. Angie has been driving the van since that time.

Psalm 15

A Psalm of David.
[1]O LORD, who may abide in Your tent?
Who may dwell on Your holy hill?
[2]He who walks with integrity, and works righteousness,
And speaks truth in his heart.
[3]He does not slander with his tongue,
Nor does evil to his neighbor,
Nor takes up a reproach against his friend;
[4]In whose eyes a reprobate is despised,
But who honors those who fear the LORD;
He swears to his own hurt and does not change;
[5]He does not put out his money at interest,
Nor does he take a bribe against the innocent
He who does these things will never be shaken.

THE VISION OF "THE DRAIN"

If we belong to the LORD then we are slaves of the LORD. Paul referred to himself in Romans 1:1 as "a doulos [Greek, translated "bond-slave"]" of the LORD. As slaves we are stewards of all that we have, all of our possessions and all that we are belongs to the LORD. Our money, our time and talents all belong to the LORD, and we need to live in light of that truth lest we rob the LORD of what belongs to Him.

I was faced with a financial question and I sought the LORD, my question to Him was "LORD this is your money do you want me to spend it in this manner? [God knows what I am referring to, and it would have been a $25/month commitment]". **The question was very specific, I sought the Scriptures and I was uncertain as how to proceed so I went to the LORD for a personal word (Greek, rhema).** I asked the LORD to please reveal His will to me while I was sleeping that day, and then I took a nap. After a very nice nap I began to wake up; I was in a place somewhere between sleeping soundly and being alert. I was lying down with my eyes closed and beginning to process my thoughts when I began seeing in my minds-eye what looked like a round shaped area in the distance and it was spinning or swirling from the outside in. As I focused in on the object I drew in very close and I clearly saw that it was a drain with water collecting to the center swirling and running into the middle and down the drain. **The most interesting thing about this vision was my ability to navigate and maneuver to every angle and look into the drain. I would literally consider any angle that I wanted to approach the drain and without saying a word and without moving I was able to maneuver fluidly, so to speak, into position.** I even moved directly over and down into the drain looking at it from every angle as the water was swirling and running into the drain; it was fascinating to watch this process. When I was done, or when the LORD was done I opened my eyes I thanked the LORD and then I asked the LORD what that was all about. **And**

331

without words the LORD reminded me of the old saying "it's like pouring money down the drain". I received that as the LORD saying "No" to my question.

Job 4

¹²"Now a word was brought to me [Eliphaz the friend of Job]
stealthily, and my ear received a whisper of it.
¹³Amid disquieting thoughts from the visions of the night,
when deep sleep falls on men,
¹⁴dread came upon me, and trembling,
and made all my bones shake.
¹⁵Then a spirit passed by my face;
the hair of my flesh bristled up.
¹⁶It stood still, but I could not discern its appearance;
a form was before my eyes;
there was silence, then I heard a voice:
¹⁷'can mankind be just before God?
Can a man be pure before his Maker?"

THE VISION OF THE SILT

As I recall I was asking the LORD about His will for me and others as I watched some brothers moving into some seemingly difficult and uncomfortable situations; my question to the LORD "LORD what are You doing-what are You up to?".

Psalm 46
[10] **He [LORD God] says, "Be still, and know that I am God; I will be exalted among the nations, I will be exalted in the earth."**

While asking the LORD, I had a vision of a large cross section of a pool of water; it literally looked like a lake divided down the middle from a side view. Looking at lake water from the side it was clear to see that toward the top the water was clear relative to the bottom as the silt was settling from top to bottom. From top to bottom the water became more and murky until the hovering particles of gook rested on the thick murky muddy lake floor. The LORD pointed to a particle deep in the mud bottom; He explained that this silt represented people in all levels of society and that there were people in these muddy areas that He wanted His people to reach. God explained that His people are like settling particles when they are still and trust Him they are able to be settled down as deep as He needs to get them. However, as is too often the case when the people of God find themselves in uncomfortable or seemingly illogical places they resist, panic, kick up silt and swim for the surface and head for comfort. In this case the LORD showed me that the last state was worse than the first as in the process of swimming to the surface things all became stirred up and the process of settling needed to begin again.

Jeremiah 17:7-8

[7]"Blessed is the man [woman or person] who trusts in the LORD and whose trust is the LORD. [8]"For he or she] will be like a tree planted by the water, that extends its roots by a stream and will not fear when the heat comes;
but its leaves will be green, and it will not be anxious in a year of drought [or difficulty] nor cease to yield fruit.

THE WHIRLWIND

On another occasion I was watching outside as a small dust whirlwind formed. It looked like a small spinning twister shaped cyclone, a "dust-devil", and it was quite impressive to me. As I was looking at the whirlwind I sensed that the LORD was calling me to focus in on it. I focused on the whirlwind looking at it move from a tightly twisted cyclone to a loosely formed swirl and then to a scattered cloud of dust and then to nothing all in a matter of a few seconds. After seeing the dusty whirlwind form from nothing into an impressive cyclone unwind and dissipate into thin air I sensed the LORD saying **"You [humans] are really not much more than this"**.

Psalm 103
[14]For He [LORD God] Himself knows our frame;
He is mindful that we are but dust.
[15]As for man, his days are like grass;
as a flower of the field, so he flourishes.
[16]When the wind has passed over it, it is no more,
and its place acknowledges it no longer.

A WORD TO AARON AND ROBERT

       I received a written text from Karen Salisbury regarding "speak the truth, be bold beyond your comfort zone". I have grown to recognize and appreciate Karen's gift of hearing from the LORD, and I trust her. At the time that I received the word from Karen I felt that it was for the near future. As I recall, it was either that day or the following day that I was called by Robert. Robert had an issue with chronic sin followed by repentance followed by sin (as we all do to some degree it seems). As we were talking I felt that the LORD came upon me and I told Robert of his need to be serious about his walk with the LORD. **I told Robert that the LORD wanted him to be diligent about the study of the Bible and that it was time for him to be boot-camp trained,** it was time to move from a milk fed state to a diet of solid food (See Hebrews 5:14). At that moment Robert said that he was reminded of a dream that he had had the previous night; he said he had a dream of seeing a hand flipping through the Bible. In his dream the Bible was then opened to Deuteronomy Chapter 20 **³"He shall say to them, 'Hear, O Israel, you are approaching the battle against your enemies today. Do not be fainthearted. Do not be afraid, or panic, or tremble before them, ⁴for the LORD your God is the one who goes with you, to fight for you against your enemies, to save you.' (Deuteronomy 20:3-4)** Robert and I both received this as a wonderful confirmation from the LORD. A day or so later I was having lunch with a group of young men that I meet with weekly for lunch and accountability. One of the young men, Aaron, had recently prepared for and presented a message to a large group at a weekend youth retreat. Aaron's topic of discussion addressed leadership, consistency and serious regard for the LORD. During our meeting this week Aaron shared that he was spending most of his time working and was not spending time with the LORD. **I recalled the word that I had received from Karen and I gently yet boldly rebuked Aaron for his choice to serve the world and neglect the LORD. I did not hear from Aaron for about one week, I was concerned that**

I may have hurt this young disciple of the LORD. I then received this text from Aaron "Hey I really appreciate what you said to me [Aaron] last week and how up-front you were in prayer. Thank you brother. The words have stuck with me this week." I rejoiced upon receiving this text.

Proverbs 27

Warnings and Instructions
[1]Do not boast about tomorrow,
For you do not know what a day may bring forth.
[2]Let another praise you, and not your own mouth;
A stranger, and not your own lips.
[3]A stone is heavy and the sand weighty,
But the provocation of a fool is heavier than both of them.
[4]Wrath is fierce and anger is a flood,
But who can stand before jealousy?
[5]Better is open rebuke
Than love that is concealed.
[6]Faithful are the wounds of a friend,
But deceitful are the kisses of an enemy.

THEIR BEST COMPARED TO OUR WORST

When the LORD reveals truth to us it becomes so real that we wonder how others fail to see in spite of the fact that we were unable to see prior to our revelation as well. God revealed to me that our condition as Christ followers, even in the worst of conditions is far better than that of the non-Christ follower even in their best of conditions. The LORD showed me that the sought-after-prize of the lost is everlasting life, immortality of the bodies. To the Christ follower this "best condition" of the lost would be utterly noxious even to consider as the Christ follower is looking forward to the day that they can shed this mortal flesh and step into our immortal, new, and sinless bodies. **Hence, the best that the lost can hope for is the worst that the follower of Jesus can imagine.**

In this culture the enemy has so distorted the truth that we have come to believe that "fun" is synonymies with "joy", or should I say that we have made choices as to replace joy with fun. Fun can be bought and paid for, fun is fleeting; fun can be paid for at an: amusement park, a ball game, a casino or anyplace that we can be distracted, used-up and entertained. The Apostle Paul described this as "dissipation". Dissipation is anything that will spread us thin, use us up, consume our time and render us useless, fruitless, unproductive, and "worthless" (See Luke 21:34). **Joy on the other hand cannot be bought, joy is internal, and joy is from the LORD, "the joy of the LORD is our strength"** (See Nehemiah 8:10).
True joy is something that we as believers in Jesus experience in spite of our difficult circumstances, joy can be experienced in spite of: unemployment, disease, homelessness... The LORD reveled to me that nothing can replace our eternal security, in spite of any physical trouble we may experience our Spirit or inner-man anticipates its release from these flesh bodies. **In fact, the more difficulty that we as believers may face in this life the reciprocal effect is true. We become more joyful, we anticipate with greater excitement and we literally grow**

to dislike these flesh bodies and identify them as a liability, we despise them and embrace the loss of our fleshly selves. We look forward to passing-yahoo!!

2 Corinthians 5

[1]**For we know that if the earthly tent which is our house is torn down, we have a building from God, a house not made with hands, eternal in the heavens.** [2]For indeed in this house we groan, longing to be clothed with our dwelling from heaven, [3]inasmuch as we, having put it on, will not be found naked. [4]**For indeed while we are in this tent, we groan, being burdened, because we do not want to be unclothed but to be clothed, so that what is mortal will be swallowed up by life.**

OUR ONE SHOT AT FAITH

Consider the statement **"without faith it is impossible to please God"** (See Hebrews 11:6). This would imply that **with faith it is possible to please God.** Think about that for a minute, **it is actually possible for us to bring pleasure to the creator-this is amazing to me.** When we consider that our opportunity to bring pleasure to the LORD is connected to our acts of faith, and it seems that faith will be a factor only while we are unable to see the LORD. Then it stands to reason that our time on earth is quite possibly our one shot at bringing pleasure to the LORD through our acts of faith. **This relatively small blip of time while on earth is our one shot at bringing the LORD pleasure though our acts of faith.** If this is the case then we would do well to live lives in an almost reckless abandon throwing care to the wind and living lives of great faith in God alone. **Consider this, if "without faith it is impossible to please God", then perhaps with faith it is possible to please God-wow!**

Hebrews 11
¹Now faith is the assurance of things hoped for, the conviction of things not seen. ²For by it the men of old gained approval. ³By faith we understand that the worlds were prepared by the word of God, so that what is seen was not made out of things which are visible. ⁴By faith Abel offered to God a better sacrifice than Cain, through which he obtained the testimony that he was righteous, God testifying about his gifts, and through faith, though he is dead, he still speaks. ⁵By faith Enoch was taken up so that he would not see death; AND HE WAS NOT FOUND BECAUSE GOD TOOK HIM UP; for he obtained the witness that before his being taken up he was pleasing to God. **⁶And without faith it is impossible to please Him, for he who comes to God must believe that He is and that He is a rewarder of those who seek Him.** ⁷By faith Noah, being warned by God about things not yet seen, in reverence prepared an ark for the salvation of his

341

household, by which he condemned the world, and became an heir of the righteousness which is according to faith.

BIBLICAL LOVE STARTS WHERE LIKE ENDS

In my opinion, Biblical love, (Greek, "agape") begins where like ends. In first Corinthians Chapter 13 we are given the definition of "agape" (God's unconditional care)

⁴ Love [agape] is patient, love [agape] is kind and is not jealous; love [agape] does not brag and is not arrogant, ⁵ [agape love] does not act unbecomingly; it does not seek its own, is not provoked, does not take into account a wrong suffered, ⁶does not rejoice in unrighteousness, but rejoices with the truth; ⁷bears all things, believes all things, hopes all things, endures all things. ⁸Love never fails…" 1ˢᵗ Corinthians 13:4-7

Inherent in the definition of "agape" is the teaching of how we are and how we are not to act in the face of feelings. To love with agape we will be led to behave, react and respond counter to our feelings. In order for "agape" to take place our difficult life experiences must be experienced. In the same way that before you can honestly report on how you dealt with piranhas in the Amazon, you need to experience piranhas in the Amazon. Before you can exercise control in the face of the fears in battle you must experience fears in battle. And before you can be faithful to your spouse in marriage you must be married. Before you can be persecuted for righteousness you must be righteous in the face of persecution. In the same vein, in order to love with agape you must have experienced hurts and suffering from the hand of the one that you treat with "agape". It seems clear that in the same way that you cannot pass the driver's test without parallel parking neither can you truly love patiently until your patients has been tested; you cannot act with patients and kindness until your patients and your kindness have been tested, and you cannot act without jealously until an act evoking jealously has occurred. You cannot be unprovoked in spite of being provoked without first being provoked; you cannot "not take into account a wrong suffered" until you have suffered wrongly at the hand of another, nor can you "bear all things" until you indeed bear the things. Love, (agape) is not about feelings, as has been represented, portrayed and propagated by Hollywood "love [agape]" has become confused with "like" and like is a response to feelings; "like", as does infatuation comes, and it goes. Recall that the Greek word "kurios" means "LORD", "Master" or "the LORD of us". If God is our master than we are to do as He is telling us to do. And if what He is telling us to do is the exact thing that we want to do then where lies the test?

God has instructed us to disregard our feeling and to love in spite of our not necessarily liking-here lies the test. Will we do as we are told?

Recall Jesus' good question. "Why do you call Me, 'Lord, Lord,' and do not do what I say..." Luke 6:46

Matthew 5

[1] **When Jesus saw the crowds, He went up on the mountain; and after He sat down, His disciples came to Him.** [2] **He opened His mouth and *began* to teach them, saying,** [3] **"Blessed are the poor in spirit, for theirs is the kingdom of heaven.** [4] **"Blessed are those who mourn, for they shall be comforted.** [5] **"Blessed are the gentle, for they shall inherit the earth.** [6] **"Blessed are those who hunger and thirst for righteousness, for they shall be satisfied.** [7] **"Blessed are the merciful, for they shall receive mercy.** [8] **"Blessed are the pure in heart, for they shall see God.** [9] **"Blessed are the peacemakers, for they shall be called sons of God.** [10] **"Blessed are those who have been persecuted for the sake of righteousness, for theirs is the kingdom of heaven.** [11] **"Blessed are you when *people* insult you and persecute you, and falsely say all kinds of evil against you because of Me.** [12] **Rejoice and be glad, for your reward in heaven is great; for in the same way they persecuted the prophets who were before you.** [13] **"You are the salt of the earth; but if the salt has become tasteless, how can it be made salty *again*? It is no longer good for anything, except to be thrown out and trampled underfoot by men.** [14] **"You are the light of the world. A city set on a hill cannot be hidden;** [15] **nor does *anyone* light a lamp and put it under a basket, but on the lampstand, and it gives light to all who are in the house.** [16] **Let your light shine before men in such a way that they may see your good**

344

works, and glorify your Father who is in heaven... ³⁸ "You have heard that it was said, 'AN EYE FOR AN EYE, AND A TOOTH FOR A TOOTH.' ³⁹ But I say to you, do not resist an evil person; but whoever slaps you on your right cheek, turn the other to him also. ⁴⁰ If anyone wants to sue you and take your shirt, let him have your coat also. ⁴¹ Whoever forces you to go one mile, go with him two. ⁴² Give to him who asks of you, and do not turn away from him who wants to borrow from you. ⁴³ "You have heard that it was said, 'YOU SHALL LOVE YOUR NEIGHBOR and hate your enemy.' ⁴⁴ But I say to you, love [Greek, the root word "agape"] your enemies and pray for those who persecute you, ⁴⁵ in order that you may be sons of your Father who is in heaven; for He causes His sun to rise on *the* evil and *the* good, and sends rain on *the* righteous and *the* unrighteous. ⁴⁶ For if you love those who love you, what reward do you have? **Do not even the tax collectors do the same?** ⁴⁷ **If you greet only your brothers, what more are you doing** *than others*? **Do not even the Gentiles do the same?** ⁴⁸ **Therefore you are to be perfect, as your heavenly Father is perfect.**

REEL TO REAL, TONY AND
THE VCR/DVD PLAYER

Tony is a young Viet Nemeses man that I have been meeting with and we have been studying through the New Testament together. Tony and I have recently worked through: the Books of Matthew, 1st John, and James. The LORD has been providing for Tony in great ways and He has answered our prayers for a job for Tony in spite of our tough economy and in spite of his language barrier. The LORD had given Tony some DVDs recently that covered the life of Jesus, THE JESUS FILM. Tony had been sharing the Good News of the LORD with his family and there seemed to be a lot of interest in the things of the LORD by his family. Shortly after sharing these DVDs with his family he reported that two of their DVD players had been broken. It seemed clear that the enemy did not want Tony sharing the Good News with others. Tony said that he needed to replace the DVD players and I encouraged him to pray for a DVD player-he agreed. We asked the LORD for a DVD player, and Tony added that he wanted a VCR player as well. A few days later my Dad asked me to replace his DVD/VCR player and then asked if I wanted his current DVD/VCR player, I shared the prayer request with my Dad and I look forward to giving the DVD/VCR player to Tony tomorrow. Thank you LORD.

Psalm 144:15
How blessed are the people who are so situated;
How blessed are the people whose God is the LORD!

TUNNELS

I had a dream that I was in an underground labyrinth of tunnels; the tunnels were large enough to crawl through but it was very cramped. The tunnels all lead to similar common areas that were roughly 12-15 feet square with cement walls and a cement ceiling, there were no windows. I recall that these cement common areas were underground and cramped. While I was trying to escape I became fearful and claustrophobic and I used my cell-phone to call my Pastor/mentor. While talking to my Pastor/mentor I was asking him to "please stay on the line" as I was in need of support. At that moment our phone connection began to crack and break up and I could feel demons begin to move in on me from every side, and then the connection was completely broken-I was afraid. As soon as the connection was broken I felt that the demons were moving in very quickly and it became very uncomfortable, I opened my mouth and I was unable to scream at first then I forced out "JESUS!" **As soon as the name of Jesus was spoken the demons began to retreat and I immediately felt empowered. One seemed to feed on the other, the demons were running in fear and I became increasingly more bold and empowered. I began to speak louder and then yelling "WHATS THE MATTER? YOU DON'T LIKE THAT NAME? JESUS! JESUS!"**

Mark 3:13-15

And He [Jesus of Nazareth] went up on the mountain and summoned those whom He Himself wanted, and they came to Him. And He appointed twelve, so that they would be with Him and that He could send them out to preach, and to have authority to cast out the demons.

349

WALKING IN THE SPIRIT AND STEPPING OFF THE PATH

It is December 1ˢᵗ 2011 and a light layer of snow had fallen overnight and I went on an early morning walk. The path that I typically walk on had about an inch of fresh flaky lightly packed snow. As I walked along the path I sensed that the LORD was speaking to me about: staying on the path, walking with the Spirit, and the danger of stepping off of the path. All of this was of course in reference to His Spiritual path. As I walked I was pondering the schemes of the enemy as he coerces us to walk off of God's path and trust in our own abilities rather that trusting in the LORD. As I walked I noted that the terrain of the physical path that I was walking changed, I was walking up hill, and I became concerned that I would slip and fall while on the path. Though I was walking along without slipping I was looking off the path and thinking that the grass would offer a more stable surface to walk on. I decided to walk off the path and onto the grass as it appeared to be more stable. As I stepped away from the path and onto the grass I lost my footing and I slipped and went head-over-heels tumbling down the hill covered with snow. As I tumbled I was aware of the spiritual parallels of what had just taken place. I had allowed myself to be coerced, distracted and convinced that the greater security for me was off of the path. The LORD had first instructed me regarding the importance of staying on the path and He then gave to me a real life example of the dangers of stepping off. God is a practical teacher.

Psalm 32:8-10

"I [LORD God] will instruct you and teach you in the way which you should go; I will counsel you with My eye upon you. Do not be like the horse [impulsive] or as the mule [stubborn] which have no understanding, whose trappings include bit and bridle to hold them in check, otherwise they will not come near to you. Many are

351

the sorrows of the wicked, but he [or she] who trusts in the LORD, lovingkindness shall surround him [and her]."

JOB 5:17-18

"Behold, how happy [Blessed] is the man [or woman] whom God reproved [corrects, disciplines], so do not despise the discipline of the Almighty. For He [YHWH, LORD God] inflicts pain, and gives relief; He wounds, and His hands also heal."

WE ARE NOT HERE LONG

It may have been William Barkley that commented regarding the most effective lies of the enemy. Barkley was convinced that the lie whispered into the ears of mankind **"YOU HAVE PLENTY OF TIME" is a lie from hell itself.** Our spirit or "inner-man" knows that we will live on, and on, and on, however our flesh, that is, the "outer man" is very temporary, "man's days on earth are like shadows" **(1ˢᵗ Chronicles 29:15, Psalm 102:11, Ecclesiastes 6:12)** and Scripture bears out that, "we [humankind] are a mist" **(James 4:14)**, "we are like the grass [here and gone]"**(Psalms 90:4-6, 103:15, Isaiah 40:6-7, 1ˢᵗ Peter 1:24, et al.)**, "like a phantom [tenant or sojourner]" **(1ˢᵗ Chronicles 29:15)**, "like the flowers that wither" **(Job 14:2, Psalm 103:15, 1ˢᵗ Peter 1:24)** All of us are here today, and gone tomorrow.

I believe that this is precisely what the author meant when he said that God has put eternity in the hearts of mankind, **"He [LORD God] has made everything appropriate in its time He has also set eternity in their [mankind's] heart, yet so that man will not find out the work which God has done from the beginning even to the end" (Ecclesiastes 3:11).** Perhaps the spirit of man knows well that we are eternal beings, and perhaps "the lost" in their blind state are unable to grasp that the flesh is temporary and failing. That is, though we have the knowledge of our eternal existence, perhaps "the lost" attach that eternal existence to the flesh, they are perhaps unwilling or unable to accept the brevity of life while in these bodies-our "earth-suits". While we are in the process of life the illusion of a long life in these bodies is supported by the myth of long life. In the process the lost are caught off guard and mankind perishes in his or her pursuits along the way. Consider your past, consider the decades that you, like me, have passed thorough. Now, consider that if our past has passed in a blink of an eye then our present and future will as well pass with the blink of an eye. One day to the next with hardly a clue of where the time has gone, and in the flesh we have no promise for another minute in these bodies let alone for tomorrow.

Psalm 49

¹Hear this, all peoples; give ear, all inhabitants of the world, ²both low and high, rich and poor together. ..

⁵Why should I fear in days of adversity, when the iniquity of my foes surrounds me,

⁶Even those who trust in their wealth and boast in the abundance of their riches?

⁷No man can by any means redeem his brother, or give to God a ransom for him--

⁸For the redemption of his soul is costly, **and he should cease trying forever--**

⁹**That he should live on eternally, that he should not undergo decay.**

¹⁰**For he sees that even wise men die; t**he stupid and the senseless alike perish and leave their wealth to others.

¹¹Their inner thought is that their houses are forever and their dwelling places to all generations;

they have called their lands after their own names. ¹²But man in his pomp will not endure; he is like the beasts that perish.

¹³This is the way of those who are foolish, a**nd of those after them who approve their words. Selah.**

¹⁴**As sheep they are appointed for Sheol [the place of the dead]; death shall be their shepherd; and the upright shall rule over them in the morning, and their form shall be for Sheol to consume so that they have no habitation.**

¹⁵**But God will redeem my soul from the power of Sheol, for He will receive me. Selah.**

¹⁶Do not be afraid when a man [or woman] becomes rich, when the glory of his house is increased;

¹⁷For when he dies he will carry nothing away; his glory will not descend after him.

¹⁸Though while he lives he congratulates himself--and though men praise you when you do well for yourself--

¹⁹he shall go to the generation of his father's; they will never see the light.

²⁰**Man in his pomp, yet without understanding, is like the beasts that perish.**

354

WHERE IT IS THAT WE SOW

The LORD has shown me that the teaching of Jesus as recorded by Luke **"for where your treasure is, there your heart will be also." (Luke 12:34)** is not simply a statement-it is a promise. Personally speaking, I seemed to have been looking at this passage as though it was simply a statement. That is, I seemed to be waiting for my heart to be invested in God's work and I would then give to where my burden seemed to be. However, this is not what Jesus seems to be saying. The truth implied is that we are to let God lead us, we are to follow that lead and then our heart will later follow. We are to let God instruct as to where we are to put His: money, time, effort…, we are to obey, to sew into whatever area He might dictate and trust that our heart or our desire will follow, this is the promise of the LORD, **"[Jesus said] for where your treasure is [presently], there your heart will be also" (Luke 12:34).** At the risk of being redundant, we are to ask God, where LORD do You want this treasure (material and spiritual) placed? In His word we are told that He is Master and we are "steward overseers" which means that we oversee what belongs to the Masters and we act on His behalf, (See Luke 16:20, 1st Cor. 9:17, Col 1:25). This principle goes far beyond the tithe (a tenth) in my opinion. Be assured that it will not be about what we want, in fact it will often be what we don't want, as here lies the test. **The take-home message is that we search the Scriptures and the heart of the LORD in prayer, we give generously if not all that we have to the people and places that are important to the LORD and we can be sure that before long we will be vested as our hearts will follow. What we did out of sheer obedience will soon be accompanied by our heart; that is, what began begrudgingly will soon be infused with excitement, love and joy. "Where your treasure is [present tense] your heart will be also"** Quite frankly, where we are sowing is a tangible representation of where we are persuaded to trust, value and believe in, and it goes both ways. Where we put our treasures speaks to what we value and where we put our treasures is where we will become more vested. This seems to be a Scriptural Kingdom principal, a Kingdom treasure, a truth revealed regarding the hardwire make up of human beings. Therefore the implication is similar to the process behind addiction as one starts with a taste and is soon followed by an emotional and even a physical need or drive. **We need to be careful as to what it is that we sow into, we need to be aware that this principal works to the good and to the bad, and that we will become more vested as more time, money, energy are put into whatever place that we value. That is, if we sow into the world we will become more attached to the world. We need to be: deliberate, mindful, and "on guard" as the implication is that we humans tend to be swept away, and attached to the places that we place our treasures. Our hearts are not static nor do they passively observe, they become "tied-into" the places that we sow into. Therefore, let us be cautious; let us be swept away into the things of God rather than into the things of the world and the system of the world.**

Luke 12

[15]Then He said to them, "Beware, and be on your guard against every form of greed; for not even when one has an abundance does his life consist of his possessions." [16]And He [Jesus of Nazareth] told them a parable, saying, "The land of a rich man was very productive. [17]"And he began reasoning to himself, saying, 'What shall I do, since I have no place to store my crops?' [18]"Then he said, 'This is what I will do: I will tear down my barns and build larger ones, and there I will store all my grain and my goods. [19]'And I will say to my soul, "Soul, you have many goods laid up for many years to come; take your ease, eat, drink and be merry."' [20]"**But God said to him, 'You fool! This very night your soul is required of you; and now who will own what you have prepared?' [21]"So is the man who stores up treasure for himself, and is not rich toward God."**

[22]And He said to His disciples, "For this reason I say to you, do not worry about your life, as to what you will eat; nor for your body, as to what you will put on. [23]"For life is more than food, and the body more than clothing. [24]"Consider the ravens, for they neither sow nor reap; they have no storeroom nor barn, and yet God feeds them; how much more valuable you are than the birds! [25]"And which of you by worrying can add a single hour to his life's span? [26]"If then you cannot do even a very little thing, why do you worry about other matters?

²⁷"Consider the lilies, how they grow: they neither toil nor spin; but I tell you, not even Solomon in all his glory clothed himself like one of these. ²⁸"But if God so clothes the grass in the field, which is alive today and tomorrow is thrown into the furnace, how much more will He clothe you? You men of little faith! ²⁹"And do not seek what you will eat and what you will drink, and do not keep worrying. ³⁰"For all these things the nations of the world eagerly seek; but your Father knows that you need these things.

³¹**"But seek His kingdom, and these things will be added to you.** ³²"Do not be afraid, little flock, for your Father has chosen gladly to give you the kingdom. ³³**"Sell your possessions and give to charity; make yourselves money belts which do not wear out, an unfailing treasure in heaven, where no thief comes near nor moth destroys.** ³⁴**"For where your treasure is, there your heart will be also.**

WATER AND OIL

WATER

This may sound arrogant at first glance however I do not take credit for the understanding of this information; this was revealed to me by the LORD and it makes perfect sense to me. The LORD showed me that within our world there is a perfect accounting of all minerals and every drop of water. In fact if we follow a single drop of water we will see it recycled as it goes from the air to the ground then to plants and into the bodies of animals and humans and then the cycle continues. **Every drop of water that is within our body will be returned when we dry and return to the dust.** The most interesting thing to me is that there was no need for the LORD to continue to create more water, once it was created it is simply reused. This may be obvious to others, however it was cool when I got it - call me Captain Obvious.

Job 36

²²"Behold, God is exalted in His power;
Who is a teacher like Him?
**²³"Who has appointed Him His way,
And who has said, 'You have done wrong'?
²⁴"Remember that you should exalt His work,
Of which men have sung.
²⁵"All men have seen it;
Man beholds from afar.
²⁶"Behold, God is exalted, and we do not know Him;
The number of His years is unsearchable.**
²⁷"For He draws up the drops of water,
They distill rain from the mist,
²⁸Which the clouds pour down,
They drip upon man abundantly.

[29]"Can anyone understand the spreading of the clouds,
The thundering of His pavilion?
[30]"Behold, He spreads His lightning about Him,
And He covers the depths of the sea.
[31]"For by these He judges peoples;
He gives food in abundance.
[32]"He covers His hands with the lightning,
And commands it to strike the mark.
[33]"Its noise declares His presence;
The cattle also, concerning what is coming up.

YOU ARE EVERYTHING THAT IS BRIGHT AND CLEAN

On one occasion my daughter Hannah and I were in the car backing out of the garage and I felt the Spirit of the LORD prompt me to faith. I said to Hannah "let's ask the LORD to tell us something about how He feels about you [Hannah] in the next song". Hannah and I agreed together to pray, and we asked the LORD to do just that, "please LORD speak to us about how you feel about Hannah in this song" **We turned on the radio and heard these very words "you [Hannah] are everything that is bright and clean". Hannah and I were thrilled, her grin was so cute.** God is good and He is so good to these kids.

Psalm 45:9-14
"⁹Kings' daughters are among Your noble ladies;
at Your right hand stands the queen in gold from Ophir.
¹⁰Listen, O daughter, give attention and incline your ear…

¹³The King's daughter is all glorious within;
her clothing is interwoven with gold.

YOU'RE MY YANKEE DOODLE DANDY

The LORD has a wonderful sense of humor. The other morning I was walking around the pond as I do most days. For some reason on this day I began to sing the song "I'm your Yankee Doodle Dandy" in a James Cagney voice. As I was walking and singing I began to think "what am I doing singing I'm your Yankee Doodle Dandy?" That made no sense to me though it seemed quite funny that I would even be thinking of such a song. As I walked, sang and laughed I envisioned people welcoming home solders in a parade, and then I rounded the corner of the path. As I walked I looked up over to the left and I saw a statue of a soldier holding and waving a flag in one hand and saluting with the other as if he were involved in such a parade and he would be singing "I'm your Yankee Doodle Dandy" with great enthusiasm. When I saw this guy holding and waving the flag and saluting as I was singing I cracked up even more than I had been singing this odd little old tune that was so appropriate for the moment. God, You are a hoot.

LAMENTATIONS 3:37-38

"Who is there who speaks and it comes to pass, unless the LORD has commanded it? Is it not from the mouth of the Most High [YHWH, LORD God] that both good and ill go forth?"

YOU ARE TURNING IT
THE WRONG WAY, AGAIN!

We have heard it said "you need to be careful what you pray for". We have had the great pleasure of getting to know Joann P. Joann is living with her daughter and son-in-law and their two small children, Page and Avery. Prior to their living together Joann and her daughter have been on difficult terms and their living together has been a great opportunity to reestablish their relationship. Joanne and I have been praying for opportunities to serve their family as a way to reach out with the love of the LORD. The other day Joann told me that her daughter's hot water heater was "out of commission" and needed to be replaced. We looked into a new hot water heater and a new unit would be about $900. I sensed that the LORD was leading us to action and we were able to find a good used hot water heater online, we then brought the unit over and began to remove the old hot water heater. Removal went relatively well until we attempted to remove some old bolts; we worked on them to the point that we were looking at each other for answers. As we worked I told my ministry partner Eric about a time that I was in a similar situation. I had worked for hours to remove a bolt and in frustration I stopped and prayed asking God what I was doing wrong. As I prayed I clearly heard, "you are turning it [the bolt] the wrong way", Eric and I laughed and took a break and shared the details with Joann who asked if we were turning it the right way? As it turned out my son Philip called or texted at that moment and after telling him of the details he asked "are you turning it the right way?" Again we laughed and felt that we were turning the bolt the correct way, until the light seemed to go in Eric's head and he stated **"we are turning it the wrong way", so we changed direction and all was well.** We laughed, and agreed that the LORD is good and He is funny, and He certainly was making the effort to get His message across to us. Thank You again Lord!

Psalm 27:4, 9

[4] "One thing I have asked from the LORD, that I shall seek:
that I may dwell in the house of the LORD all the days of my life,
to behold the beauty of the LORD
and to meditate in His temple...
Your face, O LORD, I shall seek.
[9]Do not hide Your face from me..."

30 MINUTES IN THE SPIRIT

As I recall, this experience occurred on a very typical day, I was not fasting, and as far as I could tell, the LORD simply choose to bless me beyond measure with this great experience.

I was driving in Saint Paul and I felt the Spirit fall on me while I was at a stoplight. While in my car I felt like I was downloading information from the Lord into my mind. While driving I listened and observed what the Spirit was doing and saying. I had never before or since heard the LORD say so many words to me at one time. I do not recall driving my car (though I'm sure that I was) and I felt like an observer; it was much like being on a railed ride at an amusement park on which you simply sit back, hold on and observe. As I drove the traffic lights before me turned green and I passed right through, I passed through them as though the rules that govern the world did not apply at that time and I seemed to have had great favor. While moving about, I received a phone call from my Pastor/mentor and he said that "he doubted that he would be able to make our scheduled meeting", I responded that "we will meet if it is God's will", I smiled and knew that we would be meeting as planned. As I was driving, things looked brilliant, and the LORD was reminding me of things that He had done and taught me in the past. I recall listening and acknowledging the Lord's review of my past by saying "O I remembered that [LORD]". The LORD specifically reminded of the "open door" experiences that He had shown me, and again I responded "Oh yes, I remember [that]" and it seemed that "opened doors" was a theme. Toward the end of the time I found myself pulling into the Perkins restaurant where I had originally planned to meet with my Pastor/mentor, I happened to be pulling into the restaurant at the exact moment as the Pastor and I recall pulling in behind him. As I got out of the car I was smiling at all that the LORD was showing me and that we indeed were meeting as planned. As it turned out I "just happened" to be about one step behind the

367

Pastor and reviewing the theme of my time with the LORD, that is, the LORD's "opened doors" in my life. As I approached the door at Perkins I heard the LORD say "let Me get that for you", and my Pastor/mentor reached out and opened the door and I walked through grinning ear to ear.

Isaiah 42

⁵Thus says God the LORD,
Who created the heavens and stretched them out,
Who spread out the earth and its offspring,
Who gives breath to the people on it
And spirit to those who walk in it,
⁶"I am the LORD, I have called You [His Christ] in righteousness,
I will also hold You by the hand and watch over You,
And I will appoint You as a covenant to the people,
As a light to the nations,
⁷To open blind eyes,
To bring out prisoners from the dungeon
And those who dwell in darkness from the prison.
⁸"I am the LORD, that is My name;
I will not give My glory to another,
Nor My praise to graven images.
⁹"Behold, the former things have come to pass,
Now I [LORD God] declare new things;
Before they spring forth I proclaim them to you."
¹⁰Sing to the LORD a new song,

THE BIBLES-GOD'S TIMING-THE MAN ON THE PLANE-MY HEART BELONGS TO DADDY

This morning the LORD was reminding me of His perfect timing with regard to answered prayers. As I listened He reminded me of a time (around 1985) when He had prompted me to send hundreds of Bibles into a country that was closed to the Gospel of Christ. For weeks after being prompted I resisted as the cost seemed far beyond what I was able. **The prompting of the LORD continued and I began to lose sleep as I was constantly reminded of the mission that I was given-I needed to send those Bibles.** After weeks of running from my mission I decided that I would do whatever I needed to do, I would put all bills and commitments aside and make this my priority. I collected all of the necessary information regarding what was needed to: purchase the Bibles (in the desired language and translation), cover postage and any other necessary expenses related to this shipment. I filled out the order form and I calculated the total. I do not recall the exact amount though it was a lot. As I was sitting at my grandma's kitchen table, I took a breath and then a step of faith, I wrote and signed the check. A few seconds after I signed the check, my Grandma who I was living with at the time yelled from the mailbox "Todd you have something in the mail and it looks like a check from the government"- though I was not expecting a refund or any check for any reason (in fact I was self-employed and I paid in at the end of the year, as I recall I had never had a refund as there was nothing to refund) When my grandma said "it looks like a check" my first thought was "this must be for the Bibles". I opened the envelope **and quickly realized that it was a check and that the check that I had just received a few seconds earlier was for the same amount as the check that I had written and signed a few seconds earlier.** I held one check in my right hand and one check in my left hand and **they were for the exact amount-to the penny!** I showed my wife and my grandmother and I said **"look at this you guys, there**

will be a day that we will question whether this really happened". My grandma then gave me a stamp to send the check for the Bibles, the-deal-was-done, paid for in-full by the LORD God Himself-what He had started He completed.

"Now He who supplies seed to the sower and bread for food, will supply and multiply your seed for sowing and increase the harvest of your righteousness" 2 Corinthians 9:10

God then reminded me of the time that He had asked me to go to Papua New Guinea in about 1990. As I prepared to go to Papua New Guinea (PNG) everything fell into place as: my wife was supportive, the money came in, I had my passport, and I had the time freed up... Everything fell into place, with the exception of the signature of a government official from a certain office in PNG. This signature marked the permission of the PNG government for me to be wandering around in their jungles. As I recall there were no fax machines available and it was getting close to the departure date and no written response had arrived. As my departure date approached I had no permission to be in PNG. I decided to move forward without permission. I boarded the plane in MN and I flew to California, then onto to Hawaii then to Guam for a layover and then to Port Moresby, PNG. On the long flight from Hawaii to Guam I had plenty of time to talk with the man sitting next to me, and he made note of my Bible... Sometime in the course of our conversation we talked on a deeper level about our mission's plans and our destination. I recall inquiring of the man's destination, he said that he was from PNG and I asked if he could please direct me to the city that I would need to travel to in order to find the man that needed to sign my document. He asked me where I needed to go, I told him and he replied that he knew the area well as he lived and worked there. **I gave him the specific office location and the name of the official and he told me that there was no need for me to travel to this office as he was the man that I was looking for. The one man in the world that I needed to sign my document before landing in PNG was the very man that the LORD had sitting in the seat next to me. That man gladly signed the document and then we landed.** Once again, what the LORD had started He provided for and He completed with great precision. **Praise the LORD!**

While I was reflecting on God's timing and those great memories I received a call from a friend who lives quite a distance east of me in Saint Paul. As we were talking he mentioned that he was in a tunnel traveling west and that our communication may be breaking up. I thought it was interesting as I too was heading toward a tunnel while traveling east and I inquired as to which tunnel it was. It turned out to be the same tunnel. As it turned out, as we were talking and praying; as God had just reviewed His great acts of sovereignty and timing with me we were now at about the same place, my friend headed in my direction on the freeway and me headed in his direction. I said over the phone "Joe where are you right now?" he explained and I said "Joe look to your left I see you now". As it turned out he looked left, I looked left as we shot past each other on the freeway we were looking and waving at each other and we both received the blessing from the LORD. What fun it was, and what a blessed reminder of Who it is that we serve and Who is in charge. Signs upon signs LORD, thank you!

It is my sincere desire and the purpose of this book that you the reader will appreciate that God is very personal and that He is interactive with us, if we will open our hearts to Him. I pray that you too will open your heart to Him. This has been a wonderful experience for me.

1st Chronicles 16:8

"Oh give thanks to the LORD, call upon His name; make known His deeds among the peoples."

Made in the USA
Monee, IL
28 January 2020